"MAKE-BELIEVES"
IN PSYCHIATRY

OR

The Perils of Progress

Clinical and Experimental Psychiatry

Monograph Series of the Department of Psychiatry
Albert Einstein College of Medicine of Yeshiva University
Montefiore Medical Center
New York, N.Y.

Clinical & Experimental Psychiatry Monograph No. 7

"MAKE-BELIEVES" IN PSYCHIATRY

OR

The Perils of Progress

Herman M. van Praag, M.D., Ph.D.

Department of Psychiatry
Albert Einstein College of Medicine/Montefiore Medical Center
New York, N.Y.

Presently at
Academic Psychiatric Center
University of Limburg
Maastricht, The Netherlands

BRUNNER/MAZEL *Publishers* • NEW YORK

Library of Congress Cataloging-in-Publication Data
Praag, Herman M. van (Herman Meïr)
   "Make-Believes" in psychiatry or the perils of progress / Herman
M. van Praag.
      p.   cm. — (Clinical and experimental psychiatry ; 7)
   Includes bibliographical references and indexes.
   ISBN 0-87630-680-6 (hardbound)
   1. Mental illness—Classification.   2. Mental illness—Diagnosis.
3. Biological psychiatry.   4. Diagnostic and statistical manual of
mental disorders.   I. Title.   II. Series.
   [DNLM: 1. Biological Psychiatry—methods.   2. Mental Disorders—
diagnosis.   3. Psychiatry—trends.   4. Psychopathology.   W1
CL664EH v.7 / WM 100 P8955m]
RC455.2.C4P73   1992
616.89'0014—dc20
DNLM/DLC
for Library of Congress   92-23744
                                                                        CIP

Published by
BRUNNER/MAZEL, INC.
19 Union Square West
New York, New York 10003

Manufactured in the United States of America

10 9 8 7 6 5 4 3 2 1

To those who are the raison d'être of my life:
my wife, children and my grandchildren

To qualify as folly for this inquiry, the policy adopted must meet three criteria: it must have been perceived as a counter-productive in its own time, not merely by hindsight. . . . Secondly a feasible alternative course of action must have been available. To remove the problem from personality, a third criterion must be that the policy in question should be that of a group, not an individual ruler. . . .

—Barbara W. Tuchman, *The March of Folly* (1984)

A Note on the Series

Psychiatry is in a state of flux. The excitement springs in part from internal changes, such as the development and official acceptance (at least in the U.S.A.) of an operationalized, multiaxial classification system of behavioral disorders (the DSM-III), the increasing sophistication of methods to measure abnormal human behavior and the impressive expansion of biological and psychological treatment modalities. Exciting developments are also taking place in fields relating to psychiatry; in molecular (brain) biology, genetics, brain imaging, drug development, epidemiology, experimental psychology, to mention only a few striking examples.

More generally speaking, psychiatry is moving, still relatively slowly, but irresistibly, from a more philosophical, contemplative orientation, to that of an empirical science. From the fifties on, biological psychiatry has been a major catalyst of that process. It provided the mother discipline with a third cornerstone, i.e., neurobiology, the other two being psychology and medical sociology. In addition, it forced the profession into the direction of standardization of diagnoses and of assessment of abnormal behavior. Biological psychiatry provided psychiatry not only with a new basic science and with new treatment modalities, but also with the tools, the methodology and the mentality to operate within the confines of an empirical science, the only framework in which a medical discipline can survive.

In other fields of psychiatry, too, one discerns a gradual trend towards scientification. Psychological treatment techniques are standardized and manuals developed to make these skills more easily

vii

transferable. Methods registering treatment outcome—traditionally used in the behavioral/cognitive field—are now more and more requested and, hence, developed for dynamic forms of psychotherapy as well. Social and community psychiatry, until the sixties more firmly rooted in humanitarian ideals and social awareness than in empirical studies, profited greatly from its liaison with the social sciences and the expansion of psychiatric epidemiology.

Let there be no misunderstanding. Empiricism does *not imply* that it is only the measurable that counts. Psychiatry would be mutilated if it would neglect that which is not yet capturable in numbers and probably never will be. It *does imply* that what is measurable should be measured. Progress in psychiatry is dependent on ideas and on experiment. Their linkage is inseparable.

This monograph series, published under the auspices of the Department of Psychiatry of the Albert Einstein College of Medicine/Montefiore Medical Center, is meant to keep track of important developments in our profession, to summarize what has been achieved in particular fields, and to bring together the viewpoints obtained from disparate vantage points—in short, to capture some of the excitement ongoing in modern psychiatry, both in its clinical and experimental dimensions. Our Department hosts the Series, but naturally welcomes contributions from others.

Bernie Mazel is not only the publisher of this series, but it was he who generated the idea—an ambitious plan which, however, we all feel is worthy of pursuit. The edifice of psychiatry is impressive, but still somewhat flawed in its foundations. May this Series contribute to consolidation of its infrastructure.

—HERMAN M. VAN PRAAG, M.D., PH.D.
Silverman Professor and Chairman
Department of Psychiatry
Albert Einstein College of Medicine
Montefiore Medical Center
Bronx, New York

Contents

Preface

I had the good fortune to start my career in psychiatry in the late fifties when this discipline was about to be shaken by two major revolutions—one biological and the other psychological. Fortuitously, a variety of drugs were discovered with psychotropic actions: LSD, minute amounts of which induced psychotic features without clouding consciousness; drugs effective in certain types of depression; antipsychotic drugs; the benzodiazepines, reducing anxiety quite selectively; and lithium, a true prophylactic agent in episodic mood disorders. This amazing spectacle gave the impulse to a revival of the study of biological determinants of abnormal behavior and of the means to treat them via direct intervention in the brain. As accurate description and ascertainment of the object of study was an absolute prerequisite for studies of this kind, the biological revolution in psychiatry was accompanied by a renewed interest in the diagnosis, differential diagnosis, and assessment of abnormal behavior. Biological psychiatry is the single most important factor in the revival of psychopathological research in the past three decades.

The second revolution was psychotherapeutic in nature. Until well into the fifties long-term, individual, dynamic psychotherapy was *the* treatment modality in psychiatry, and psychoanalysis was the absolute gold standard of psychotherapy. Then, almost simultaneously with the biological discoveries, the psychotherapeutic sky opened up. New strategies were introduced, most notably the behavioral and the cognitive techniques. The sacrosanctity of the individual was relativised when group, family, and couple approaches developed, signifying a salutary broadening of the psychotherapeutic horizon.

My career as clinician and researcher was profoundly influenced by these developments (Chapter 1). In research, diagnosis and biology of mental disorders have been my major areas of interest. As a clinician and teacher, I have strongly emphasized the importance of judging the psychiatric patient both as an individual and as a social being, as well as the need to include intrapersonal, interpersonal, and societal processes in diagnostic and therapeutic considerations.

In this book I speak as a researcher and will reflect on developments in our discipline from the formative years of modern biological psychiatry onwards. Diagnosis and classification are placed in the center, quintessential as they are for successful biological research in psychiatry. I will linger on what I see as the negative side of these developments rather than on the progress they produced. My main concerns are of three sorts.

First, they relate to the taxonomy as proposed by the third and subsequent editions of the Diagnostic and Statistical Manual of the American Psychiatric Association (DSM). The acceptance of a standardized and operationalized diagnostic system of psychiatric disorders in the USA and much of the rest of the world was a major step forward. The way the principle was put into practice, however, I consider to be disastrous for psychiatric research in general and for biological research in particular (Part I).

Moreover, I am concerned about the revival of classical nosology, generating an ever expanding system of discrete and defined "disorders" that actually seem largely the products of our own making (Part II).

I am, finally, uneasy about the overreliance on the easily objectifiable phenomena in diagnosing behavioral disorders, at the expense of the subjective domains of psychopathology. This has initiated a regrettable impoverishment of the diagnostic process (Part III).

I am not a pessimist reveling in misfortunes; not a reactionary obstructing progress; not a cynic who mistakes destructive criticism for scientific creativity. Why, then, do I dwell on the adverse effects of the biological revolution? The reason is that I consider those effects to be scientifically dangerous. Revolutions might ultimately seriously harm, even destroy, their own objectives.

It was, thus, not disappointment that made me write this treatise, but the wish to further the scientific maturation of our profession, a process I do thoroughly admire.

Abbreviations used in this book are: DA (dopamine), 5-HT (5-hydroxytryptamine, serotonin), NA (noradrenaline), MA (monoamine), CA (catecholamines), HVA (homovanillic acid), 5-HIAA (5-hydroxyindoleacetic acid), MHPG (3-methoxy-4-hydroxyphenylglycol), DOPA (dihydroxyphenylalanine), 5-HTP (5-hydroxytryptophan), PCPA (para-chlorophenylalanine), MCPP (m-chlorphenylpiperazine), DMI (desmethylimipramine), CNS (central nervous system), CSF (cerebrospinal fluid).

—1—

Self-Portrait

1. PROLOGUE

This book is a reflection of the ideas that have shaped my academic life and, taken as a whole, make up my professional identity. My professional viewpoints and corresponding goals were set early on in my career, actually in the first years of my residency. I have cultivated and elaborated them, but I have adhered to the basic tenets unswervingly. Before I clarify my credo, let me first in a few rough strokes paint the circumstances that molded it.

2. CIRCUMSTANCES

When I started my residency in early 1958, research, that is to say, empirical research, was virtually nonexistent in psychiatry. Psychiatry's knowledge base had two major components.

The *first* was philosophy, by which I mean a system of theories, often brilliant, daring, and thought-provoking, in essence based on individual case histories, but going far beyond the scope of the original observations. Freud (depth psychology), Jaspers (phenomenology), and Binswanger (anthropology) were the undisputed trustees of that body of knowledge.

The *second* component of the psychiatric knowledge base went back to Kraepelin. It comprised the results of often keen and detailed clinical observation of cohorts of patients over long time periods.

The masters had made major contributions, the followers were often bogged down in fruitless discussions of unsystematized observations, made without operationalized criteria in highly selected

1

populations. Psychiatrists of psychoanalytic persuasion diagnosed in a strictly individualized, nongeneralizable manner, geared almost exclusively towards psychogenesis and largely disregarding symptomatology. Psychopathologists, spiritual descendants of Kraepelin, stood on the other extreme. They were obsessed by symptoms, often at the expense of considerations about their (psycho)genesis. Symptoms had the tendency to be overvalued and to assume a pathognomonic weight they actually do not have. Diagnoses were often incomplete, not standardized, and not based on operationalized criteria. The result was a confusion of tongues that seriously detracted from psychiatry's scientific credibility. By and large, the profession was thought-oriented, rather than action-oriented. The blatant lack of research was rationalized and covered up by an overemphasis on the heterogeneity of mankind in both health and disease, precluding, so it was asserted, any valid generalizations about (abnormal) human behavior.

On the one hand, I felt at ease in this literary, philosophical setting. It provided the study of abnormal behavior with a dimension that was absent in the rest of medicine and that I had sorely missed. On the other hand, the interminable tattle, the unwavering reliance on words rather than on facts, the plethora of theories, and the readiness to heap one hypothesis on the other and to consider these edifices as bastions instead of houses of cards made me profoundly uncomfortable. As is the case for other medical disciplines, empirical research is the lifeline of psychiatry, without which it will never reach maturation, will never become accepted in medical circles, and will progressively lose ground to neighboring disciplines that do esteem research, such as neurology and experimental psychology.

3. FIRST DOMAIN OF CONCERN: DIAGNOSIS

3.1. Standardization/Operationalization of Diagnosis and Assessment of Abnormal Behavior

Understandably, then, my first domain of concern was diagnosis and my first order of priority was standardization of diagnosis and assessment of abnormal behavior. During the first year of my residency in 1958, prompted by a research interest in mood disorders,

I proposed a standardized and operationalized classification system for depression (van Praag, 1962). Assessment instruments at that time were few. The Hamilton Scale for Depression had just been introduced, but did not allow for syndromal differences to be measured. It occurred to me at the time that no one had tried to standardize *the* instrument of psychiatric examination: the interview. So we decided to do so and published in 1965 the first standardized, structured interview for the recognition of various syndromal types of depression (van Praag, Uleman & Spitz, 1965).

Today, those activities appear rather commonplace. In the late fifties and early sixties, they were perceived as sacrilegious. I was accused of destroying psychiatry; the methods I advocated would damage the very roots of psychiatry that had been so carefully cultivated in the years gone by.

3.2. Multi-axial Diagnoses

Another concern I entertained in those years had to do with the structure of psychiatric classification. The taxonomic ideal at the time was strictly Kraepelinian: a categorical diagnostic system of discrete and separable disorders, each with its own etiology, symptomatology, and course. Textbooks were organized that way, each chapter discussing a separate disorder. It was understood, if not stated outright, that the clinical boundaries drawn reflected specific underlying pathophysiological processes. Almost automatically these alleged processes became the target of biological research.

Early on, I had grave difficulties in accommodating to this viewpoint. In day to day practice I rarely saw textbook cases; instead, patients usually showed (parts of) several syndromes. It was obvious that etiological factors did not reliably predict symptoms, nor did a particular syndrome indicate a particular etiology. I observed that the same syndrome could occur in all grades of severity, that its duration is likewise a variable, that its long-term outcome is hard to predict, and that the relation between personality structure and psychopathology does not seem to follow simple rules. When one used psychotropic drugs, it soon became obvious that existing diagnoses were relatively poor predictors of therapeutic response. Yes, schizophrenia might respond to neuroleptics, but so do other types of psychoses. Imipramine is an antidepressant, but was shown to be effective in panic disorder as well. Monoamine oxidase inhibitors are helpful in endogenous depression, but likewise in atypical depression.

In short, I felt that the textbook chapters delineated castles in the sky instead of real entities. If diagnostic criteria were conscientiously applied, many patients would not be classifiable. One could not escape the conclusion that patients were often forced into existing diagnostic boxes. As far as I was concerned, that amounted to diagnostic malpractice. This practice was excused, however, through introduction of hierarchical decision rules. Behavioral disorders were ranked according to severity. If a higher-ranking disorder was diagnosed, lower-order pathology could be ignored. A deus ex machina that never appealed to me.

Nosological skepticism became, thus, part of my professional identity. As for the units of classification, delineation of syndromes is as far as one can legitimately go (van Praag & Leijnse, 1965). Other clinically relevant variables such as severity, duration, course, and etiology should be assessed and documented independently of each other and of the syndromal diagnosis. I became a very early and staunch advocate of multi-axial classification (van Praag, 1962).

3.3. Functional Psychopathology

It will come as no surprise, then, that the ideas of Claude Bernard appealed more to me, even as a student, than those of Virchov, the prominent 19th century pathologist who provided medicine with the foundations of a nosological taxonomy. It was he who fostered Kraepelin's dream of a nosological psychiatry of which (neuro)pathology would be the godfather. Bernard, on the other hand, was the protagonist of physiology. The understanding of physical disease, he maintained, is predicated on our ability to analyze and measure disturbances in functional systems such as the cardiovascular, digestive, and respiratory systems. Ascertaining dysfunction presupposes familiarity with normal functions. Physiology thus became a major force in the advancement of medicine. Bodily diseases are seldom confined to one functional system, but rather consist of a composite of dysfunctions in various organ systems. Thus, for a functional analysis of a particular medical disorder, the boundaries set by nosology can easily obstruct our view.

Psychiatry would gain, I contended, by adopting the Bernardian model. Psychopathological symptoms are not entities sui generis. They are the behavioral manifestations of underlying psychological dysfunctions that are seldom, if ever, typical for a particular disorder. As it is in medicine, analyzing and measuring the (in this case, psychological) dysfunctions that constitute the basic elements of a behavioral disorder is a crucial step in a comprehensive diagnosis and conceivably a productive starting point for human brain and behavior research. I called this approach *functional psychopathology*, substituting the term "functional" for "physiological" because the latter inevitably refers to bodily processes. A comprehensive psychiatric diagnosis, then, in my evolving conception became a three-tiered structure.

Tier one is the nosological diagnosis representing no more than a broad general diagnostic outline.

Tier two depicts the syndromal composition of the disorder and an assessment of other relevant variables, such as severity, duration, course, and etiology on independent axes.

Tier three represents the dissection of the syndrome into its basic components—the psychological dysfunctions—and includes a detailed assessment of functions that are disturbed and those that are still intact.

I came to believe that a three-tiered diagnostic system would substantially contribute to the scientific maturation of psychiatry.

4. SECOND DOMAIN OF CONCERN: THE BRAIN AND BEHAVIOR MIRACLE

Most surprising to me in those early days of my career was psychiatry's blatant lack of interest in the brain. Yes, we had to perform physicals and carry out lumbar puncture in all patients with severe psychopathology, and an electroencephalogram was routine. The rationale of all these interventions was exclusion or demonstration of what was called "organicity," a term alluding to severe morphological brain injury: a tumor, infection, hemorrhage, and so on. Most psychiatric cases, however, were "functional": the depressions, the schizophrenias, anxiety disorders, personality disorders, addiction disorders, but one had to keep in mind, so we learned, that in sporadic cases organic brain disease masqueraded as a functional disorder.

These "functional" psychiatric disorders were considered to develop somehow beyond the brain. They were thought to be the product of intrapsychic rather than intracerebral processes. Mainstream psychiatry, at that time, dismissed the brain.

I had the good fortune of passing through my residency when the psychotropic agents were revolutionizing psychiatry. These agents clearly demonstrated that "functional" interference in the brain could induce significant changes in "functional" behavioral disorders. The prophylactic potential of lithium in unipolar and bipolar depression had just been demonstrated, followed by the discovery of the neuroleptics. In the first month of my residency, the group of the antidepressants was introduced, with no fewer than two dissimilar prototypes: imipramine, the first tricyclic antidepressant, and iproniazid, the first MAO inhibitor. A few years later, the benzodiazepines initiated a new generation of anxiolytics. Psychotropic drugs became the core of testable brain and behavior hypotheses; LSD's effect on serotonin generated the serotonin hypothesis of schizophrenia. Dopamine receptor blockade by neuroleptics prompted the dopamine hypothesis of schizophrenia. The ability of antidepressants to increase monoamine availability in the brain became a cornerstone of the monoamine hypotheses of depression. I was profoundly moved by these developments intellectually, even emotionally. The study of brain and behavior became my major research interest and pushing biological psychiatry from an underdog position into mainstream psychiatry became a major goal.

As a child of my time, my point of departure was initially nosology. We studied vital (endogenous) depression and schizophrenia, but soon became dissatisfied. Diagnostic categories in psychiatry seemed to be no more than broad basins containing a variety of more or less related syndromes, not genuine disease entities. Nosological taxonomy seemed an unreliable partner for biological psychiatric research, largely responsible for the fact that much of the "biology" uncovered in mental disorders, seemed to be devoid of diagnostic specificity.

As a result, I moved from a categorical to a dimensional vantage point. Our goal became not the finding of nosological markers and, eventually, causes of, for example, schizophrenia, panic disorder, and antisocial personality disorder, but rather the search for the biological determinants of psychological dysfunctions such as mood dysregulation, heightened anxiety, anhedonia, lack of drive, and disturbances in impulse control (van Praag & Leijnse, 1965; van Praag et al., 1975, 1987c).

This strategy proved to be much more productive than the nosological approach. In this context, one example may suffice. Serotonin (5-hydroxytryptamine; 5-HT) disorders were first discovered in depression. They could not be linked to a particular type of depression, nor could the concept of a 5-HT depression—a depression characterized by its pathogenesis, i.e. a cerebral 5-HT disorder—be made plausible. Today, it seems likely that the 5-HT ergic be a dysregulation in depression relates to components of the depression, particularly to anxiety and increased aggression, components that might or might not be prominent in depression and which are by no means specific for depression.

Conducting brain and behavior research, I was earmarked as a "biological psychiatrist," a distinction I never felt comfortable with. *First,* because I did not want to unduly "biologize" and objectify psychiatry. My inaugural professorial address in 1968 was entitled: "The complementary relation between biological and psychodynamic psychiatry" (van Praag, 1969). Though devoted to the study of brain and behavior, I have, at the same time, never ceased to caution against the dangers inherent in this approach: coarsening of diagnosis; preoccupation with the obvious; disregard for the subjective constituents of the psychopathological spectrum; horizontalism, i.e. a system of diagnosing mainly grounded on symptoms and detached from etiology, particularly from determinants of a psychological nature; oversimplification, i.e. classification of roughly comparable but actually dissimilar syndromes into broad, general categories (e.g. van Praag 1971, 1972, 1979a, 1979b, 1981, 1986c, 1990a).

A *second* reason to feel uncomfortable with the designation "biological psychiatrist" was that it seemed to imply disinterest in psychological and social determinants of abnormal behavior. In my case, that implication was wrong! In 1964, I qualified the distinction between "biologists" and "psychicists" as a fallacy. I contended that psychiatry should distinguish, as the rest of medicine does, between *etiology* and *pathogenesis* (van Praag & Leijnse, 1964). Abnormal behavior presupposes disturbed cerebral functioning, elucidation of which would reveal the *pathogenesis* of the disorder. The disruption of cerebral functioning, in its turn, can be caused by a multitude of factors, biological, psychological, and social in nature, constituting the *etiology* of the disorder. Both pathogenesis and etiology are of legitimate concern to psychiatry.

The separation of etiology and pathogenesis in the exploration of the origins of mental disorder prevented me from becoming a biological diehard and made me into a convinced "generalist."

5. THIRD DOMAIN OF CONCERN: PSYCHOTHERAPEUTIC ECLECTICISM

Defining myself as a generalist had practical consequences. I could not but regard psychological interventions as an inalienable component of the psychiatric armamentarium. Psychotropic drugs are aimed at normalization of the neuronal dysfunctions underlying abnormal patterns of behavior. Psychotherapy, on the other hand, is meant to eliminate or alleviate etiological factors of a psychological nature. Drugs are unable to do that. Even in a biological utopia, I wrote in 1964 (van Praag & Leijnse, 1964), in which brain and behavior relationships would have been fully clarified and the tools developed to remedy every set of neuronal dysfunctions, psychotherapy would remain an indispensable and, hence, respectable therapeutic strategy.

When I entered the profession, psychological intervention was, practically speaking, synonymous with long-term, individual, psychodynamically oriented psychotherapy. The present could be understood if the past was known. Understanding the past was key in the regulation of dysfunctional behavior. I felt intuitively that this view, though enlightening, was unduly restrictive. Being a war child and a Holocaust survivor, I had witnessed that there are other forces than those historically determined that shape human behavior. Reward and punishment, for instance, and fright and relief. I had seen the behavior of my friends change dramatically when the Jews were outlawed soon after the German invasion of Holland. Friendship turned into detachment; intimacy gave way to estrangement. Self-protection transformed perceptions as well as behavior on very short notice. I got to know mind-set as another powerful force in shaping human behavior. In the concentration camp, hope, even hope against better judgment, had significant survival value; defeatism, on the other hand, proved to be a sure way to death.

And, finally, I had learned that human interaction is as revealing a way to self-knowledge as introspection is. The group to which one belongs mirrors significant provinces of one's inner life and can, thus, serve as a vehicle to reshape individual behavior according to social expectations. What seemed to be true for normal individuals in abnormal circumstances should also be valid for individuals behaving abnormally in relatively normal circumstances.

Then, soon after I finished my residency, the psychotherapeutic horizon suddenly opened up. Strategies other than interpretation and insight, such as behavioral modification and cognitive therapy, were introduced. The involvement of others in the treatment process, such as family members or other patients, acquired legitimacy as therapeutic techniques. For me, this was a major revolution, one of the same magnitude as the psychopharmacological one.

With a spectrum of techniques now at our disposal, training in psychotherapy should be broadened accordingly. A psychotherapist should master at least several psychotherapeutic strategies in order to be able to meet the needs of the patient, rather than requiring that the patient adjust to the technique the therapist happens to master. Hence, psychiatric residents should be thoroughly exposed both to psychopharmacology and to several modalities of psychotherapy. Training should not put the psychiatrist under restraint. I have subscribed to this adage all my life.

6. FOURTH DOMAIN OF CONCERN: THE STATUS OF PSYCHIATRY

In the medical community, psychiatry was not held in great esteem at the time of my residency. It tended to be qualified as a profession based on words rather than on facts, versed in theory formation rather than in empirical investigation, speaking in tongues rather than in medically intelligible phrases, unreliable in diagnoses, and in large measure impotent when it came to treatment. In truth, psychiatry was the black sheep in the family of medicine.

I found that a most uncomfortable situation to which I never could acquiesce and to whose reversal I devoted a good deal of energy. Closer association of psychiatry with the rest of medicine could be accomplished, I felt, via various routes. Consultation psychiatry had to be developed as our advanced bastion in medicine. Standardization of diagnoses and assessment would make psychiatry more accept- able. Biological psychiatry, furthermore, could generate the proper vocabulary and ambiance for rapprochement; for that reason alone, it should be hailed.

For the same reason, I considered the marriage of psychiatry and neurology—still intact at the time of my residency—to be of fun- damental importance. In the seventies, however, the trustees of both professional organizations decided to separate and to virtually uncouple training in neurology and psychiatry, precisely at the juncture when study of the living brain started to become relevant for psychiatry; when psychopharmacology was blossoming; when the neuropsychi- atric interface began to grow. The decision of our elders, therefore, I considered to be of such stupidity that every effort should be made to undo it and to train psychiatrists in such a way as to free them from fear of the body in general and of the brain in particular, as well as from feelings of alienation while sojourning in the medical com- munity. This is another training goal I have pursued in my academic career.

7. FIFTH DOMAIN OF CONCERN: EQUAL THERAPEUTIC OPPORTUNITY

The last component of my credo pertains to patient care. To my consternation, I learned early on in my training that in psychiatry a broad distinction was made between "good" and "bad" patients. "Good" were those deemed suitable for longer-term, insight- oriented psychotherapy. To qualify for this designation, one had to be fairly young, quite intelligent, and introspective, and deliber- ately chosen for this form of treatment. "Bad," on the other hand, were the somewhat older patients, not bountifully blessed with intelligence, seemingly not so self-reflective, and not eagerly embracing this treatment modality. In other words, the patient had to fit the treatment, rather than the treatment being adjusted to the patient.

This attitude had rather disastrous effects. Large groups of psychiatric patients were seriously neglected therapeutically, among them the chronic schizophrenics, the drug addicts and alcoholics, the organically disabled. Those psychiatrists who dared to defy the *Zeitgeist* and decided to take care of the therapeutically dispossessed were looked down on as professional misfits. Psychiatric hospitals were frequently not much more than storehouses for the more seriously disturbed. The antipsychiatric uprising in the sixties and seventies woke up a profession enmeshed in doctrines justifying unethical behavior. The awakening was rough, allied with harmful side effects, but in essence it was needed.

Another surprising circumstance at the time was the self-image of psychiatrists as healers. Healing is a process leading to restoration or institution of health. Indeed, psychoanalytic theory considered intrapsychic conflicts originating in early developmental phases as *the* fundamental cause of mental disturbance and psychoanalytic therapy as a causal treatment. A treatment apparently suited to eliminate the cause of a disease cures. Those healing fantasies led psychiatrists to look down upon treatment forms openly avowing that adjustment, not healing, was their primary aim; adjustment to psychological defects. The most poignant target of the condescension was rehabilitation, encompassing such therapeutic methods as: social skill learning, training in daily living and vocational rehabilitation.

I soon discovered that we in psychiatry were fooling ourselves. We seldom cure; we treat and, in many cases, are remarkably successful if all therapeutic modalities available are used without prejudice. Greater understanding of the psychological processes that made us what we are may alleviate psychic distress; dysfunctional behaviors can be unlearned and replaced by more adequate behaviors; self-defeating thoughts can be corrected; surviving psychological functions can be strengthened, and those affected can be rehabilitated. Symptoms diminish, quality of life is enhanced, a labile equilibrium is established. Relapse is common, as it is in the rest of medicine. "Bad" patients are the scapegoats of therapeutically impotent psychiatrists.

Psychiatry in those days was a narcissistic, self-centered discipline. The self-glorification at the expense of the patient's needs was embarrassing. I have honestly tried to resist the temptation of exclusivism.

8. EPILOGUE

These, then, are the major components of the credo that budded during my residency years and has guided my professional life ever since—the life of a convinced generalist with a profound interest in the brain and behavior enigma, the life of someone who has witnessed the most abhorrent of human pursuits, yet never stopped believing in the plasticity of the mind. Thus, for me psychiatry has been a spiritual and intellectual home of great delight.

In this book I reflect on the biological revolution in psychiatry with both awe and disquietude. It is both a loyalty pledge and a critique. It is partly a retrospective and partly a look ahead. It does not, however, get stalled in ambivalence. The adverse side effects of that revolution are set forth, but at the same time I outline ways to avoid the pitfalls. The credo laid down in this chapter should clarify the provenance of my viewpoints.

SECTION I

The Right Destination, But the Wrong Direction

—2—

Codified Disorder in
Psychiatric Taxonomy

In 1958, when I started my residency training in psychiatry, diagnostic confusion reigned in the realm of behavioral disorders. Diagnostic concepts were not operationalized, nomenclature was not standardized, and no taxonomy was generally accepted. This made systematic research virtually impossible, dependent as it is on precise definition and demarcation of the object of study. What is the situation today, some 30 years later? Now we work under the patronage of the DSM-III classification of behavioral disorders, a system in which diagnostic concepts *are* operationalized and nomenclature *is* standardized; it is a system that *is* officially accepted in the U.S. and de facto in numerous countries all over the world. Did that system provide order where chaos reigned? The answer has to be in the negative and I will explain this conclusion on the basis of two examples—depression and schizophrenia.

1. SYNDROMAL FOGGINESS

1.1. Depression

The DSM-III holds the view of depression as being syndromally heterogeneous and recognizes two basic entities: major depression and dysthymic disorder. In delineating these entities, it utilizes the "choice-principle": No fixed set of symptoms has to be present in order to qualify for either diagnosis. All that is needed are y symptoms out of a series y + x, no matter which ones. As a consequence, the same term covers a diversity of depressive syndromes. Moreover,

15

TABLE 2:1
Symptomatological Characteristics of Depression According to DSM-III (1980)

MAJOR DEPRESSION	DYSTHYMIC DISORDER
Dysphoric mood	Depressed mood
or	or
Anhedonia	Anhedonia
+	+
$\frac{4}{8}$ symptoms	$\frac{3}{13}$ symptoms

SIMILAR SYMPTOMS

Anhedonia	Anhedonia
Loss of energy; fatigue	Low energy level or chronic tiredness
Insomnia or hypersomnia	Insomnia or hypersomnia
Diminished ability to think or concentrate	Decreased attention, concentration, or ability to think clearly
Suicidal ideation or suicide attempt	Recurrent thoughts of death and suicide
Feelings of worthlessness, self-reproach, or excessive guilt	Feelings of inadequacy, loss of self-esteem, or self-depreciation
Psychomotor agitation or retardation (not only subjectively)	Feels slowed down or restless

DIFFERENTIATING SYMPTOMS

Poor or increased appetite	—
Weight loss or gain	—
—	Irritability or excessive anger
—	Tearfulness or crying
—	Decreased effectiveness at school, work, and home, and social withdrawal

van Praag, 1989

the majority of symptoms listed under major depression are similar to those listed under dysthymic disorder; discriminating symptoms are few, both in the DSM-III and the DSM-III-R (Tables 2:1 and 2:2). The proposed dichotomy resembles two poorly focused slides, projected simultaneously and largely overlapping. The symptom pattern of the depressive episodes in cyclothymia is identical with that of major depression. Obviously, clarity is fictitious.

This state of affairs is detrimental for research, especially for biological research, as well as for clinical practice. In biological psychiatry, the search is for the biological underpinnings of specific syndromes or specific psychopathological dimensions, as well as for specific biological

TABLE 2:2
Symptomatological Characteristics of Depression
According to DSM-III-R (1987)

MAJOR DEPRESSION	DYSTHYMIC DISORDER
5/9 symptoms at least one of them either	Depressed mood
	+
1) depressed mood or 2) anhedonia	2/6 symptoms

SIMILAR SYMPTOMS

Insomnia or hypersomnia	Insomnia or hypersomnia
Fatigue or loss of energy	Low energy or fatigue
Feelings of worthlessness or excessive guilt	Low self-esteem
Diminished concentration or indecisiveness	Poor concentration or difficulty making decisions
Recurrent thoughts of death, or suicide plan, or suicide attempt	Feelings of hopelessness
Decrease or increase of appetite; weight loss or gain	Poor appetite or overeating

DIFFERENTIATING SYMPTOMS

Anhedonia	(All dysthymic symptoms feature in
Psychomotor retardation or agitation	major depressive syndrome)

van Praag, 1989

interventions to eliminate them. These goals are ill served by diagnostic ambiguities. For the practitioner, the DSM system may seem handy, but it does not serve him or her well either. Psychotropic drugs acquire ever greater biochemical specificity and, thus, probably a more narrowly focused therapeutic action. Working with unfocused diagnostic concepts, one could easily fail to discern specific therapeutic indications. It is true that many depressed patients do not fit rigidly defined diagnostic concepts, but it is better to recognize that and categorize them for the time being as "mixed states," or as "double depressions," or as "not yet classifiable with some degree of certainty" than to use labels that for all intents and purposes are meaningless and only provide pseudo-certainty.

When in the early sixties I introduced the operationalized concepts of vital and personal depression, I rejected the "choice-principle," defined these syndromes rigorously (Table 2:3), and categorized the patients in between the endpoints of the spectrum as mixed depres-

TABLE 2:3
Symptomatological Characterization of Vital (Endogenous, Melancholic) and Personal
(Neurotic, Dysthymic) Depression

Vital Depression	Personal Depression
1. DEPRESSED MOOD	DEPRESSED MOOD
Meaningless: i.e. no, for patient, understandable connection between mood and precipitant (if any)	Experiences congruence between mood and life experiences or personality make-up
Often experienced "Leib-nah" rather than "Geist-nah"	Experienced as "Geist-nah"
2. MOTOR DISTURBANCES	MOTOR DISTURBANCES
Retardation	Agitation (usually not very pronounced)
Agitation	
Both	
3. SLOWING DOWN	THOUGHT PROCESSING: UNDISTURBED
Thought	
Time experience	
4. ANHEDONIA	EMOTIONAL RESPONSIVITY UNDISTURBED
	(Sometimes depersonalization)
5. SOMATIC DISTURBANCES	SOMATIC DISTURBANCES
Fatigue, lack of energy	Somatic anxiety equivalents (e.g. palpitations, atypical precordial pain)
Decreased appetite	
Early morning awakening	Multiple sleep disturbances
Disturbed sexual functions (impotence; decreased libido; disturbances of menstrual cycle)	Sexual functions not disturbed
6. DIURNAL FLUCTUATION	NO OR IRREGULAR FLUCTUATIONS
7. ANXIETY	MANIFEST ANXIETY
Not manifest in retarded vital depression	
Manifest in agitated vital depression, often linked to delusional thinking (e.g. poverty, guilt, hypochondriasis)	
8. SIGNS OF MANIFEST OUTWARD DIRECTED HOSTILITY NOT PROMINENT	IRRITABILITY AND MANIFEST HOSTILITY
9. TAEDIUM VITAE	TAEDIUM VITAE
10. INABILITY TO CRY	CRYING SPELLS
11. GUILT FEELINGS; SELF-REPROACH	FEELINGS OF INADEQUACY; BLAMES OTHERS
12. ONCE GENERATED, THE COURSE IS INDEPENDENT OF PRECIPITANTS	PRESENCE OF SYMPTOMS CLOSELY RELATED TO PERPETUATION OF PRECIPITATING FACTORS

sions (van Praag et al., 1965; van Praag, 1989). Vital and personal depressions are the specified and operationalized equivalents of the syndromes described until then under the headings of endogenous and neurotic depression. The best fitting DSM-III diagnoses are major depression, melancholic type, and dysthymic disorder, respectively. In Chapter 3, I will discuss these depression concepts more extensively.

1.2. Schizophrenia

Syndromal fogginess is by no means confined to the group of depressions. Schizophrenia and the group of the schizophrenia-like psychoses provide other striking examples (Table 2:4) (see also Chapters 4 and 5). I use the term schizophrenia-like psychoses to capture the DSM-III-R diagnoses of schizophreniform disorder, schizoaffective disorder, delusional disorder, and brief reactive psychosis. The rationale for the term schizophrenia-like is that in these disorders, as in schizophrenia, a variety of psychotic symptoms occur with intact consciousness as opposed to organic psychoses in which consciousness tends to suffer.

The symptomatological criteria for schizophrenia and *schizophreniform disorder* are identical. One qualifies for the diagnosis *delusional disorder* if delusions are present, nonbizarre in nature, or hallucinations, considered to be nonprominent. In addition, behavior should not be obviously odd or bizarre. On exactly the same grounds, however, the diagnosis schizophrenia or schizophreniform disorder is permitted. The diagnosis *brief reactive psychosis* is based on the same symptoms as those regarded indicative of schizophrenia, the only discriminating feature being emotional turmoil. The differential diagnostic power of that criterium is not great. Identifying schizophrenia—even chronic schizophrenia—with flat affect and emotional blunting results in a misconception. In the earlier phases of schizophrenia, episodes of psychosis may generate profound emotional turmoil and in the more advanced stages of the disease emotional upheaval is by no means uncommon.

Schizophrenia and *schizoaffective disorder* are discriminated through cross-sectional analysis of symptom patterns, the latter diagnosis being appropriate if schizophrenia and affective disorder occur con-

TABLE 2:4
DSM-III-R Symptomatological Criteria for Schizophrenia and Other Schizophrenia-like Psychoses

Schizophrenia	Schizophreniform Disorder	Brief Reactive Psychosis	Delusional Disorder	Schizoaffective Disorder
Either (1), (2), or (3) (1) At least two of the following symptoms: -Delusions -Hallucinations -Incoherence or loosening of associations -Catatonic behavior -Flat or inappropriate affect (2) Bizarre delusions (3) Prominent hallucinations	As in schizophrenia	Both (1) and (2) (1) At least one of the following symptoms: -Delusions -Hallucinations -Incoherence or loosening of associations -Catatonic or disorganized behavior (2)Emotional turmoil	Both (1) and (2) (1) Non-bizarre delusions Nonprominent auditory or visual hallucinations might be present (2) Behavior is not obviously odd or bizarre	Both (1) and (2) (1) Same symptoms as in schizophrenia (2) At some time major depression or manic syndrome concurrent with schizophrenia

TABLE 2:5
Symptom Overlap in Schizophrenia and Major Depression

DSM-III-R Criteria for Major Depression	Does that Symptom Commonly Occur in Schizophrenia?
Minimal 5 symptoms, one being depressed mood *or* anhedonia	
Depressed mood	Yes
Anhedonia	Yes
Weight loss	No
Sleep disorders	No
Psychomotor symptoms	Yes
Fatigue or loss of energy	Yes
Feelings of worthlessness or guilt	No★
Diminished ability to think and concentrate	Yes
Suicidal ideations	Yes

★Though many young schizophrenics feel very embarrassed and handicapped by the disease, and the distinction with depressive feelings of worthlessness might be difficult.

currently. The differential diagnosis is, however, less obvious than it seems. First, major depression may occur in "nuclear schizophrenia" (Elk et al., 1986). Second, schizophrenic episodes can be accompanied by profound despondency and hopelessness. Thirdly, several components of major depression other than mood lowering are also observed in schizophrenia per se, particularly anhedonia, psychomotor symptoms, loss of energy, diminished ability to think and concentrate, and suicidal ideation. Actually, no less than six of the nine symptoms mentioned as indicative for major depression occur in schizophrenia as well (Table 2:5). Since only five out of those nine suffice for the diagnosis of major depression, the diagnostic decision of "pure schizophrenia" or schizophrenia concurrent with major depression, that is, schizoaffective disorder, can in a given case be wholly arbitrary. Fourthly, depression concurrent with or following a schizophrenic episode can be hard to distinguish from (residual) negative symptoms (Siris et al., 1988).

Of the few *subtypes of schizophrenia* distinguished in the DSM-III-R (Table 2:6), only the catatonic subtype stands clearly on its own, the mandatory presence of catatonic symptoms being the anchorpoint. The disorganized and undifferentiated subtypes largely overlap. Only one symptom differentiates the former from the latter and that is flat or grossly inappropriate affect. Chronic, severe forms of schizophre-

TABLE 2:6
DSM-III-R Symptomatological Criteria for Subtypes of Schizophrenia

Catatonic Type	Disorganized Type	Undifferentiated Type	Residual Type	Paranoid Type
Prominent catatonic symptoms	-Incoherence; marked loosening of association or grossly disorganized behavior -Flat or grossly inappropriate affect -Nonsystematized delusions or hallucinations	-Prominent delusions; hallucinations;	-No prominent psychotic symptoms, though nonprominent delusions and hallucinations might be present Incoherence or grossly disorganized behavior -Residual symptoms, such as social withdrawal, illogical thinking, and mild loosening of associations	-One or more systematized delusions or auditory hallucinations -No incoherence, marked loosening of association, flat or grossly inappropriate affect, catatonic behavior, or grossly disorganized behavior

nia might be meaningfully divided into forms with or without seriously disturbed emotionality, but nothing in the text seems to suggest that that is the viewpoint the DSM-III holds, nor does one find support for that viewpoint in the literature. The distinction seems fortuitous rather than deliberate. The paranoid subtype is characterized by systematized delusions or auditory hallucinations in the absence of other symptoms characteristic of schizophrenia. The overlap with the symptom pattern of delusional disorder is, thus, virtually 100 percent. The diagnosis of residual type of schizophrenia is made in the presence of two out of at least nine symptoms, while "typical" schizophrenic symptoms such as delusions, hallucinations, incoherence, or grossly disorganized behavior are absent, making this category the wastebasket of the various manifestations of chronic schizophrenia.

Again, syndromal fogginess is by no means confined to the group of depressions.

2. NOSOLOGICAL CURTAILMENTS

2.1. Depression

The DSM-III aspires to be more than a syndromal depression classification and aims at delineation of disease entities, not only characterized by symptoms but by criteria such as intensity, duration, and underlying personality structure as well. For example, dysthymic disorder is defined by symptoms as well as by mild intensity (at least less severe than major depression), chronicity, and disordered personality. The diagnosis of major depression, melancholic type, is justified when certain symptoms are present and when the depression is severe and the premorbid personality basically normal. Cyclothymia is defined as a chronic mood disorder of at least two years duration involving numerous hypomanic and depressive episodes. In other words, the DSM-III classification is firmly rooted in nosological soil. That soil is traditionally polluted with wishful thinking, i.e. the hope that mental disorders will turn out to be classifiable as neat, separable packages, each with its characteristic psychopathology, causation, and course.

I consider the nosological concept in depression classification as a mirage. Syndromal distinctions are as far as one can go (van Praag

& Leijnse, 1965). We demonstrated that factors like duration, intensity, and personality structure do not relate specifically to a particular depressive syndrome, but vary within one syndrome. Hence, they should be assessed on independent axes, that is, independent of syndromal diagnosis. I will illustrate this statement with three examples (van Praag, 1982a, 1989). (For a more extensive discussion, see Chapter 3.)

1. A syndromally mixed group of depressive patients was independently assessed by two clinicians, one determining the type of syndrome, the other the severity of the syndrome. The syndrome of vital depression (major depression, melancholic type) was shown to occur in all degrees of severity, from mild to very severe. The same turned out to be true for personal depression (dysthymic disorder). According to these data, severity is not a syndromal characteristic.

Symptomatologically, major depression and dysthymia are largely overlapping. The DSM-III made severity a major differential diagnostic criterion. According to our studies, however, this criterion has no validity. Assuming our data to be correct, mild major depression would not be distinguishable from dysthymia, nor severe dysthymia from major depression. *Ipso facto*, the depressive phase of cyclothymia is, in cross-sectional perspective, undistinguishable from dysthymia, since the only remaining difference is duration.

2. It is generally accepted that the duration of a vital (major) depressive episode varies tremendously from a few weeks to several years. We showed the same to be true for personal (dysthymic) depression. In 76 percent of patients diagnosed as such on syndromal grounds, the duration of the last depressive period had been less than a year, in 47 percent six months or less, and in 19 percent of the sample three months or less. The duration of the symptom-free (or symptom-reduced) intervals varied from less than a week to 6–12 months. Thus, it seems erroneous to define dysthymia as a chronic depression.

In cyclothymia, the depressive episodes are defined as being of short duration, but they can be similarly short-lived in dysthymia. This eliminates the last remaining criterion that distinguishes a dysthymic from a cyclothymic depressive episode.

3. Personality disorders are recognized as being very prevalent in dysthymia. We demonstrated that vital depressions (major depression, melancholic type) and mixed depressions are by no means immune. Studied after remission, "character-neurosis" scores in the two latter groups were substantially higher than in a control group. Personality disorder seems to be ubiquitous in depressive disorder and not restricted to a particular subtype. This observation has important implications. Therapeutic implications: major depression, melancholic type, in most cases, is as much a target for psychotherapy as it is for biological treatment. Research implications: biological variables found in major depression are not necessarily related to (features of) the depressive disorder, but they could be the biological underpinnings of the coexisting personality pathology. For many years this was an entirely ignored consideration in affective disorder research.

By attaching nosological strings to syndromal depression concepts, one condemns many a depressed patient to be described as Depressive Disorder not Otherwise Specified; this is tantamount to not being diagnosed at all.

2.2. Schizophrenia

Since symptomatological criteria utterly fail to separate the various diagnostic schizophrenia-(like) categories, the DSM-III introduces other criteria to typify them. Thus, the impression is created that we deal at least with the precursors of nosological entities, while, in fact, what is created is a would-be nosology. The criterion of *duration* is introduced to differentiate schizophrenia from schizophreniform disorder. A duration of six months of the psychosis is the watershed. It makes sense to differentiate psychoses that, despite treatment, take a more chronic course from those that are, with or without treatment, transient. The issue at stake, however, is whether the factor of duration makes schizophrenia better identifiable or better distinguishable from schizophrenia-like psychoses; the answer is, in both cases, in the negative. The traditional view of schizophrenia as an essentially chronic, deteriorating condition, the one that has been adopted by the DSM-III, has been seriously challenged. The outcome of schizophrenia tends to be relatively heterogenous even for those samples diagnosed prospectively (Harding & Strauss, 1984; Zubin et al., 1983; Moller et al., 1988).

The second reason why duration is of little help in identifying "true" schizophrenia is that a protracted course is by no means specific for schizophrenia. Brief psychotic reaction is comparable with the European concept of reactive or psychogenic psychoses save for what the prefix indicates. Schizophrenia-like psychoses seemingly unleashed by profound emotional distress are variable as to duration, may not resolve for months, and may even assume a chronic course (see Jauch & Carpenter, 1988a, 1988b for review).

The course of delusional disorder is likewise unpredictable. The disorder may quickly remit, take a protracted course, or become intermittent, in which case psychotic episodes are interspersed with remissions of variable duration. The prognosis of schizoaffective patients may be statistically better than of those originally diagnosed as schizophrenia, yet in a substantial percentage of cases the course is unfavorable, leading to personality damage and states of chronic psychosis (van Praag & Nijo, 1984; Berg et al., 1983; Coryell & Zimmerman, 1988b; Levitt & Tsuang, 1988; Marneros et al., 1989).

A second criterion used in the DSM-III (R) to individualize schizophrenia and schizophrenia-like psychoses is the occurrence of *life events preceding the psychoses*. It is a particularly important criterion in the delineation of brief reactive psychosis. In that disorder, the psychotic symptoms appear shortly after one or more events with what I have called "objective valence," that is, that would have been "markedly stressful to almost anyone in similar circumstances in that person's culture." Precipitants may be typical for that diagnostic category; the specificity of that criterion is low. The traditional view that schizophrenia develops insidiously and "out of the blue" is by no means invariably true. In 14 of a group of 34 patients, cross-sectionally diagnosed as "true schizophrenics," the psychosis had developed rather abruptly, i.e. in the course of one to six weeks and subsequent to an objective life event. If subjective life events were also taken into account, the number rose to 22.★ Over time, the correlation between subsequent psychoses and life events may lessen, but that might be so only at the surface. In the psychotic world, threatening events could conceivably be enacted of which we are not cognizant. In patients diagnosed as schizoaffective

---

★See Chapter 11, Section 6.3 for a discussion of "objective" and "subjective" life events.

disorder, life events preceding psychotic episodes were even more frequent than in schizophrenia; in delusional disorders less frequent, but by no means negligible (See Table 5:2, Chapter 5).

Prodromal and residual symptoms occupy a prominent differential diagnostic role in the DSM-III. For the diagnosis of schizophrenia, it is required that the active psychotic episode be preceded and followed by a phase of clear deterioration from a previous level of social and occupational functioning; the length of those phases is not specified. Though a break in the process of growth and development is not uncommon, particularly in young schizophrenics, this criterion is neither necessary nor sufficient for the diagnosis of schizophrenia. The same is true for the postpsychotic persistence of personality changes or residual symptoms. In the group of 34 schizophrenics cited above, the notorious break in the developmental curve had occurred in a little less than 50 percent of the patients; in the same percentage of patients, resolution of the psychosis was incomplete for at least one year after the acute symptoms had subsided. The two groups overlapped for 75 percent. Though approximately half as common, prodromal and residual symptoms do occur in patients who were and had been diagnosed as schizoaffective disorder and delusional disorder respectively. The diagnostic specificity of the criterion under discussion is clearly low.

Personality structure has not been given differential diagnostic weight in the DSM-III (R) diagnosis of schizophrenia and schizophrenia-like psychoses. Schizoid and schizotypal personality disorders are only some of the variety of personality disorders that might accompany schizophrenia. Moreover, a variety of premorbid personality disorders are also discernible in those suffering from the various types of schizophrenia-like psychoses.

In conclusion, the attempts to accentuate the borders between schizophrenia and the various types of schizophrenia-like psychoses by linking each syndromal diagnosis to other than symptomatological criteria have so far failed. These criteria lack specificity, just as the psychopathological symptoms do.

2.3. Rescue Operation of the Nosological Paradigm

A recent paper by Kendler (1990) provides an illustration of the intellectual tour de force established researchers are willing to employ to salvage the nosological paradigm in general and its conceptualization in recent editions of the Diagnostic & Statistical Manual (DSM-III-R) in particular. Kendler discussed issues that, though critical for "scientific nosology," he considers as fundamentally nonempirical and defying the scientific method. The three major issues he qualifies as such are the following.

First of all, he contends, one cannot study the validity of a psychiatric disorder where there is disagreement about its proper construct. This is an odd statement in a treatise to be read as a pleading for a scientific nosology. If true, it would imply that the roads towards a scientific nosology are basically blocked, or rather are nonexistent, for there exists in psychiatry hardly any diagnostic construct about which a consensus exists. The statement is odd, also, because it disqualifies the very essence of nosological research, that is, the study of which of the various constructs of a given diagnostic entity is the most predictive in terms of, for instance, genetic loading, treatment outcome, and prognosis. If the predictive validity of each of the constructs is low, the homogeneity of that diagnostic entity has to be questioned and attempts should be made to dissect it into smaller parts. Scientific scrutiny of current nosological categories is a matter that should receive highest priority in psychiatry. For a profession claiming to be *en route* to scientific maturation, this is little less than a matter of life and death. Kendler's statement is unfortunate because it could make it legitimate to omit just that.

The example he gives of discrepant constructs of the same disorder is also illustrative of the degree of diagnostic hairsplitting towards which neonosology has drifted. Regarding schizotypal personal disorder, two positions have been articulated, termed "familial" and "clinical." The former concept defines the disorder as a nonpsychotic, schizophrenia-like syndrome that occurs commonly in relatives of schizophrenics and uncommonly in other individuals. The "clinical" construct for schizotypal personality disorder describes those patients as showing substantial schizophrenia-like symptoms, despite the absence of classic symptoms of psychosis. Even after torturing my brain, I find it hard to conceptualize the difference between a nonpsychotic schizophrenia-like syndrome and a schizophrenia-like syndrome in the absence of classic symptoms of psychosis. I have stopped this exercise in futility.

The second issue Kendler designates as "non-empirical" is the problem arising if different validators of a given diagnostic construct do not agree. As an example, he refers to schizophrenia. The DSM-III criteria succeed in defining a syndrome with relatively poor outcome. However, if familial aggregation were the main validator, then the DSM-III criteria for schizophrenia are too narrow. Which validators should be given priority, Kendler wonders. In view of the absence of objective criteria for the diagnosis of schizophrenia, this question indeed defies empirical analysis, but the question is, I think, ill-conceived. If different validators of a given diagnostic concept disagree, the relevant question to be raised is whether or not that concept indeed represents an entity or else a composite of different diagnostic entities. That question is empirically accessible, in fact, pivotal, for a scientific psychiatric nosology.

The example given is again telling in another way as well, this time of the artificiality and arbitrariness of current diagnostic criteria. The DSM-III criteria for schizophrenia succeed in defining a bad-prognosis syndrome simply by stipulating a minimum duration of six months. If a duration of 12 months had been chosen, no doubt the construct would have been even better in predicting poor outcome. To state, moreover, that familial data indicate that the DSM-III criteria for schizophrenia are too narrow is a nosological euphemism. A more realistic interpretation is that no data more clearly than the familial indicate the heterogeneity of the present-day concept of schizophrenia.

A third issue considered to be non-empirical is raised. If a given validator would indicate that two possibly related syndromes are different, what is their mutual relationship? As an example, to clarify the question, mood-incongruent psychotic depression is mentioned. This construct could be 1) a form of depression without subtype status; 2) a subtype of major depression; 3) a distinct diagnostic category within the mood disorders, or, 4) a subtype of schizophrenia. Again, it is the phrasing that is unscientific and, thus, the underlying issue *appears* to be "non-empirical." Who would be so bold as to define criteria to distinguish "a subtype of major depression" from "a distinct mood disorder," or a "subtype of major depression" from a form of "depression without subtype status." Esoteric formulations can conceal a scientific issue, which in this case poses the question of whether psychotic depression is different from either major depression or schizophrenia. This question is by no means impervious to analysis by "scientific nosologists," provided the boundary between major depression and schizophrenia is firmly defined.

In Kendler's reasoning, the nosological paradigm as it is conceptualized in the DSM-III is kept upright by proclaiming the major issues at stake as fundamentally "non-empirical." This is a sophism. Properly formulated, these issues do lend themselves to scientific scrutiny. Many current diagnostic constructs seem to be built on quicksand, as far as validity is concerned. When the major issues are declared to be scientifically inaccessible, dust is thrown in our eyes.

3. ETIOLOGICAL PRUDERY

The DSM-III aspires to be "atheoretical" and thus abstains from an etiological axis. This prudence is unnecessary. Potential etiological factors can be assessed with considerable precision: personality dysfunctions with inventories or standardized interviews; recent life events with appropriate scales; hereditary factors via a detailed family history; physical factors through a thorough medical and neurological work-up. The issue of the etiological weight of these factors in a given case is a complicated one, but a consensus opinion can be reached most of the time, much the same as one can agree regarding the presence and severity of particular psychopathological symptoms.

To make etiology a classificatory outcast is wrong. Etiology determines important therapeutic decisions, such as the initiation of systematic psychotherapy; prognosis is hard to predict without taking etiological factors into account. An etiological analysis, or hypothesis if one wishes, is an indispensable part of psychiatric diagnosis. The DSM-III as it stands now imprints the trainees with the notion that such analysis is barely feasible and that it is preferable to make incomplete diagnoses. This is a harmful imprint.

4. DIAGNOSTIC INEQUALITY

The DSM-III recognizes that the psychiatric condition of a given patient is often multisyndromal in nature. To resolve this problem, it does not recommend that each be recorded, but rather that all but one be disregarded. In other words, it resorts to a hierarchical principle whereby psychiatric disorders are rank-ordered according to severity and the more serious disorder takes precedence over the more minor one (Foulds, 1976). Major depression, for example, cannot be diagnosed in the presence of schizophrenia and generalized anxiety disorder has to be disregarded in the presence of a mood disorder. Compared to the DSM-III, the principle of multisyndromal diagnoses gained some ground in the DSM-III-R, but the hierarchical system is by no means abandoned.

Psychiatry has little to gain from hierarchical diagnostic systems and much to lose: loss of diagnostic information and loss of therapeutic opportunities, since little evidence exists that lower-order syndromes will disappear if higher-ranking syndromes have been combated successfully. Loss, finally, of validity of research, in particular biological research. How can one interpret biological findings, say in schizophrenia, if in one patient major depression coexists and in the other it does not.

5. CONCLUSION

Today's classification of the major psychiatric disorders is as confusing as it used to be some 30 years ago. All things considered, the present situation is worse. Then, psychiatrists were at least aware that diagnostic chaos reigned and many of them had no high opinion of diagnosis, anyhow. Now, the chaos is codified and thus much more hidden. It is true that the codification is not sacrosanct and is periodically adjusted; so far, however, this process is guided by experts, not by focused research. Modifications introduced today, therefore, will inevitably be followed by modifications tomorrow, creating even more confusion both practically—not every clinician keeping up with the ever changing guidelines—and scientifically, because research conducted under the jurisdiction of the various DSM editions will be increasingly hard to compare. It is ironic that a taxonomy devised to promote research relies on the least scientific of methods to further its own development—expert opinion.

There is nothing wrong in basing the first draft of an operationalized taxonomy on expert opinions. On the contrary, one should not postpone the introduction of a standardized classification indefinitely until all issues of validity and reliability have been addressed and resolved. One should abstain, however, from proceeding further on that route. Yet, this is exactly what happened; the principal vehicle for taxonomic advancement continues to be expert opinion. Thus, it remains business as usual in psychiatry.

During the past century, clinical wisdom and expertise, as encompassed in the opinion of individual experts, were the major modes for progress in psychiatry. The change introduced in preparing the third edition of the DSM was that groups of experts were deployed instead of single experts. A quantitative change, not one of principle. Does insight grow numerically, parallel with the number of discussants? Not necessarily. A single expert might generate brilliant ideas that usher in a new epoch. Freud and Kraepelin are telling examples. Though the chance of that happening is not great, it is infinitely smaller if experts are assembled in groups. The group has to reach a consensus; in order to do so, one has to compromise. The group decision makes some happy, some markedly unhappy, while the majority acquiesce in it. Decisions so arrived at are oligarchic, not scientific. Experts, of course, reckon with the existing literature. Pertinent data, however, might be scarce. Different studies have generally used dissimilar methodologies and might differ in outcome. Most studies were not designed to address questions relevant to the taxonomist and thus, provide not–to–the–point answers. Hence, a survey of the literature will rarely result in unambiguous answers, forcing one to rely on a greatest common denominator, that is, on a compromise.

The only way to pursue progress in psychiatric taxonomy is for experts to phrase the relevant questions and to design made-to-measure protocols to resolve them. A long and tedious road, but the only one that will lead us out of the diagnostic quicksand, through which we march at present, towards more solid grounds. The present procedure operates in the opposite manner. Experts decide to change a given diagnostic definition and, subsequently, researchers might or might not decide to study its validity (Zimmerman et al., 1989). This is putting the cart before the horse or, more accurately, disconnecting the two. If so inclined, the horse might move the cart, but the process is haphazard, time consuming, and inefficient.

To use experts as a source of opinions rather than as the initiators of focused research is a waste of time and talent. Consequently, I strongly feel that 1) an immediate moratorium should be laid on any further expert-opinion-based alterations in the classification of depression and schizophrenia (or any other psychiatric disorder, for that matter) and that 2) future changes should be based on research only, conducted in several centers simultaneously and specifically designed to resolve issues pertinent to the DSM classification. In organizing, conducting, and funding such a collaborative, goal-directed effort, the National Institute of Mental Health and comparable institutions in other parts of the world could play a seminal role. A tall order, but the Diagnostic Manual deserves it.

6. SUMMARY

Up to the introduction of the DSM-III in 1980, diagnostic concepts in psychiatry were not operationalized, the nomenclature was not standardized, and no taxonomy was generally accepted. With a measure of exaggeration, one could state that the number of classifications paralleled the number of psychiatric textbooks. Today, we work under the aegis of the DSM-III-R taxonomy, a system in which diagnostic concepts *are* operationalized, nomenclature *is* standardized, and this nomenclature is officially accepted in the USA and de facto accepted in numerous countries all over the world. Yet, that system failed to create order where disorder reigned. This viewpoint has been illustrated with two examples: depression and schizophrenia. In conceptualizing these disorders, very definite choices were made:

1. In symptomatological terms, depressive syndromes are loosely defined and the definitions widely overlap. The same is true for schizophrenia. The borders between the latter concept and adjacent diagnoses, i.e. schizophreniform psychosis, schizoaffective psychosis, brief reactive psychosis, and delusional disorder, are blurred.

An alternative would have been rigid symptomatological description of a few prototypes, designating the intermediate or mixed forms as an area for further diagnostic research.

2. To provide these diagnoses with at least a modicum of recognizability, nonsymptomatological variables, such as severity, duration, and premorbid personality structure, are incorporated into the definition. These variables, however, lack diagnostic specificity.

An alternative would have been scoring of these variables on separate axes, independent of the syndromal diagnosis.

3. An etiological axis was avoided rather than requesting a judgment on biological, psychological, and environmental determinants of depressive and schizophrenic disorders in every case.

4. Anxiety disorders and mood disorders are treated as independent diagnostic concepts. An alternative would have been to conceive of these groupings as highly overlapping and intertwined, scoring them dimensionally and simultaneously in each and every patient with a mood disorder.

The same holds for mood disorders and personality disorders. In the DSM-III, these two diagnostic domains are treated as independent. An alternative viewpoint sees them as strongly and often inseparably intertwined, to be scored dimensionally and simultaneously in every mood-disordered patient.

5. The problem of comorbidity is solved with the introduction of the hierarchical principle. Only the "top-diagnosis" is reported and "subordinate" ones are discounted. An alternative would have been to require that all syndromes or disorders occurring in a given patient be accurately assessed and reported.

These alternatives are regarded as preferable to the solutions that were chosen in the DSM-III for the reasons discussed.

—3—

Diagnosing Depression
Looking Backward into the Future

1. CLASSIFICATION OF DEPRESSION—THE SITUATION IN THE FIFTIES

A little over 30 years ago, the progenitors of the two classical groups of antidepressants were introduced, i.e. iproniazid (Marsilid), the first monoamine oxidase (MAO) inhibitor, and imipramine (Tofranil), the first of the tricyclic antidepressants. This occurrence coincided with the start of my residency training and ignited my interest in three related questions. What depressions or what depressive syndromes are most affected by these drugs; what is their effect on brain monoamines (MA), and is MA ergic functioning disturbed in antidepressant-responsive depressed individuals? Study of those issues presupposed the existence of a precise taxonomy of depressive disorders. Such a system, however, did not exist. Delineation of syndromes was ill-defined and neither classificatory criteria nor nomenclature were standardized. With some but not much exaggeration, one could contend that as many taxonomies existed as there were psychiatric textbooks. Schematically, three viewpoints were recognizable.

1. Only one syndromal type of depression exists and the sole relevant criterion to differentiate depressions is severity (Mapother, 1926; Lewis, 1934; Hamilton, 1982).
2. Syndromally, depressions are not classifiable, but relevant dis-

This chapter was adapted from van Praag, H.M. (1989). Diagnosing depression—Looking backward into the future. *Psychiatric Developments*, 4:375-394.

35

tinctions can be made on the basis of etiology. Thus, depression classifications came into being with many and diverse categories, reflecting the diversity of depressive etiologies. An example is Rümke's (1960) classification with categories like: psychogenic depression, characterological depression, exogenous depression, nostalgic depression, senile depression, depression after emeritus status, and several others.

3. Two basic depression types exist named "endogenous" and "neurotic," differing not only in symptoms but also in etiology and course (Gillespie, 1929; Schneider, 1959). Endogenous depression occurred without discernible precipitants and took a recurrent course. Neurotic depression, on the other hand, was psychogenically induced, and was a more chronic type of depression. Soon, however, the content of these terms was watered down. The adjective "endogenous" was used not only for a nosological entity, but also to indicate a particular depressive syndrome, or the absence of causes or precipitants, or a severe depression. "Neurotic" could mean a nosologic entity, a syndrome different from that labeled as "endogenous," presence of psychological causes or precipitants, or mild depression.

In order to permit meaningful biological and pharmacological studies, a precisely delineated and verifiable taxonomy had to be worked out. We set ourselves to do just that in the years between 1958 and 1966 (van Praag, 1962; van Praag et al., 1965; van Praag, 1965, 1966, 1977a, 1978a, 1982a, 1982b). Some 15 years later, the DSM-III was published and the depression classification it proposed was accepted throughout the USA and de facto through much of the rest of the world. Did that system mend the chaos existing in depression classification up to that time? I will address this question by first discussing the major keypoints of the depression classification we proposed, and summarizing the data on which those were based and then comparing the DSM system with the keypoints we had formulated. Using our own work as benchmark, presumptuous as it may seem, seems justified because it was the first attempt to systematize the diagnosis of depression based on empirical data. Moreover, the major findings on which this system rests have, so far, not been refuted.

2. KEYPOINTS OF OUR DEPRESSION CLASSIFICATION

2.1. Keypoint 1: Multi-axial Classification of Depressive Disorders

The classification of depressive disorders in the fifties was chaotic, first, because different classificatory criteria were used by different authors and, second, because the same adjectives—"endogenous" and "neurotic"—were used in different ways, i.e. to indicate a disease entity, a syndrome, degree of severity, and an etiology. I argued that classification of psychiatric disorders, in this case depressive disorders, had to be standardized and, based on four basic criteria, scored independently (van Praag, 1962, 1965). Thus, the concept of multi-axial classification of mental disorders was conceptualized earlier than at the WHO Seminar for Disorders of Childhood in Paris in 1967 as stated in the DSM-III-R (p. 440). The criteria I proposed were the following:

Symptomatology. The predominant depressive syndrome(s) should be indicated. Syndromes had to be delineated in detail, in terms of symptoms required and definition of the required symptoms. Syndrome and severity were considered as separate dimensions and scored independently.

Etiology. Hereditary and acquired biological, psychological, and environmental determinants have to be scrutinized independently of each other and of the prevailing syndrome(s). Recent life events and personality pathology have to be assessed independently. Reliable information on possible etiological factors could be acquired by detailed family history, stock-taking of life events preceding the behavioral disorder, personality inventories and interviews, and a thorough medical and neurological work-up. In other words, I challenged the viewpoint that etiology of psychiatric disorders is too confusing a subject to be systematized. I maintained that reliable information can be obtained and a consensus opinion can generally be reached about the etiological weight of each of these factors in a given case.

Course was advanced as the third criterion for classification of psychiatric disorders, in this case depression. First episodes were distinguished from cases in which previous episodes had occurred. The latter cases were to be subdivided in those who had recovered completely or incompletely, and in those in whom chronification had occurred after a previous episode.

Finally, as a fourth classificatory criterion, we mentioned *pathogenesis*, a factor to be distinguished from etiology. Pathogenesis was defined as the complex of cerebral dysfunctions underlying a given behavioral disorder; etiology as the composite of forces, having acted on the brain presently or in the past, that can be held responsible for these dysfunctions (van Praag & Leijnse, 1964, 1965). Nothing was known about the pathogenesis of most psychiatric disorders at the time. Yet, I added this criterion to emphasize its importance and to encourage active research.

There was no experimental data to substantiate the tenet of multiaxial classification of psychiatric disorders. Its introduction was based on common sense, applying to psychiatry what in the rest of medicine was common practice (van Praag, 1988a).

2.2. Keypoint 2: Symptomatological Classifiability of Depression

2.2.1. *The Classification*

Depressive syndromes, I maintained, differ basically in terms of symptom composition; the endpoints of the spectrum were named vital and personal depression. The two concepts were operationalized, that is, the symptoms necessary to be present for each diagnosis were listed and defined (van Praag, 1962, 1977a, 1982a). (See Tables 2:1 and 2:2, Chapter 2). We applied a "fixed system" rather than the "choice-principle" that the DSM-III would adopt later. Thus, for a particular diagnosis, all symptoms of a given set have to be present, rather than x symptoms, out of series of y, no matter which ones. The fixed system, albeit rigid, has the invaluable advantage that one term covers one well-defined syndrome. The conception of vital/personal depression was introduced emphatically as a dimension, not as a dichotomy. Vital and personal depression were seen as endpoints of a continuum with many mixed forms in between that were still to be charted.

The syndromes of vital and personal depression were kindred to the ones hitherto described as endogenous and neurotic depression, though neurotic depression was a symptomatologically ill-defined concept. I rejected those designations because they were, as said, multi-interpretable. The concepts of vital and personal depression, on the other hand, were defined in strictly symptomatological terms without any implications about etiology, severity of symptoms, duration, course, or premorbid personality functioning. Those variables were assessed independently of the syndrome and of each other. As far as symptoms are concerned, the best fitting DSM-III diagnoses for vital and personal depression are major depression, melancholic type, and dysthymic disorder. The fit, however, is highly imperfect because the DSM-III does not specify the precise outline of the syndromes.

Finally, we developed an instrument to assess the syndromes of vital and personal depression. The Hamilton Rating Scale for Depression had just been published (Hamilton, 1960) but it provided a severity index, rather than a syndromal evaluation. It occurred to us that *the* instrument of psychiatric examination, i.e. the interview, could be used as a measuring device, provided it was structured and standardized. In this vein, the Vital Syndrome Interview came into being, a standardized, structured interview and the first of its kind to be introduced in clinical psychiatry (van Praag et al., 1965). Later, the Present State Examination (Wing et al., 1974) and the Schedule for Affective Disorders and Schizophrenia (Endicott & Spitzer, 1978) would utilize the same approach in a much more elaborate form.

2.2.2. *The Data*

The data supporting this tenet were psychopharmacological in nature (van Praag, 1962, 1966, 1977). A study of the monoamine oxidase inhibitor (MAOI) iproniazid in patients suffering from various syndromal forms of depression showed the vital depressives to be significantly more responsive to the drugs than those diagnosed as personal depression. The therapeutic results in the group of mixed depression fell in between. Similar results were obtained with the MAOI isocarboxazide and with the tricyclic antidepressant imipramine. The efficacy of electroconvulsive therapy was distributed similarly. Very high improvement rates in vital depression (approximately 85 percent); poor results in the group diagnosed as personal depression (satisfactory improvement in approximately 15 percent of patients), and intermediate results in the group of mixed depression.

From the divergent results obtained with specific antidepressant drugs and with electroshock therapy in vital and personal depression, we concluded that this symptomatological distinction was valid. We underlined the importance of precise syndromal depression diagnosis to guard against antidepressants being prescribed or withheld inappropriately, and suggested that syndromal differentiation was crucial for studies in the pathogenesis of depression. Later multivariate statistical studies consistently identified a group of depressives with so-called endogenous features, as well as a group of neurotic depressives, the latter in itself probably heterogenous (e.g., Paykel, 1971, 1987; Kendell, 1976; Akiskal et al., 1978; Feinberg & Carroll, 1982; Carroll, 1984). The endogenous group, moreover, proved to be more responsive to ECT and antidepressant medication than the latter (e.g., Bielski & Friedel, 1976; Paykel, 1979; Klein et al., 1980; Nelson & Charney, 1981).

2.3. Keypoint 3: Depressive Syndromes Are Etiologically Nonspecific

2.3.1. *Etiological Factors in Depression*

The concept of endogenous depression had traditionally been linked to the absence of significant precipitating factors. The syndrome was considered to be either "ideopathic" (i.e. of unknown origin) or strongly determined by heredity. Preceding psychological stressors were considered to be incompatible with that diagnosis. In studying this issue systematically we found this viewpoint to be untenable. More often than not, the syndrome of vital depression (as said, the detailed and operationalized version of the *syndrome* of endogenous depression) proved to be preceded by psychosocial and somatic stressors.

Neurotic depression was considered to be invariably the catastrophic endpoint of psychological conflict situations. The diagnosis could not be considered in the absence of stressful psychological events. This adage, too, was shown to be inaccurate. A substantial percentage of patients indicated no precipitant, other than a general

TABLE 3:1
Precipitants in the Six Months Preceding the Depression in
Vital (Endogenous, Melancholic) and Personal (Neurotic,
Dysthymic) Depression

| | Number of Patients Indicating Precipitants | |
	Vital Depression (n = 100)	Personal Depression (n = 100)
No Precipitants	27	33
Precipitants:	73	67
Psychosocial:	59	56
Biological:	14	11

and chronic feeling of dissatisfaction with one's life and a sense of nonfulfillment.

Vital depression, we concluded, is an etiological nonspecific syndrome that may occur not only "spontaneously," without demonstrable precipitants, but also as a response to psycho-traumatic or physico-traumatic events. Personal depression (again, the defined and operationalized version of the *syndrome* of neurotic depression) might be provoked by psychological stressors, but quite often those seem to be absent (van Praag, 1962, 1982a, 1982b).

2.3.2. *The Data*

In 100 patients with vital depression and an equal number with personal depression, the occurrence of psychosocial and physical stressors in the six months prior to the depression was systematically explored. Only those events were counted that could be verified by an "important other." The absence of precipitants was noted with almost equal frequency in both groups (27 and 33 percent respectively). In the group of vital depression, stressful events were ascertained in a majority of patients (73 percent) (Table 3:1). The finding that the presence or absence of stressful events does not distinguish syndromal depression types was confirmed by Brown et al. (1979), Paykel et al. (1984), and others.

2.4. Keypoint 4: Type of Syndrome and Severity Are Independent Variables

2.4.1. *Severity Is No Syndromal Characteristic*

By definition, endogenous depression was a severe form, neurotic depression a mild form of depression. Mild endogenous depression was considered to be a contradiction in terms; mild depression, therefore, could not qualify for biological treatments, while severe depression, ipso facto, could not call for systematic psychotherapy. I found this viewpoint to be both fallacious and harmful. Both depression types were shown to occur in all grades of severity, from mild to very severe. Hence, severity and syndrome ought to be scored separately on independent axes.

> Particularly mild vital depression is often not recognized. In those cases, feelings of sadness are not the most striking feature. To the outsider, the patient often does not give a definite depressive impression. The patient himself indicates that his condition is inadequately characterized by the term "despondent." He is not so much downcast as he is filled with feelings of malaise and ill-humor. Life becomes gray. The joy of living disappears and, with that, anhedonia is foreshadowed. One might speak of a continuous sort of hangover, or, with Schneider (1959), of a *depressio sine depressione*. It is only in a later stage that the typical, massive, unchangeable melancholia develops. This stage is frequently, but incorrectly, regarded as typical for vital depression.

> In the early phases of vital depression or in mild cases, there are no objective signs of motor retardation. Those symptoms are typical for the fully developed vital depression. In an earlier phase, the retardation manifests itself exclusively in the realm of subjective experience. The patient notices that his work has become laborious. His speed is diminished. He has the feeling that something is holding him back; he is unable to complete his undertakings. Nothing goes smoothly and easily any longer; all activity begins to require voluntary effort.

> Manifest bradyphrenia is likewise a manifestation of an advanced stage of vital depression. Before that point is reached, the diminished *vis a tergo* in the thinking process manifests itself

TABLE 3:2
Syndromal-Depression Type and Severity of Depression

		Number of Patients with Severe, Moderate or Mild Depression		
	N	Severe	Moderate	Mild
Vital (Endogenous, Melancholic) Depression	100	39	48	13
Personal (Neurotic, Dysthymic) Depression	100	31	52	17
Mixed (Double) Depression	100	41	39	20

only in the realm of subjective experiences. The patient notices that it takes longer than usual before he becomes aware of things. He has difficulty in perceiving certain connections. There is a paucity of invention, of ideas. Sometimes, there is also a sort of chronic indecisiveness; the patient has severe difficulties in making choices.

In the same vein, motor agitation is a late phenomenon. In earlier stages of vital depression, agitation is experienced as anxiety and inner tension, whereas motor unrest is not observed.

The traditional viewpoint was called harmful in that it contraindicated biological treatment in patients who could profoundly benefit from it, i.e. in mild vital depression, while those treatments were prescribed for patients with slight chance of benefit, i.e. in severe personal depression. Syndrome, I submitted, is the primary criterion for treatment choice, not severity (van Praag, 1962, 1966).

Mood lowering, moreover, proved to be a variable hard to gauge reliably. In their assessment of the depth of a depression, clinicians regularly use symptoms that are easier to assess, particularly anhedonia and motor symptoms, rather than to try to judge the mood state per se. Since both anhedonia and motor pathology are much more pronounced in vital than in personal depression, this could explain the persistence of the myth that vital depression is by definition severe, while personal depression is a mild form of depression.

2.4.2. The Data

One psychiatrist assessed syndromal type of the depression, another, independently, its severity. The groups so studied each comprised 100 patients with various forms of depression. No correlation was found between type of syndrome and severity of depression. High and low severity scores occurred with equal frequency in all depression types (Table 3:2).

Apart from a global severity rating, we asked the second clinician to rate, in addition, the severity of a number of depression components. Global severity ratings correlated highly with the severity ratings of anhedonia, motor inhibition, and agitation, not with the degree of mood lowering.

2.5. Keypoint 5: Personality Disturbances Occur with Comparable Frequency in Both Vital and Personal Depression

2.5.1. *Personality Disturbances in Depression*

Neurotic depression was, as discussed, linked to a "neurotic personality." In endogenous depression, on the other hand, premorbid personality structure was thought to be non-neurotic (Rosenthal & Klerman, 1966), even "syntonic," i.e. well in tune with the environment, though a certain lability of mood was acknowledged (Kretschmer, 1951). This standpoint had therapeutic consequences. If personality disorder occurred in depression, psychotherapy was thought to be indicated and biological treatment contraindicated. In studying the matter systematically, we found this thesis to be false. Indeed, personal depression coexists frequently with personality disturbances, but those traits appear in comparable rates in other depressive syndromes (van Praag, 1962, 1977a, 1978a). Personality disorder appeared to be not a reliable indicator of a particular depressive syndrome. The old thesis was harmful therapeutically and scientifically. Therapeutically, because it led to the withholding of biological treatment in cases of vital depression with personality disorder. Scientifically, because most biological studies in vital depression attributed their findings to the affective disorder and disregarded abnormal personality traits as a possible behavioral correlate.

2.5.2. *The Data*

Instead of relying on questionnaires, we used, in this study of personality disorder in depression, structured interview techniques focusing on phenomenological phenomena in the sense of Jaspers

(1948). Thus, we concentrated on the individual's own inner experiences. In this case, we tried to explore whether the patient experienced his or her personality make-up as being neurotic, that is, as a source of dissatisfaction and displeasure. We were particularly interested in the occurrence of "character neurosis." Such patients report signs of personality disorder, but they do not experience them as pathological, but rather as part and parcel of their personality make-up ("It is just the way I am"). This condition contrasts with "symptom neurosis," in which the signs of personality disorder are felt as definitely abnormal (for instance, severe anxiety or mood lowering, obsessions, and compulsions). The diagnosis of "character neurosis" was made if, in a structured interview, the following experiential qualities were thought to be present by at least two independently scoring clinicians:

1. Basic *feeling of discontent* with one's own life situation and one's own psychological make-up. Feelings that life has treated one unfairly, in that it had blessed most others with more pleasure and satisfaction than oneself.

2. Unhappiness with one's *personal relations*, ranging from parental relations and school and work experiences to marital relations and relations with one's children. Others are felt to be not forthcoming, distant, threatening, cold, abrasive, or in other ways not meeting the individual's expectations and needs. As a consequence, a chronic feeling of loneliness and solitude has developed.

3. *Emotional instability*, in that the basic discontent ignites a range of emotions varying from mood lowering to guilt, anger, despair, and anxiety. These emotions are generally intense and vary abruptly and frequently, sometimes ignited by traceable events in the life situation, sometimes not clearly so.

Each of the three factors was scored on a 5-point scale ranging from 4 to 0 so that a maximum score of 12 and a minimum score of 0 could be obtained. Interviews were done when the patients were either free of depressive symptoms or in a much better condition than before treatment (Hirschfeld et al., 1983b).

The average score on the three items was 8.0 in the group of vital depression, 10.2 in the personal depressives, 7.9 in the mixed forms, and 0.9 in the normal controls (Table 3:3). Personality disorder with-

TABLE 3:3
Syndromal Depression-Type and Personality Structure

	N	Score on Semistructured Interview Focused on Self-experience		
		Basic Feelings of Discontent	Unhappiness with Personal Relations	Emotional Instability
Vital (Endogenous, Melancholic) Depression	20	8.2	8.9	7.0
Personal (Neurotic, Dysthymic) Depression	20	10.3	9.8	10.5
Mixed (Double) Depression	20	8.8	7.9	6.9
Normal Controls	20	0.8	0.5	1.2

out ego–dystonic symptoms, i.e. without elements the patient himself considers as pathological (one could say asymptomatic personality disorder corresponding, as stated, to the classical Freudian concept of character neurosis), was diagnosed in a majority of depressed patients, irrespective of syndromal type. The impossibility of distinguishing syndromal depression types on the basis of the presence or absence of personality disorders has been confirmed by several authors (e.g. Matussek & Feil, 1983; Hirschfeld et al., 1983b; Zimmerman et al., 1988; Pilkonis & Frank, 1988; Ainaes & Torgensen, 1988; Wetzler et al., 1990).

2.6. Keypoint 6: The Multisyndromal Nature of Psychiatric Disorders

2.6.1. *The Nosological Ideal*

In the first half of the century, well up into the sixties, nosological principles were ingrained in European psychiatry. Psychiatric disorders were conceived of and, hence, generally perceived as discrete entities, each with its own etiology, typical symptom pattern, course, and prognosis. If a given disease state did not meet nosological criteria, the conclusion was drawn that the proper nosological diagnosis was not yet known. The nosological principle itself was not questioned.

In studying symptom patterns in depression systematically, it became clear to us that the nosological principle was untenable. Not only is etiology not predictive of syndrome and syndrome not of etiology, but many patients show simultaneously (parts of) different syndromes. Mixed depression is a typical example, but we additionally recorded frequent coexistence of anxiety disorders and depression. Rather than explain these facts by assuming as yet unknown nosological entities, we postulated that psychiatric syndromes overlap and that in an individual patient the behavioral state is frequently multisyndromal in nature (van Praag, 1962; van Praag & Leijnse, 1964, 1965). The component syndromes of the disorder, we argued, were each to be diagnosed and recorded.

2.6.2. *The Data*

Patients with vital depression, personal depression, and mixed depression along with normal controls (n = 25 in each group) were assessed, independently and on the basis of the same interview by two clinicians, as to the occurrence of anxiety symptoms. Anxiety and depressive syndromes were shown to strongly overlap. This was especially true for the group of personal depression in which the rate of generalized anxiety disorder (called free-floating anxiety, at the time), panic disorder (known as hyperventilation syndrome, at the time), and phobic anxiety was 76 percent, 12 percent, and 16 percent respectively. The corresponding figures for the group of vital depression were lower: 48 percent, 8 percent, and 12 percent respectively, but still considerable. In the group of mixed depression, the rates were 68 percent, 8 percent, and 16 percent; in a normal control group, 12 percent, 0 percent, and 4 percent (Table 3:4). Whether the syndromes relate causally or exist independently (co-morbidity) remained an open question, which it still is today. The co-occurrence of anxiety disorder and mood disorder has been repeatedly and convincingly shown by various investigators (e.g. Gurney et al., 1972; Roth et al., 1972; Roth & Mountjoy, 1982; Sanderson & Wetzler, 1991).

3. THE DSM-III CLASSIFICATION OF DEPRESSION

3.1. Evaluation via the Comparative Approach

In 1980, the DSM-III was published, a taxonomy of psychiatric disorders based on five criteria (axes) and describing in considerable

TABLE 3:4
Co-occurrence of Depression and Anxiety Disorders

	N	Free-Floating Anxiety (Generalized Anxiety Disorder)	Phobic Anxiety	Hyperventilation Syndrome (Panic Disorder)
		Number of Depressed Patients also Meeting Criteria for an Anxiety Disorder		
Vital (Endogenous, Melancholic) Depression	25	12	3	2
Personal (Neurotic, Dysthymic) Depression	25	19	4	3
Mixed (Double) Depression	25	17	4	2
Normal Controls	20	3	1	0

detail the symptoms that might be observed in each entity. The system is largely based on expert opinions and clearly grafted upon the nosological tradition, considering psychiatric disorders as discrete and separable entities.

This bold attempt to standardize and operationalize psychiatric diagnoses was a true landmark and a necessary prerequisite for the process of scientification psychiatry is undergoing. Having said that, I want to discuss the question whether the DSM-III has clarified the diagnosis of depression: Did it create order where chaos reigned? I will do so by comparing the DSM-III system with ours. The hypotheses I formulated will serve as guidelines.

3.2. Keypoint 1: Multiaxial Classification

The DSM-III adopted the principle of multiaxial diagnosis; the nature of the axes, however, was different from ours. Syndromal typology (DSM-III Axis I) is shared. Since the DSM-III wants to be "atheoretical," no etiological axis is introduced, at least not openly. Covertly, etiology pops up in Axis II, III, and IV. Personality disorder and physical disorder are assessed "atheoretically," i.e. irrespective of their etiological weight. Psychosocial stressors (Axis IV), on the other hand, should be scored only if judged to have been a significant contributor to the development or exacerbation of the current disorder. Definitely, a "theoretical" approach. Hereditary factors are not accounted for. Course is treated, not as an independent axis but as a diagnostic criterion, characterizing together with the symptoms a particular type of depression. For example, one of the diagnostic criteria for major depression is having had one or more major depressive episodes and no manic episodes.

Having the syndromal axis in common, the two systems differ in other respects. Our system carries an axis etiology, while the DSM-III avoids the term, though not the substance. Etiological considerations are introduced, but ambivalently and incompletely. Course, which we considered as a separate axis, the DMS-III treats as a diagnostic criterion, making it impossible to score variations in the "official course," such as first episode, partial recovery, or chronicity. Axis 5 (recording the level of adaptive functioning) is an important axis we had omitted. Naturally, pathogenesis is lacking in a taxonomy aspiring to be "atheoretical."

3.3. Keypoint 2: Syndromal Heterogeneity of Depression

The DMS-III holds the view of depression being syndromally heterogeneous and recognizes two basic entities: major depression and dysthymic disorder. As mentioned, it utilizes the "choice-principle." No fixed set of symptoms has to be present in order to qualify for either diagnosis, but only y symptoms out of a series of y + x, no matter which ones. As a consequence, the same term covers a diversity of depressive syndromes. Moreover, the majority of symptoms listed under major depression are similar to those listed under dysthymic disorder; discriminating symptoms are few (See Tables 2:1 and 2:2, Chapter 2). The proposed dichotomy resembles two poorly focused slides, projected simultaneously and largely overlapping. Clarity is minimal.

This state of affairs is detrimental for research, in particular biological research, as well as for clinical practice. In biological psychiatry, the search is for the biological underpinnings of specific syndromes or specific psychopathological dimensions, as well as for specific etiological interventions to eliminate them. Those goals are ill served by diagnostic ambiguities. For the practitioner, the DSM

TABLE 3:5
Syndromal Depression-Type, Hedonic Functioning and Response to
Antidepressants

| | | Number of Patients with Anhedonia and Vital (Endogenous, Melancholic) Depression or Personal (Neurotic, Dysthymic) Depression | | | |
| | | Anhedonia | | Depression-Type | |
	N	PRESENT	ABSENT	VITAL	PERSONAL
Strong Response to Antidepressants	50	39	11	41	9
No or Weak Response to Antidepressants	50	14	36	16	34

system may seem handy, but in fact it does not serve him or her well
either. Psychotropic drugs acquire ever greater biochemical specificity and, thus, probably a more narrowly focused therapeutic action
(van Praag et al., 1991). Working with unfocused diagnostic concepts, one could easily fail to discern specific therapeutic indications.
It is true that many patients do not fit rigidly defined diagnostic concepts, such as those of vital and personal depression, but it is better
to recognize that and categorize them for the time being as "mixed
states" or as "double depressions" (see 3.6), or as "not yet classifiable
with some degrees of certainty" than to use labels that are for all
intents and purposes meaningless and provide only pseudocertainty.

A particularly puzzling aspect of the DSM-III depression classification is anhedonia being regarded as a symptom of both major
and dysthymic depression. Anhedonia is defined as loss of interest
or pleasure in activities that used to be interesting and rewarding.
Von Gebsattel (1937a, 1937b), amongst others, regarded anhedonia
as a key symptom of endogenous depression. This viewpoint was
later shared by Klein (1974) and Carroll (1983), and corroborated by
Fawcett et al. (1983). We found empirical evidence substantiating that
view. In patients who recovered or had improved substantially on
antidepressant drugs (mainly the monoamine oxidase inhibitor
iproniazid), anhedonia had been recorded before treatment in 78 percent of cases while 82 percent were diagnosed as vital depression.
The latter is to be expected since anhedonia is included in the diagnostic criteria for vital depression. Two months later, however, a final
therapeutic evaluation was made by a clinician blind to the initial

TABLE 3:6
Most Cumbersome Symptom of the Depressed Condition

	Percentage of Patients Indicating that Symptom	
	Vital (Endogenous, Melancholic) Depression (n = 50)	Personal (Neurotic, Dysthymic) Depression (n = 50)
Anhedonia	43	16
Mood-Lowering	31	70
Motor Phenomena	11	0
Fatigue	9	4
Sleep Disturbances	5	7
Affective Disturbances	1	0
Irritability	–	3

diagnosis. The results indicated that vital depression, anhedonia, and good therapeutic response are indeed interrelated. Among the poor responders, anhedonia was uncommon (28 percent of patients) and the predominant diagnosis was personal depression (68 percent) (Table 3:5).

A second argument suggesting diagnostic specificity is the fact that in a cohort of 50 patients with vital depression 43 listed anhedonia as the most cumbersome symptom, in contrast to patients with personal depression in whom this number was only 16. In the latter group, mood lowering was indicated to be the predominant symptom (70 percent) (Table 3:6).

In the aggregate, it seems to be a fair conclusion that the syndromal depression classification according to the DSM-III augmented diagnostic confusion rather than resolving it.

3.4. Keypoint 3: Etiological Aspecificity of Depressive Syndromes

The DSM-III is called a "descriptive" system, describing the manifestation of the disorder, but generally not how it came about. The "atheoretical" line, however, is not sustained; thus, the approach to etiology, as was stated in Section 3.2, is better characterized as ambivalent.

There is no good reason, I felt, to shy away from promoting etiology to a legitimate diagnostic axis in its own right. The occurrence of personality disorders, stressful life events, physical ailments, and familial occurrence of the disorder can be documented properly and reliably and their etiological weight in a given case at least be approximated. Assessment by several raters of the presence or severity of a particular symptom is often also an approximation. Opinions diverge, but a consensus opinion can generally be reached. My experience is that the same is true if possible etiological factors are weighted. To make etiology a classificatory outcast is harmful for several reasons.

First, it detracts from what could be called psychodynamic awareness, that is, the notion that the past is reflected in the present, that the present is often puzzling if the past is not taken into account, that the past has to be explored in order to obtain a grasp of existing psychopathology in the present. We would be back to Kraepelin's days if that historical notion is neglected or ignored.

Second, the fact that Axis II, describing lasting personality pathology, is detached from Axis I in which incidental psychopathology is summarized engenders the danger that the question of the extent to which the Axis II diagnosis has contributed to the Axis I diagnosis will not be raised. Indeed, this question remains, nowadays, often unanswered, notwithstanding the fact that a pronouncement about this issue is essential for all spheres of psychiatry, biological psychiatry included. The answer is, for instance, of immediate relevance for the question whether a particular biological variable relates to the Axis I diagnosis or to (underlying or concomitant) personality traits.

Third, evading the question of a possible linkage between the Axis I and II diagnoses leaves the decision whether or not to institute one or the other form of psychotherapy hanging in air. The hypothesis that such a linkage exists constitutes a major justification for psychotherapy.

Fourth, the separation of an Axis I from an Axis II diagnosis, thus circumventing the issue of psychogenesis, consolidates the present inclination to "medicalize" psychiatry, that is, to give up the psychological and social aspects of abnormal behavior and withdraw to biology. The damage that this retreat would inflict on our profession is immeasurable.

In a word, then, an etiological hypothesis is an indispensable part of psychiatric diagnosis. By de-emphasizing this fact, the DSM-III brings damage to psychiatry.

3.5. Keypoint 4: Independence of the Severity Dimension

Major depression and dysthymia are introduced as discrete syndromal entities, but for the greater part they overlap and the major criterion that seems to properly differentiate them is *severity*. Curiously, that variable is wanting in the definition of major depression, but emerges in that of dysthymia where it is stipulated that "the symptoms are not of sufficient severity to meet the criteria for major depression."

Actually, the DSM-III classification reflects two traditional but opposite viewpoints. First is the unitary concept that postulates symptomatological homogeneity of depressive syndromes and considers severity as the only relevant differentiating criterion. Second is the dichotomous view that distinguishes two syndromal depression types, differing both in symptoms and severity (the original endogenous/neurotic dichotomy). Both standpoints, as we saw, are questionable. Heterogeneity of depressive syndromes is a more plausible concept than the unitary view, while severity is a freestanding dimension independent of depression type. But even apart from that, the very attempt to unify two basically opposite concepts is a logical inconsistency that is bound to generate confusion.

Duration was not included in our classification system, but it is in the DSM-III, albeit in a somewhat ambiguous way. I mention the variable here because duration in the DSM-III, like severity, is used as a criterion differentiating major and dysthymic depression. According to the definition of major depression, the symptoms should be present "nearly every day for at least two weeks." Under dysthymic disorders, however, one reads that a minimum duration of two years is required; the symptoms, it is added, are not only of insufficient severity but also of insufficient duration to meet the criteria for major depression. The duration of vital depression, i.e. the nearest equivalent of major depression, has been shown to be highly variable (Angst et al., 1973; Scott, 1988). The suggestion that a depression should have lasted for at least two years before qualifying as a major depression is confusing and fallacious.

We excluded duration as a diagnostic criterion for a particular depression type because duration was found to be highly variable, not only in vital depression but in personal depression as well (see 4.2).

3.6. Keypoint 5: The Nonseparability of Personality Disorder and Mood Disorder

The frequent coexistence of depression and personality disorder is recognized for dysthymia in DSM-III. "Often the affective features of this disorder are viewed as secondary to an underlying personality disorder." The issue is ignored as far as major depression is concerned, though it is clear that personality disorder is not uncommon in that category, as well. This disregard is unfortunate, first, because it perpetuates the erroneous idea that patients with major depression are not proper candidates for systematic psychotherapy and can be properly treated with psychotropic drugs alone. Moreover, disregard for the frequent coexistence of personality disorder and major depression left aside the question of whether or not biological variables observed in major depression are to be attributed to (components of) major depression or to underlying or concomitant abnormal personality traits.

3.7. Keypoint 6: Diagnostic Equality in Diagnosing Psychiatric Disorders

The DSM-III implicitly recognizes that the behavioral disorder of a given patient is infrequently monosyndromal, more often a composite of several syndromes occurring integrally or in incomplete form. To resolve this problem, it does not recommend that each be recorded, but resorts to a hierarchical principle (Boyd et al., 1984). Diagnostic classes are rank ordered according to alleged severity, whereby the more serious disorder takes precedence over the more minor one. A disorder high in the hierarchy may have features found in disorders lower in the rank order, but not the reverse. If a psychiatric condition is multisyndromal in nature, the DSM-III guideline is to ignore all syndromes but the one that is supposed to override all others. In other words, if major depression occurs in, for instance, schizophrenia (rank ordered higher than depression), it cannot be diagnosed as such, while "lower-order conditions," like panic disorder, generalized anxiety disorder, and obsessive compulsive disorder, if occurring jointly with depression, will remain undiagnosed.

Psychiatry has little to gain from hierarchical diagnostic systems, as they were advocated by Foulds (1976), and much to lose. Foremost is the loss of diagnostic information. Sets of symptoms may indeed be overridden by others, namely derivative symptoms by those directly related to the pathogenesis of the disorder. The trouble is that in psychiatry pathogenesis is largely unknown, rendering all hierarchical models speculative. Boyd et al. (1984) demonstrated that people with a "dominant disorder" have high odds of having symptoms of a "subordinate disorder." A causal relationship, however, seems unlikely since little evidence exists that lower-order syndromes disappear if higher-ranking syndromes have been successfully treated. Consequently, applying a hierarchical system could easily lead to neglect of therapeutic opportunities.

Finally, the hierarchical system could diminish validity of research, particularly biological research. How can one interpret biological findings, for instance, in schizophrenia if in one patient major depression coexists, but not in the other. The DSM-III does not apply the hierarchical principle consistently. The possibility of major depression coexisting with dysthymic disorder is recognized and named double depression. In this case, the allegedly more severe disorder (major depression) apparently does not override the one considered to be less severe.

Parenthetically, the question remains whether the term double depression is appropriate or whether such conditions are better described as mixed forms of depression, as we have suggested. In case of double depression, three types of interrelations are conceivable: dysthymia as the result of major depression, or the reverse, or both syndromes occurring independently. The first possibility is unlikely since dysthymia generally remains if major depression is successfully combated. For lack of specific medication, it is unknown what impact successful treatment of dysthymia would have on major depression. The study of the third option also awaits the availability of antidepressants specific for dysthymia.

The concept of mixed depression, as we defined it, entails the presence of both depression forms (vital and personal depression) simultaneously, each often to an incomplete extent. An observation favoring that concept is that patients diagnosed as mixed depression responded modestly to antidepressants (see Section 2.2.2) and that after six weeks of treatment the diagnosis was: mixed depression, improved, not dysthymic disorder.

The issue under discussion is not purely "academic." If two syndromes are independent but superimposed, one could in principle study the pathogenesis of one and disregard the other. If two syndromes are mixed, such patients are unsuitable for biological studies. One has, for the time being, to carefully select and study monosyndromal patients.

4. THE DSM-III-R CLASSIFICATION OF DEPRESSION

The DSM-III-R, introduced in 1987, retained the principle of multiaxial depression classification (Keypoint 1) and no etiological axis was added (Keypoint 3). The changes that were introduced will be discussed below, again by contrasting them with the tenets I had formulated.

4.1. Keypoint 2: Syndromal Differentiation

The principle of syndromal heterogeneity of depressive disorder is upheld in DSM-III-R and the description of major depression remained virtually unchanged. The symptom profile held to be characteristic for dysthymic disorder, however, underwent significant modifications. For no apparent reason, two out of six instead of three out of 13 symptoms are now required, making comparability of research based on DSM-III and DSM-III-R criteria illusory.

All symptoms listed under dysthymia are also found under major depression. Anhedonia, however, is removed from the listing of dysthymic symptoms and the presence of motor pathology has also acquired differentiating power. Diagnostic haziness does persist, though some clearing has occurred.

4.2. Keypoint 4: The Severity Issue

The *severity* of major depression is now recognized to be variable and an axis to rate this dimension is added. This addition does improve

TABLE 3:7
Duration of Present Dysthymic Episode and of the Preceding Symptom-
Free or Symptom-Reduced Interval

| | *% of Patients Indicating that Time Interval* (n = 100) | |
	Duration of the Present Dysthymic Episode	*Duration of the Preceding Symptom-Free (-Reduced) Interval*
< 1 Week	–	6
1 Month	6	38
1–3 Months	19	35
3–6 Months	22	19
6–12 Months	29	2
12–24 Months	14	–
< 24 Months	10	–

the sensitivity of the diagnosis of major depression, but it lessens the differentiability of dysthymic and major depression based as it is, in large measure, on differences in severity. The dysthymic group remains defined as mild, perpetuating the fallacy of excluding severe forms from a proper diagnosis.

The diagnostic role of *duration* is better specified in the DSM-III-R. For the diagnosis of major depression, a duration of at least two weeks is required. The length of the period is unspecified and one can agree with that because it varies tremendously. A requirement for the diagnosis of dysthymia is a duration of two years during which depression has been present "most of the day, more days than not." This requirement is at odds with our clinical data. The duration of dysthymic episodes is capricious (Table 3:7). In a cohort of 100 patients, a majority (76) indicated a duration of less than one year, 14 a duration of 1–2 years, and 10 a duration of more than two years. Duration ran from a few days to months or years in a row, sometimes interspersed with symptom-reduced or symptom-free intervals, sometimes not. The duration of the latter, if occurring, is also variable; it varied from one month to a year. The occurrence of symptomatic and asymptomatic or less symptomatic episodes often coincides with stressful and more tranquil phases in life, respectively. The DSM-III-R forces one to categorize many patients with dysthymia as "Depressive disorder not otherwise specified" and I see no reason for doing so.

4.3. Keypoint 5: Personality Disorder and Depression

The overlap of dysthymic disorder and personality disorder is once more stressed and the issue continues to be ignored in major depression. In major depression melancholic type, however, a new criterion is added, i.e. absence of significant personality disturbances before the first major depressive episode. This is a classical conception, reaching back to Kretschmer, but a misconception. Carrying this criterion through would leave many melancholic patients misdiagnosed.

4.4. Keypoint 6: Against Diagnostic Hierarchies

The principle of multisyndromal diagnoses gained some ground in the DSM-III-R. Panic disorder and major depression are now considered to be "compatible." In the description of phobia and obsessive-compulsive disorder, the incompatibility rules for cases in which these anxiety disorders coexist with a mood disorder have disappeared. Psychotic disorders, however, still "override" major depression and mood disorders take precedence over generalized anxiety disorder. The hierarchical system is apparently phased out, but yet by no means abandoned.

5. THE OFFICIAL DEPRESSION CLASSIFICATION TODAY: SUMMING UP

The decision to standardize and operationalize diagnostic concepts in psychiatry was a landmark in the development of our profession. Having said that, I add that the depression classification as adopted in the DSM-III shows major shortcomings.

1. The principle of syndromal heterogeneity of depression is accepted, but diagnostic distinctions are foggy.
2. Etiological considerations are treated with trepidation. They are neither left out nor covered comprehensively. The system aspires to be "atheoretical," fails to be and is instead ambiguous.
3. The factor of severity is used as a diagnostic characteristic, not

as a separate dimension. This is a serious flaw that has haunted depression taxonomy for many years.

4. The frequent coexistence of major depression with personality pathology is not acknowledged, fueling diagnostic confusion of major depression with dysthymia.

5. An ill-conceived hierarchical model is used, albeit not consistently, leading to considerable loss of information and flawing of data obtained in biological research of depression and coexisting mental disorders.

The DSM-III classification of depression is not the end product of systematic research into the anchorpoints on which this classification rests, but evidently a product of compromise of a diversity of expert opinons. Hence, the situation is chaos now, as it was some 30 years ago. All things considered, the present situation is worse. Then, psychiatrists were at least aware that diagnostic chaos reigned and many of them had no high opinion of diagnosis anyhow. Now, the chaos is codified and thus much more hidden. It is true that the codification is not sancrosanct and is periodically adjusted. So far, however, it has been guided by experts, not by focused research. Modifications introduced today, then, will irrevocably be followed by modifications tomorrow, creating even more confusion both practically—not every clinician keeping up with the ever changing guidelines—and scientifically, because research conducted under the jurisdiction of the various DSM editions will be increasingly hard to compare.

6. SOME REMEDIES

What steps could be taken to turn the tide of proliferating confusion?

1. Prototypes of depressive syndromes should be clearly and unambiguously defined with as little overlap as possible. The intermediate forms would be indicated as"mixed"or"double" depressions and recognized as a group still in need of detailed charting. This would mean elimination of the "choice-principle" and contrasting of the symptom clusters held to be characteristic for major depression and dysthymia.

2. Definition of the various forms of depression should be based on symptoms *only* and the variables of severity and duration assessed independently.
3. The same is true for the factor course, which is so variable in most syndromal depression forms that it should not be handled as a trademark of a particular syndrome, but rather scored separately on an independent axis. An exception is seen in depressions alternating with (hypo)-manic episodes. Bipolar disorder seems to approach the qualifications of a distinct nosological entity.
4. Since premorbid personality disturbances seem not to be restricted to a particular syndromal form of depression, personality disorders, too, ought not to be part of the diagnostic definition of a depression, but instead assessed independently of syndromal diagnosis.
5. Etiology is to be handled as a legitimate and independent axis. Physical disorders, personality disorders, psychosocial stressors, and familial factors have to be carefully documented and estimated as to their etiological weight.
6. If the behavior disorder of a given patient is composed of more than one syndrome, each of them should be documented. Hierarchical rank–ordering of psychiatric disorders, whereby one overrides the other, is a nonvalidated and harmful construct, with no heuristic value, that can lead only to tremendous loss of information.

The keypoints I formulated some 30 years ago, then, seem still to be valid; certainly, the author of this book has not changed his mind. Is he perhaps another expert hoping to see his views eternalized in the next DSM edition? In all sincerity, the answer is: Not at all. Let me once more specify my point of view. Unless we had been prepared to wait for decades, there was only one way to develop an operationalized taxonomy, namely via expert opinion. However, the necessity of developing a classification system on short notice, did not make that method virtuous. It remained what it is: scientifically invalid. Further changes in the DSM-III should, therefore, not have been based on learned discussions, but rather on research specifically designed to answer questions raised by DSM-III taxonomy. The ongoing bickering with diagnostic criteria is destroying the very fabric that should give psychiatric research its durability. Already, data collected before 1980 are not comparable with those obtained after the DSM-III was introduced, which are in their turn not comparable with those that were gathered under the aegis of the DSM-III-R.

There is no end to this confusion in sight. Diagnostic uncertainty is not the soil in which a medical science can thrive. It is tragic that a system developed to bring order where chaos reigned has become a boomerang, harming the very enterprise for which it was developed. It is for those reasons that I recommend that an immediate moratorium should be laid on any expert-opinion-based alterations in the DSM-III classification of depression (or, for that matter, in that of any other psychiatric disorder). To the best of my knowledge, this item is not on the agenda of the trustees of that most precious component of our professional estate: the taxonomy of psychiatric disorders. For me, that is reason for great concern.

7. SUMMARY

Before the advent of antidepressants, no generally accepted and operationalized classification of depression existed. In the late fifties and sixties, I proposed a multiaxial and operationalized depression taxonomy in order to be able to study systematically the clinical and biochemical action of antidepressants and the biological characteristics of depressive patients responsive to antidepressants. The keypoints of that system and the data on which it was based are discussed, after which it is compared with the depression classification proposed by the DSM-III and DSM-III-R. Though it is recognized that a system based on consensus opinion can never be completely acceptable to everyone, the conclusion is reached that the DSM-III depression classification is outright unsatisfactory and contributes to diagnostic confusion rather than to reducing it. It is recommended that an immediate moratorium should be placed on expert-opinion-based alterations in the classification of depressions and that future changes be based only on research specifically designed to resolve issues pertinent to that classification. The fact that this approach is apparently not seriously considered should be reason for great concern for those who take psychiatric research to heart.

—4—

Against the Unitary Concept of Schizophrenia

PART I: THE GREAT ILLUSION

1. INTRODUCTION

Kraepelin's concept of dementia praecox brought a number of diagnostic categories that had been hitherto recognized, under one denominator. The entities were: Hecker's hebephrenia, Morel's démence précoce, and Kahlbaum's catatonia. The common denominator was supported by two observations: absence of external and internal precipitants, along with a chronic progressive course leading to "psychichen Siechtum" (psychic sickness). In retrospect, the basis for this unitary concept looks remarkably thin. Recognition of precipitants, in particular of stressful life events, is codependent on the sensitivity of the interviewer and his readiness to take personality make-up into account. Seemingly innocuous events can be quite devastating for a vulnerable personality. Furthermore, many behavioral disorders may occur without obvious provocation. Spontaneous, or seemingly spontaneous occurrence is by no means specific for schizophrenia. Nor is downhill course a criterion to base a disease entity on, even if the terminal stage would be similar. Many heart diseases, for instance, lead ultimately to heart failure, but it would have been scientifically disastrous if they, consequently, would have been lumped together in a unitary "heart failure disease." Besides, the residual schizophrenic state is by no means homogenous, but rather a collective term for a variety of syndromes. As such, it constitutes rather an argument favoring a heterogeneity hypothesis rather than a unitary model.

It is true that Kraepelin (1899) relativized his unitary schizophrenia concept by calling it tentative, but on the other hand he consolidated its nosological status by postulating that a single morbid process explained the downhill course: "Dementia praecox on the whole represents a well-characterized form of disease . . . the expression of a single morbid process." Bleuler (1911) was in this respect his counterpart. He coined the term schizophrenia, used the word in the plural in his seminal book *Dementia Praecox or the Group of Schizophrenias* (1911), and stated emphatically that the concept of schizophrenia included several diseases.

The question of what the taxonomic status of schizophrenia is remained unresolved and, thus, an issue for animated discussion. In 1980, the third edition of the DSM-III was introduced and it basically endorsed the Kraepelinian position: Schizophrenia was seen as an entity, not as a blanket term for a heterogeneous group of psychoses. In the description of subtypes, the DSM-III also stuck quite closely to Kraepelinian tracks. Since the classification proposed by the DSM-III was accepted *de jure* in the USA and *de facto* in most of the rest of the world, the discussion about the nature of schizophrenia came practically to a standstill. Consequently, the DSM-III invites us to study such topics as the genetics, the biological determinants, the outcome of a singular concept: schizophrenia, along with the antecedents and the response to pharmacological and psychological interventions of a particular group of patients: schizophrenics. What a waste of money and energy if after all Bleuler were to be right!

In 1976, I published a paper entitled *About the Impossible Concept of Schizophrenia* in which I scrutinized the unitary concept of schizophrenia and reached the conclusion that it was untenable. Now, 16 years later, I want to tackle this crucial subject again and evaluate whether there is reason for a change of mind. In other words, is the symptomatology of that disorder homogenous, are the causal mechanisms involved comparable on a case-to-case basis, is the treatment response uniform and the outcome predictable to a degree that a unitary hypothesis is arguable?

2. REVIEW OF THE UNITARY CONCEPT

2.1. Phenomenology

2.1.1. *Symptoms*

Symptoms described under the heading of schizophrenia span practically the entire spectrum of psychopathology. Disturbances in cognition may occur, in perception, volition, level of initiative, concentration, motoricity, emotionality, regulation of mood, anxiety, and aggression, and bonding, to mention only the major psychological domains that may be affected. Comparing individual patients, the variation in symptomatology is striking, as Table 4:1 illustrates. Patients with encapsulated delusions, functionally intact and with no significant defects in intellectual and emotional communication, and those with massive delusions and hallucinations, incoherent, completely dysfunctional and with a variety of motor disturbances, all sail under the same flag. The syndromes in between these two extremes are countless.

As a consequence of conceptualizing schizophrenia as a unitary disorder, those patients that do not recover from the disease but continue to show substantial residual symptoms are thrown together under the general diagnosis of chronic schizophrenia. This does not make much sense. As far as symptomatology is concerned, this group is as heterogeneous as the more acute forms of schizophrenic psychoses. The degree of impairment is likewise variable. As an illustration, Table 4:2 sums up the major symptoms of a group of 15 patients who had showed schizophrenic symptoms uninterruptedly for at least three years in spite of treatment and who had been diagnosed as chronic schizophrenics. Obviously, the symptom patterns are extremely variable. Delusions and hallucinations may be prominent or virtually absent. Apathy and avolition may be in the center of the clinical picture or at the margin. Emotionality can be substantially reduced, but also it can be intensified, although strange. Social adjustment is most frequently injured; however, that is hardly specific for schizophrenia, and is a common trait in most chronic psychiatric conditions.

TABLE 4:1

Symptom Pattern in 15 Randomly Selected Patients Diagnosed as Schizophrenics*

Patient	Delusions	Hallucinations	Diminished Drive	Reduced Speech	Emotional Impoverishment	Disinterest in Other People	Unintelligible Speech	Neologisms	Depression	Unkempt at Admission	Involuntary Movements
1	+	-	+	-	+	+	+	-	+	-	-
2	+	+	+	-	-	-	+	-	+	-	-
3	±	±	+	-	±	-	+	-	+	+	-
4	+	+	-	-	±	±	±	-	+	+	±
5	+	+	-	+	±	±	-	-	-	+	±
6	±	-	-	±	-	±	-	±	-	+	-
7	+	-	±	±	+	±	-	±	±	-	-
8	+	-	+	±	+	±	+	±	±	±	+
9	+	±	+	-	+	±+	+	-	-	+	+
10	±	-	+	+	±	+	±	-	+	+	-
11	+	-	+	+	±	-	+	+	+	+	-
12	+	+	+	-	±	-	-	-	±	-	-
13	+	±	±	-	±	±	+	-	-	-	±
14	+	+	±	-	±	-	+	±	+	+	-
15	+	+	+	+	±	±	+	±	+	+	-

*Symptom is clearly present (+), absent (−), or there is no consensus about its presence (±)

TABLE 4:2

Symptom Pattern in 15 Randomly Selected Patients Diagnosed as Chronic Schizophrenics*

Patient	Delusions	Hallucinations	Diminished Drive	Reduced Speech	Emotional Impoverishment	Disinterest in Other People	Unintelligible Speech	Neologisms	Depression	Unkempt at Admission	Involuntary Movements
1	+	−	−	−	±	±	−	−	+	+	−
2	±	−	+	±	±	±	−	−	+	+	−
3	−	+	+	±	±	±	+	−	±	+	−
4	−	+	±	±	−	−	+	±	−	+	±
5	+	−	±	−	−	−	+	+	−	−	−
6	−	±	−	−	−	−	−	−	−	−	+
7	+	±	+	+	±	−	+	−	±	+	+
8	+	±	+	+	+	−	−	−	+	+	+
9	−	−	+	±	+	+	−	−	+	−	−
10	+	−	+	±	+	+	±	±	−	±	±
11	+	+	−	−	±	±	−	+	−	±	+
12	+	±	±	+	−	−	+	±	−	+	−
13	±	±	±	±	±	±	−	−	−	−	+
14	±	±	±	−	−	+	−	−	±	−	±
15	±	−	−	−	−	−	±	+	+	+	−

*Symptom is clearly present (+), absent (−), or there is no consensus about its presence (±)

2.1.2. *Syndromes*

Kraepelin (1899, 1919) distinguished five schizophrenic syndromal subtypes. *Hebephrenia* is an exuberant psychiatric syndrome with massive hallucinations and/or delusions, loss of contact with the environment, and loss of initiative; it usually starts at an early age— during puberty or early adolescence. In *paraphrenia*, the patient develops systematized but encapsulated paranoid delusions, but shows no overall disintegration of the personality. Unlike paraphrenia, *dementia paranoides* is characterized by unsystematized paranoid delusions and progressive deterioration of the entire personality. The predominant features in *dementia simplex* are autism and loss of initiative, while delusions and hallucinations are not very pronounced. *Catatonia*, finally, is a psychotic syndrome characterized by predominance of motor disorders such as stereotypies, stupor, grimacing, etc. Not by any stretch of the imagination can these syndromes be brought under the same phenomenological denominator. They seem to be as dissimilar as the symptoms of circulatory shock and those of jaundice.

The DSM-III-R distinguishes five schizophrenic subtypes. Two of them, the *catatonic* and the *paranoid* subtypes, are borrowed from Kraepelin. The *disorganized* and *undifferentiated* subtypes are novel conceptions that, however, largely overlap. Both syndromes are characterized by grossly disorganized behavior and nonsystematized delusions and hallucinations. Only one symptom is discriminating, that is, flat or grossly inappropriate affect, a symptom that is notoriously hard to assess reliably. The category of *residual* type of schizophrenia encompasses the multitude of chronic forms of schizophrenia and, hence, is utterly heterogeneous.

Again, there seems to be no common core discernible in these syndromes to lend the unitary concept of schizophrenia a degree of face validity, nor has it been demonstrated that they possess any predictive validity (See Table 5:1, next Chapter).

2.1.3. *Pathognomic Symptoms?*

Symptomatological heterogeneity does not preclude the possibility that symptoms exist that are characteristic for schizophrenia and occur across syndromes. Kraepelin (1899) listed as basic symptoms of schizophrenia: poor insight, decline of mental flexibility and performance, blunting of affect, and a loosening of internal unity. He considered them as obligatory, that is, they had to be present in every case diagnosed as schizophrenia. As features of more or less secondary diagnostic importance, he listed hallucinations, delusions, depressive mood, motor pathology, volitional disturbances, negativism, and "Befehlsautomatie" (automatic response to commands). Those he considered to be facultative; they may, but need not, be present in schizophrenia.

Bleuler (1911) considered loosening of associations and "splitting of the personality" essential for the diagnosis of schizophrenia. Splitting means dissociation—dissociation of emotions from ideas, of expression from emotion, of conduct from intentions, and so on. He regarded these so-called "primary symptoms" as direct consequences of a supposed underlying brain disease. He dismissed such symptoms as hallucination, delusion, confusion, twilight states, manic and depressive changes of mood, and catatonic symptoms as "secondary" and not essential to the diagnosis; they were simply psychological reactions to the primary manifestations.

Both Kraepelin and Bleuler showed little finesse in operationalizing the diagnostic criteria for schizophrenia. Moreover, several of the symptoms they deemed characteristic cannot be diagnosed without a fair amount of subjective interpretation, and this impedes their transferability. The most carefully elaborated attempt to describe symptoms pathognomonic for schizophrenia was made by Schneider (1959). He described 11 of them, which he called symptoms of the first rank. The presence of any of these symptoms was sufficient to warrant a diagnosis of schizophrenia, unless gross anatomic abnormalities were present in the brain. Schneider's list included audible thoughts; thought broadcasting, extractions and insertions; third person auditory hallucinations; passivity phenomena of made thoughts, made impulses, and made feelings; and delusional perceptions: a normal perception is followed by an erroneous interpretation with a very special, patient-oriented significance.

The reported frequency of one or more first-rank symptoms in schizophrenia varies from as high as 73 percent (O'Grady, 1990) to 28 percent (Taylor, 1972). Moreover, the specificity of first-rank symptoms has been seriously challenged. Carpenter et al. (1973), for instance, found them in 23 percent of those with affective disorders; we observed first-rank symptoms both in schizoaffective psychosis (46 percent) and psychogenic psychosis (33 percent). The presence of first-rank symptoms has not been shown to indicate chronicity of illness or poor outcome (Radhakrishnan et al., 1983; Brockington & Leff, 1978).

Schneider's choice of the symptoms of the first order was not based on theoretical considerations, but was entirely pragmatic; they could be most readily diagnosed in a patient. On the other hand, there were psychiatrists with a diagnostic preference for symptoms that are difficult to objectify, i.e. those that can be established only in communicative contact with the patients. They focused primarily on the patient's ability to enter in an affective relationship with another person and on the extent to which he shows affective "resonance" in such a contact. Riimke's (1967) thinking provides a typical example. He maintained that there are no symptoms specific to schizophrenia. The diagnosis is, in fact, made on the basis of a feeling that the patient evokes in the investigator, the so-called praecox feeling. He tried to define this as a sense of estrangement—one senses that one's own overtures meet an obstacle. The patient accepts nothing of what the investigator offers—contact, warmth, understanding. Recognition of this praecox feeling requires a well-developed empathic ability on the part of the investigator. There have been no empirical studies conducted to try to validate this criterion.

2.1.4. *Conclusions*

Symptomatologically, then, there is no compelling reason to consider schizophrenia as a diagnostic entity. On the contrary, if so many psychological domains can be affected and individual syndromes differ as widely as they do (both in acute and chronic forms of schizophrenia), one rather suspects schizophrenia to be a blanket term for a pathogenetically diverse group of psychoses loosely bound together by the criterion of intactness of sensorium.

Yet, as of this day, respected schizophrenia researchers are prepared to play around with symptoms in a desperate attempt to salvage the unitary character of a disease entity called schizophrenia (Andreasen & Flaum, 1991). It is an exercise as embarrassing for the scientific credibility of psychiatry as it is futile.

2.2. Course

Kraepelin (1899) defined schizophrenia as a functional psychosis with a deteriorating course, though later in his life he did qualify his opinion when he observed that six patients, of a cohort of 127 he had studied over a long period of time, had fully recovered. Bleuler's (1911) viewpoint was ambiguous from the beginning. On the one hand, he maintained that the disease can recede or be arrested in any stage; on the other hand, he stated that schizophrenia is incurable, or at least that *restitutio ad integrum* does not occur. "For the most part, although one may not notice any advance in the deterioration as long as one is in constant daily contact with the patients, I am usually struck by the increased decline when I have occasion to see the patients again after an interval of many years."

In subsequent years, the natural history of schizophrenia continued to generate controversy. Some authors remained faithful to Kraepelin's original view, using the term schizophrenia only if the outcome had been obviously unfavorable, and they considered complete recovery to be incompatible with that diagnosis. Those patients that did recover or substantially improved were reclassified as, for instance, schizophreniform psychosis (Langfeldt, 1937) or pseudoschizophrenia (Riimke, 1967). Others discarded the prognostic criterion as unreliable and diagnosed schizophrenia on symptomatological grounds, disregarding outcome; they claimed significant psychotherapeutic successes in the treatment of this disorder. The DSM-III leans towards the Kraepelinian view in stipulating that a diagnosis of schizophrenia requires a duration of the psychosis of at least six months. When one uses this approach, those remitting spontaneously and the treatment-responsive cases are sifted out, since neuroleptics, if effective, will show results well within a six-month range.

Well designed longitudinal studies leave little doubt that when the diagnosis of schizophrenia is made cross-sectionally, the bad-prognosis criterion is invalid. Shepherd et al. (1989) gave a detailed account of the relevant literature. I will merely summarize the conclusions of a few representative studies. Bleuler (1978) studied 208 patients personally treated over a 5–20 year follow-up period and reported clinical recovery in 20 percent of the cases and poor outcome in 24 percent. Moller et al. (1982) followed up 103 cases and found that five years after hospitalization 10 percent were in clinical remission, 31 percent

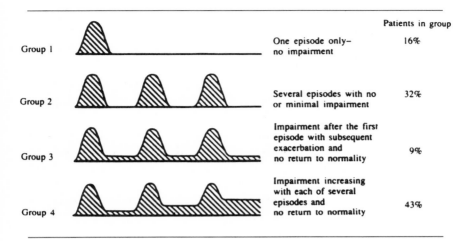

		Patients in group
Group 1	One episode only– no impairment	16%
Group 2	Several episodes with no or minimal impairment	32%
Group 3	Impairment after the first episode with subsequent exacerbation and no return to normality	9%
Group 4	Impairment increasing with each of several episodes and no return to normality	43%

Figure 4:1. Graded course of illness for a cohort of 107 schizophrenics during five years as indicated by episodes of illness, symptomatology and social impairment at assessments (Shepherd et al., 1989).

showed a poor outcome, and more than half the patients were considered to exhibit satisfactory social functioning. The World Health Organization (WHO) collaborative study (Sartorius et al., 1986) studied 811 schizophrenic patients from nine countries over a period of five years. In developing countries, 45 percent were considered to be in remission and 29 percent had a poor outcome. The corresponding figures in the developed countries were 25 percent and 50 percent.

Harding et al. (1987), in a retrospective study of 269 patients who had been hospitalized a mean of 16 years prior to the beginning of the study, reported that at follow-up 32 years later, 68 percent of the patients had no schizophrenic symptoms and 45 percent were free of any psychiatric symptoms. Shepherd et al. (1989) reported on 121 schizophrenic patients followed up over a five-year period. The outcome was considered to be good for 48 percent of the cohort. Sixteen percent of the cohort had during the five-year period one episode only and no impairment afterwards; 32 percent had several episodes with no or minimal impairment between episodes; 9 percent experienced several episodes, with impairment after the first episode, but no progression after subsequent episodes; 43 percent went through several psychotic episodes, with increasing impairment after each episode (Fig. 4:1). Of the follow-up studies conducted after 1950, no one reported poor clinical outcome in more than 50 percent of the cohorts studied, though the rates vary considerably between individual studies.

The reason for the discrepancies between Kraepelin's original prognostic observations and the results of later outcome studies is unknown. Conceivably, Kraepelin's cohort represented a negative selection in that psychiatric hospitals in his days were places of last resort, for the most part admitting patients whose condition had become unbearable for their families and in whom spontaneous remission was not forthcoming. Another possibility is that modern treatment approaches prevent or retard progression of the schizophrenic "process," a theory for which there exists indeed some scattered evidence (Wyatt et al., 1988).

Be this as it may, data on the course of schizophrenia do not support a unitary hypothesis, but rather favor a heterogeneity hypothesis. If an ostensibly similar condition, for instance a tumor, can take a benign or a malignant course, it is ill conceived to hypothesize the malignant form to be merely the "nuclear variant" of the same disease and to consider the pathogenesis of the two connections as basically similar. This is exactly what today tends to happen regarding schizophrenia.

2.3. Causation: Etiological Factors

Is there any consistency in the variables related to the occurrence of schizophrenia? In this respect, I distinguish between etiological and pathogenetic factors (van Praag & Leijnse, 1964). The complex of cerebral dysfunctions underlying a particular behavioral disorder is named: pathogenesis, the factors that have contributed to the cerebral dysregulation are characterized as etiology. Etiological factors may be biological, psychological, or environmental in nature, and biological factors can be acquired during life or genetically transmitted. I will first discuss potential etiological factors in schizophrenia.

2.3.1. *Exogenous Factors*

Kraepelin defined schizophrenia as a functional psychosis, that is, as a psychosis occurring with no signs of an organic brain disease, though he emphasized repeatedly that the disease in all likelihood was rooted in a "tangible disease process in the brain" that was as yet, however, obscure. The DSM-III, being more royalistic than the king, requires for the diagnosis of schizophrenia "that it cannot be established that an organic factor initiated and maintained the disturbance." This view is overly restrictive. Anatomical damage of the brain does occur in schizophrenia, as manifested in enlarged ventricles on the CT scan, while postmortem studies revealed anatomical changes though they are unspecific and variable as far as location is concerned (see section 2.4.1.).

The point to be stressed in this context is that morphological damage may or may not occur in schizophrenia, and that we know of no psychopathological correlates of these phenomena. Conversely, known brain diseases may be accompanied by psychoses symptomatologically undistinguishable from schizophrenia. Examples are encephalitis (Crow, 1984), cerebral tumors in the diencephalic and limbic regions (Davison & Bagley, 1969), temporal lobe epilepsy (Trimble, 1991), and Huntington's chorea (Davison & Bagley, 1969). Recently, O'Callaghan et al. (1991) reviewed the birth dates of schizophrenic inpatients in eight health regions in the U.K. for any effect of the 1957 A2 influenza epidemic. Five months after the peak infection prevalence, the number of births of individuals who later developed schizophrenia was 88 percent higher than the average number of such births in the corresponding periods of the two previous and the next two years.

No correlation has been established between the occurrence of a psychosis and the localization of the anatomical lesion. Thus, the label "organic schizophrenia" is probably inappropriate. On the other hand, neither family history nor disturbances in premorbid personality structure or adjustment suggest that we deal with organically worsened or precipitated forms of schizophrenia. The nature of organic schizophrenia is obviously unresolved.

2.3.2. *Hereditary Factors*

Kraepelin counted dementia praecox among the chiefly hereditary psychoses. There is indeed little doubt that schizophrenic psychoses might run in families, while twin and adoption studies suggest that that phenomenon can be better explained by genetic than by environmental factors (McGuffin et al., 1987). However, genes are not equally important in all cases. Though the concordance for schizophrenia is much higher in monozygotic twins (20–40 percent) than in dizygotic twins (8–20 percent), it is far from 100 percent. Moreover, a substantial proportion of cases diagnosed as schizophrenia is sporadic, in that there are no other reported cases of schizophrenia in the family. Some studies even failed to demonstrate any increased risk of schizophrenia or "schizophrenia spectrum" personality disorders in relatives of schizophrenics versus never-ill controls (Kendler, 1988). Schizophrenics with a positive family history and sporadic cases seem to differ in a number of seemingly unrelated variables, such as electrodermal responsiveness, theta activity in the electroencephalogram, CT scan abnormalities, and concentration of the serotonin metabolite, 5-hydroxyindoleacetic acid in the cerebrospinal fluid (Dalen & Hayes, 1990).

Not only is the genetic contribution variable, it is also unclear what actually is being transmitted. Adoption studies showed that children of schizophrenic mothers, adopted by nonschizophrenic families shortly after birth, had a higher incidence of schizophrenia than adopted children of nonschizophrenic mothers (Heston, 1966; Kety, 1983). Among the biological relatives of the adoptees from schizophrenic mothers, however, schizophrenia was overrepresented, but so were conditions that were considered as schizophrenia-related, such as borderline schizophrenia, reactive schizophrenia, schizoid and paranoid personality disorders, and "eccentric" and "odd" behavior (Kety et al., 1978). There is, however, no consensus as to which conditions make up the "schizophrenia spectrum." Using stricter diagnostic criteria, Kendler et al. (1981) demonstrated that the prevalence of schizotypal personality disorder was significantly higher in the biological relatives of schizophrenic adoptees than in controls.

It thus seems likely that what is being transmitted is not the disposition for a discrete illness, for a *morbus schizophrenicus*, but rather for a (set of) psychological dysfunction(s) that might occur in the "schizophrenic spectrum," but might be absent as well, or the disposition for the development of a personality trait that sensitizes for the occurrence of schizophrenic spectrum disorders, but which is not necessary for their development.

Sherrington et al. (1988) reported a susceptibility gene for schizophrenia on the chromosome 5q11—q13 region, but three subsequent studies failed to corroborate that finding (McGuffin et al., 1990). Genetic heterogeneity of schizophrenia could be the explanation, but at least as likely is again the possibility that the locus on chromosome 5 is not transmitting a discrete illness, but rather a component of the syndrome or a personality trait acting as a vulnerability factor that might occur in schizophrenic disorders, but is not essential for their occurrence.

It is fair to conclude that the genetic data utterly fail to substantiate the notion of a discrete, unique *morbus schizophrenicus.*

2.3.3. *Psychological Factors*

Kraepelin underplayed the possible role of psychological factors in the causation of schizophrenia. "The sometimes excellent psychological passages in his (Kraepelin's) textbook succeeded as it were against his intention: he considers them temporary stopgaps until experiment, microscope or test tube will have made everything accessible to objective investigation" (Jaspers, 1948). Bleuler, in the fourth edition of his textbook, brought the psyche back in schizophrenia by differentiating between "process schizophrenia" and "reactive schizophrenia," the former with largely organic etiology, whereas the latter should be largely psychogenic. Others followed his example, but used different names, such as true schizophrenia versus pseudoschizophrenia (Rümke, 1967) and true schizophrenia and schizophreniform psychosis (Langfeldt, 1939).

In Europe the concept of psychogenic psychosis was introduced, alluding to a condition with schizophrenic symptomatology, relatively good prognosis, and interpretable as the catastrophic nadir of neurotic development, that is, as the extreme consequence of unresolved psychological problems (Faergeman, 1963). The DSM-III recognizes a group of psychoses closely associated with psychotraumatic events and named them brief psychotic reactions. It is stipulated that the psychotic symptoms generally subside in a day or two and that "by definition, this diagnosis is not applicable if the psychotic symptoms persist for more than one month." The time restriction seems arbitrary since the duration of psychoses called psychogenic is quite variable and unpredictable (Jauch & Carpenter, 1988a).

It has been shown, both in retrospective (Lukoff et al., 1981) and prospective studies (Ventura et al., 1989), that stressful life events may occur in close temporal proximity to the beginning of the schizophrenic episode. In other cases, however, the temporal linkage is not so clear or severe psychosocial stress is not easily demonstrable at all. Often, moreover, it is hard to establish whether the distress preceded the breakdown or rather was a consequence of the imminent psychosis. The relationship of life events to the onset of schizophrenia is unknown. They could play a formative or a triggering role (Brown & Harris, 1978), contributing significantly to the causation of the psychosis or merely aggravating a strong preexisting tendency that would sooner or later have manifested itself anyhow. In the long run, episodes seem to occur more and more "spontaneously."

In the fifties and sixties, theories were in vogue postulating that disturbed family relations might give rise or could contribute to schizophrenia. The double bind theory of Bateson et al. (1956) is a typical example. No family pattern, however, has been found that consistently could predict the occurrence of schizophrenic psychoses, whereas family patterns thought to be specific for schizophrenia have been found in other psychiatric conditions as well. Familial factors definitely have an impact on relapse risk. Criticism, hostility, and overinvolvement of the patient's family members, in short, undue negative stimulation, can have an unfavorable impact on the course of the disease (Fallon et al., 1982).

Personality functioning before the first psychotic episode is often found to be disturbed, but the disturbances are far from consistent. In some cases, personality development seems to have been normal up to a relative brief period—months up to a few years—before the manifestation of the psychosis. A developmental break has occurred after which the patient becomes progressively "strange." In other cases, we hear that the patient has been "odd" or "eccentric" from early childhood on. The kind of "strangeness" is also variable. Sometimes it takes the form of inactivity, withdrawal, and remoteness. In others, the behavior is described as eccentric with odd beliefs and signs of magical thinking. Other types of personality dysfunctions that may precede the psychosis are paranoid features and a global retardation of personality development. In short, personality pathology is frequent, but variable in its manifestations and its time of occurrence. Schizotypal symptoms, moreover, are not specific for "preschizophrenics," but are also observed in other behavioral disorders, such as borderline personality disorder (George & Soloff, 1986) and schizoaffective disorder (Coryell & Zimmerman, 1988).

Obviously, then, schizophrenic psychoses often do not occur "out of the blue" and can be closely interwoven with signs of disturbed personality structure, premorbid maladaptive functioning, and psychosocial stress. Consistency in the occurrence and nature of these variables, however, is lacking and we are completely in the dark about their etiological weight.

2.3.4. *Conclusion*

It thus seems fair to conclude that the etiology of schizophrenic psychoses does not involve a single factor, but is determined by a pattern of factors and that that pattern is capricious and variable from subgroup to subgroup and from patient to patient. The etiological data thus fail to provide any support for a unitary view.

2.4. Causation: Pathogenetic Factors

2.4.1. *Structural Defects*

A quite consistent finding in schizophrenia has been a decrease in brain weight and an increase in size of the cerebral ventricles, particularly in the frontal and temporal horns. Reviewing the literature, Weinberger and Kleinman (1986) found that 24 of 29 studies using computer axial tomography (CAT or CT) scanning reported this anomaly. The overlap with control values, however, is substantial. Enlargement of cortical sulci was reported in 14 out of 17 studies. In accordance with these findings, magnetic resonance imaging (MRI) studies have revealed a smaller temporal lobe gray matter volume in patients with schizophrenia than in normal controls (Suddath et al., 1989), while postmortem studies reported a decrease in cerebral tissue in the temporal lobe (Bogerts et al., 1985; Brown et al., 1986). The medial temporal lobe structures (hippocampus and parahippocampal gyrus) are preferentially affected (Roberts, 1991).

It is unknown whether increased ventricular size represents a failure of neural development or an acquired loss of brain tissue, or whether the ventricular enlargement is caused by the loss of brain tissue or is obstructive in nature and, thus, the cause of the tissue loss. The structural changes are probably nongenetic in origin, since, in monozygotic twins discordant for schizophrenia, they were found in the affected twin, not in the normal one (Suddath et al., 1990). Ventricular enlargement has not been found to correlate with length of hospital stay, length of illness, or current or past dosage of neuroleptics (Weinberger et al., 1980a, 1980b). Some authors reported increased ventricular size in first-break schizophrenics, but others could not confirm this.

It is clear, however, that abnormalities in ventricular size occur only in a minority of schizophrenic patients, varying in different studies from 10–40 percent. Only Suddath et al. (1990) reported enlargement of the lateral and third ventricles in the great majority of the cases they studied. The structural changes are, moreover, not specific for schizophrenia, but have also been reported in other behavioral disorders, such as manic–depressive disorder and Alzheimer's disease (Pearlson et al., 1984; Woods et al., 1990).

Neuropathological studies have reported structural brain abnormalities, such as neuronal loss and aberrant architecture in the cingulate gyrus and prefrontal cortex, in the basal limbic structures of the forebrain, and atrophy in temporolimbic structures, such as the hippocampus and amygdala (Stevens, 1982; Mesulam, 1980; Roberts, 1990). However, the findings are inconsistent and nonspecific, vary from study to study, and, more importantly in this context, occur only in a subset of schizophrenic patients.

Cognitive impairment and poor premorbid and social functioning appear to be related to loss of brain weight, increased ventricular size, and abnormalities of cyto-architecture (Bruton et al., 1990; Pakkenberg, 1987), suggesting that those structural abnormalities are not specific for schizophrenia, but related to particular psychopathological dimensions of the syndrome that may or may not be present in a given case.

2.4.2. *Functional Disturbances*

Positron emission tomography (PET) and regional cerebral blood flow (RCBF) studies have found relatively decreased levels of metabolism in the frontal cortex of schizophrenic patients (Andresen, 1988; Cleghorn et al., 1989; Weinberger & Kleinman, 1986). Since the frontal lobe syndrome and so-called negative schizophrenia overlap to some extent, this seemed to support Crow's (1980) theory that this form of schizophrenia is caused by morphological brain damage. However, these findings have not been confirmed by some authors (Sheppard et al., 1983), while medication effects have not been excluded. For example, Cleghorn et al. (1989) reported relative *hyper*-metabolism of the frontal lobe in schizophrenic patients who had never received medications. More important, however, hypofrontality is certainly not a hallmark of schizophrenia, but has been reported to occur only in a subgroup of patients carrying this diagnosis.

Neurophysiological dysfunctions have been reported to occur in schizophrenia, one of the most intriguing being eye-tracking dysfunctions. Eye-movement disorders consist of the following components: 1) a larger-than-expected number of saccadic intrusions, including square wave jerks and saccadic pulses during pursuit movements and during fixation eye movements; 2) saccadic smooth-pursuit tracking, indicating low-gain pursuit; or 3) large saccadic substitutions for smooth pursuit (Holzman et al., 1988). The dysfunctions, however, are not universal in schizophrenia, but have been reported in 51 percent to 85 percent of schizophrenic patients. Moreover, the same disturbances are encountered in 30 percent to 50 percent of patients with affective disorders. Other neurophysiological dysfunctions, such as abnormalities in electrodermal activity and in event-related potentials, proposed as markers for schizophrenia, likewise lack diagnostic specificity (Szymanski et al., 1991).

2.4.3. *Neurotransmitter Disturbances*

Dopamine. Several theories exist about the cerebral dysfunctions that might underlie schizophrenic psychoses. First among equals is the dopamine (DA) hypothesis, postulating DA hyperactivity as an important mechanism in the generation of schizophrenic symptoms. A somewhat more sophisticated variant of this hypothesis holds that the primary DA lesion in schizophrenia is hypofunction of the mesocortical DA system, leading to the complex of negative symptoms. Hypofunction of this DA system would lead to disinhibition of the mesolimbic DA system, a process thought to be responsible for the positive symptoms (Review: Losonczy et al., 1987).

The DA hypothesis rests largely on the observation that all neuroleptics attenuate DA ergic activity; direct supportive evidence is scarce and largely derived from postmortem studies. Dopamine-2 receptors have been found to be increased in the brains of schizophrenic patients, both in postmortem and in PET

studies. In the former, the impact of preceding neuroleptic treatment could not be excluded, while the PET results have not been
confirmed. DA disturbances are also suggested by the findings of
increased DA concentration in the nucleus accumbens and the
anterior perforated substance, but, again, the effect of neuroleptic
treatment could not be excluded. Consistent changes in the cerebrospinal fluid level of homovanillic acid (HVA), the major metabolite of DA, have not been found, though some schizophrenic
patients do show abnormal HVA levels. The same can be said of
plasma HVA, likewise a crude indicator of DA metabolism in the
CNS. Moreover, there is some evidence that the most symptomatic patients have the highest plasma HVA, but it has not been
established which symptoms in particular might be DA-linked.

The major point I want to make in this context is that signs of
central DA dysfunctions, if at all demonstrable, are inconsistent in
that they occur in some, but are absent in other, patients diagnosed as schizophrenics, and that in an entirely unpredictable
fashion.

Noradrenaline. A second theory relates noradrenaline (NA) dysfunction to schizophrenia, a major argument again being psychopharmacological: Neuroleptics are effective blockers not only of DA
receptors, but of NA receptors as well. In support of this hypothesis
is tentative evidence of an elevated NA level in the nucleus accumbens of chronic schizophrenics, as well as in the CSF (Van Kammen
et al., 1989). Without going into detail, I would note here that these
phenomena were by no means universal in schizophrenia, but
seemed to correlate with the existence of paranoid symptoms (Kendler & Davis, 1981).

Serotonin. Recently, some evidence has emerged that implicates the
serotonin (5-hydroxytryptamine, 5-HT) system in the pathogenesis
of schizophrenia (van Praag, 1992b). Clozapine, as well as some
other atypical neuroleptics like rispiridone, are potent blockers of
$5-HT_2$ and $5-HT_{1C}$ receptors in the brain, a feature that might
explain their apparent superiority vis à vis classical neuroleptics in
chronic schizophrenia. Blockade of $5-HT_3$ receptors likewise seems
to exert antipsychotic effects (van Praag, 1992b).

Moreover, challenge tests with the relatively selective 5-HT agonist M-chlorophenylpiperazine (MCPP) have revealed disturbances in 5-HT receptor sensitivity in schizophrenia. In chronically relapsing, nonhospitalized and still more or less functional schizophrenics, Iqbal et al. (1991a, 1991b) found both signs of hypersensitive 5-HT receptors, i.e. worsening of symptoms after MCPP, and signs of hyposensitive 5-HT receptors, i.e. blunting of hormonal responses. Apparently, the various subpopulations of 5-HT receptors are unevenly affected. A similar dissociation of MCPP effects has been reported in obsessive-compulsive disorder. MCPP worsened psychopathological symptoms, in particular obsessions and anxiety, while at the same time the hormonal responses were found to be blunted (Zohar et al., 1987). The similarity of 5-HT dysfunctions indicates that they are not specific for a particular disorder, but probably related to a psychopathological component common to both disorders. I have suggested that this common denominator should be sought in the sphere of cognition (van Praag, 1992b). In severe, chronic schizophrenics who had been hospitalized for many years, MCPP has been reported to improve certain schizophrenic symptoms (Kahn et al., 1991b; Lindenmayer et al., unpublished).

Obviously, then, 5-HT disturbances are not ubiquitous in schizophrenia. They seem to vary in nature and preliminary evidence suggests that at least some of them are related to components of the schizophrenic syndrome, not to the disorder itself.

Endorphins. The endorphin system has been implicated in the pathogenesis of schizophrenia. The most sophisticated hypothesis is the one proposed by De Wied (1978). He demonstrated that certain endorphin fragments, particularly des-tyrosine-γ-endorphin (DTγE) and des-enkephaline-γ-endorphin (DEγE) had lost their opiate effects and in test animals demonstrated neuroleptic-like properties. Alpha-endorphines, on the other hand, were shown to have behavioral effects comparable with those of the central stimulants. Based on those findings, De Wied proposed that a disturbed balance between α- and γ-endorphines, resulting in a decreased availability of γ-endorphines, could play a role in the pathogenesis of schizophrenia. Direct evidence supporting this hypothesis is lacking, but it derived some indirect support from studies showing that DTγE and DEγE might have therapeutic potential in schizophrenia. No effect across the board has been demonstrated, however, but a relatively modest effect has been seen in some schizophrenic patients, so far not psychopathologically identifiable in advance (Manchanda et al., 1988; Verhoeven & Van Ree, 1988).

GABA. The last system to be mentioned here, implicated in the occurrence of schizophrenia, is the gamma aminobutyric acid (GABA) system. A feedback loop involving GABA inhibitory effects on DA ergic neurons has been proposed in the nigrostriatal, mesolimbic, and mesocortical DA ergic pathways. A reduction in the activity of GABA ergic neurons would decrease inhibition, resulting in DA ergic hyperactivity (Davis & Greenwald, 1991). In support of this theory, some researchers have found GABA levels to be decreased in the brains of schizophrenics. Some reported a lowering of GABA levels in the CSF as well. Psychopharmacological data are contradictory in that some GABA agonists have been found to be beneficial in schizophrenia, while others reportedly lead to deterioration of the psychosis. Whatever the significance of these findings might turn out to be, no author claimed their universal occurrence in schizophrenia. They were demonstrable only in a subgroup and the psychopathological identity of that subgroup is not known.

2.4.4. *Conclusions*

In sum, the limited data available on possible pathogenetic mechanisms in schizophrenia lend no support to a unitary hypothesis. They rather suggest the existence of different disorders, each with its own pathophysiology. An alternative explanation is that the biological findings in schizophrenia are linked not so much to particular syndromes, but to discrete psychopathological dimensions that may occur in schizophrenia, but may be absent as well (van Praag et al., 1987c; van Praag, 1990b).

2.5. Pharmacotherapy

Neuroleptics are a mainstay in the treatment of schizophrenic psychoses. Are they likewise a mainstay for a unitary hypothesis? By no means. First of all, neuroleptics are antipsychotic, not antischizophrenic, drugs, effective in all types of psychoses whatever the etiology and whatever their symptomatology. Therapeutic response to a broad-spectrum antibiotic allows the conclusion of an infectious disease, but no specification of the infectious agent. Similarly, therapeutic response to a neuroleptic suggests the existence of a psychosis, but provides no information about its phenomenology or nature (Table 4:3).

Moreover, the therapeutic efficacy of neuroleptics in schizophrenic psychoses is highly variable. Some patients remit completely—fast, that is, within a couple of days, or gradually in the course of weeks to months. In others, the recovery is incomplete and certain symptoms do persist. In a minority of cases, the drugs seem to exert hardly any therapeutic effect at all (Table 4:3).

To avoid relapses, most patients need neuroleptics; some, however, do not relapse on long-term treatment with placebo. Maintenance treatment might be required for life while other patients improve over time and can eventually manage without medication.

In sum, then, treatment results in schizophrenia obtained with neuroleptics are quite variable and unpredictable; they do not support a unitary hypothesis about the pathogenesis of this disorder.

3. RENOUNCING THE UNITARY HYPOTHESIS

The unitary hypothesis is an albatross around the neck of schizophrenia research. It leads to findings that are inconsistent, hard to reproduce, impossible to generalize. After 30 years of modern schizophrenia research, not a single finding in schizophrenia has been unequivocally established as a marker of that disease. I believe the unitary hypothesis is largely responsible. In short, it is a gigantic barrier on the road to progress in schizophrenia research. This is the inevitable conclusion to be drawn from the data discussed in the foregoing. Lip service paid to the heterogeneity concept is widespread, but the reality is that most schizophrenia research is executed in schizophrenics, period. Attempts to subclassify schizophrenia should have the highest priority in schizophrenia research, but they obviously do not.

TABLE 4:3

Short-term Treatment Results Obtained with Neuroleptics in a Group of 138 Patients with Schizophrenia and Schizophrenia-like Psychoses

	N	Spontaneous Remission Within 1 Week of Admission	Remission Within Max. 2 Weeks of Neuroleptic Treatment		Remission Within Max. 3 Months of Neuroleptic Treatment		No Remission After 3–6 Months of Neuroleptic Treatment
			Complete	Incomplete	Complete	Incomplete	
Schizophrenia	54	1	7	12	14	18	2
Schizoaffective Psychosis	38	3	5	14	10	6	–
Psychogenic Psychosis	46	5	17	8	11	4	1

Against the Unitary Concept of Schizophrenia

PART II: SUBCLASSIFICATION OF SCHIZOPHRENIA: AN OUTLINE FOR A NEW BEGINNING

In the previous chapter, I qualified the unitary concept of schizophrenia as the great illusion of psychiatry, as the entry to a blind alley. Subclassification of this presumably heterogeneous disorder should have, it seems to me, the highest priority in schizophrenia research.

1. SUBCLASSIFICATION OF SCHIZOPHRENIA: THE DSM-III SYSTEM

Two subclassifications of schizophrenia are currently in use: the one proposed by the DSM-III-R and the positive/negative schizophrenia dichotomy. Of the subtypes of schizophrenia distinguished in the DSM-III-R, only the *catatonic subtype* stands clearly on its own, the mandatory presence of catatonic symptoms being the anchorpoints. The *disorganized* and *undifferentiated subtypes* largely overlap. Only one symptom differentiates the former from the latter and that is flat or grossly inappropriate affect.

Chronic, severe forms of schizophrenia might be meaningfully divided into forms with or without seriously disturbed emotionality, but nothing in the text seems to suggest that that is the viewpoint the DSM-III holds, nor does one find support for that viewpoint in the literature. The distinction seems fortuitous rather than deliberate. The *paranoid subtype* is characterized by systematized delusions or auditory hallucinations in the absence of other symptoms characteristic of schizophrenia. The overlap with the symptoms pattern of delusional disorder is, thus, virtually 100 percent. The diagnosis of *residual type* of schizophrenia is made in the presence of two out of at least nine symptoms, while "typical" schizophrenic symptoms, such as delusions, hallucinations, incoherence, or grossly disorganized behavior are absent, making this category the wastebasket of the various manifestations of chronic schizophrenia.

Schizotypal personality disorder is defined by the DSM-III-R as a condition having many symptoms in common with schizophrenia, including ideas of reference, paranoid ideation, unusual perceptual experiences, and eccentricity. Those symptoms, however, should not be "severe enough to meet the criteria for schizophrenia" (p. 340). However, the criterion of severity is not included in the definition of schizophrenia.

The clearness of the DSM-III-R subclassification of schizophrenia is obviously low and so is its predictive power (Table 5:1). There is some evidence that the paranoid subtype has a better short-term and long-term prognosis than the other schizophrenic subtypes (Kendler et al., 1984). In terms of short-term outcome, however, our own data do not confirm this observation. If anything, the patients diagnosed as paranoid schizophrenia did worse on neuroleptics than the other subtypes (Table 5:1). In terms of family loading, premorbid adjustment, and CSF concentration of HVA, this subdivision has no predictive value either. Family studies have not provided evidence that the different subtypes "breed true." Moreover, patients often meet criteria for different subtypes at different stages in their lives. The DSM subtyping seems to have been dictated more by reverence for Kraepelin's legacy than by scientific arguments.

An important prerequisite for subdivision of a diagnostic entity is the careful demarcation of that concept from adjacent diagnostic entities. Has at least that condition been fulfilled in the DSM-III-R operationalization of schizophrenia? I will turn to this issue first, before discussing the merits of the positive/negative schizophrenia distinction.

TABLE 5:1
DSM-III-R Schizophrenia Subtype and the Occurrence of Family Loading, Premorbid
Maladjustment, Disordered Central Dopamine Metabolism and Treatment Response to
Neuroleptics.

(The Four Subtypes Do Not Vary Significantly on any One of These Variables)

| | | *Number of patients scoring positive on the following variables* | | | | |
| | | *Family* | *Premorbid* | *Abnormal* | *Substantive Remission After:* | |
	N	*Loading*★	*Maladjustment*	*CSF HVA*	*2 Weeks*	*3 Months*
Catatonic Type	8	3	2	2	4	3
Disorganized Type	25	11	12	5	7	13
Paranoid Type	19	10	8	3	3	7
Undifferentiated Type	16	9	8	4	6	7

★At least one relative with documented schizophrenia

2. THE BOUNDARIES BETWEEN SCHIZOPHRENIA AND ADJACENT DIAGNOSTIC ENTITIES

2.1. Syndromal Fogginess

Symptomatologically, the DSM-III-R does not sharply demarcate borders between schizophrenia and related psychoses. I use the term schizophrenia-like psychoses to capture the DSM-III-R diagnoses of schizophreniform disorder, schizoaffective disorder, delusional disorder, and brief reactive psychosis. The rationale for the term schizophrenia-like is that in these disorders, as in schizophrenia, psychotic phenomena occur with intact consciousness, as distinct from the organic psychoses in which consciousness is usually clouded.

The symptomatological criteria for schizophrenia and *schizophreniform disorder* are identical. One qualifies for the diagnosis of *delusional disorder* if delusions are present, nonbizarre in nature, or hallucinations considered to be nonprominent. In addition, behavior should not be obviously odd or bizarre. On exactly the same grounds, however, the diagnosis of schizophrenia or schizophreniform disorder is permitted. The diagnosis of *brief reactive psychosis* is based on the same symptoms as those regarded as indicative of schizophrenia, the only discriminating feature being emotional turmoil. The differential diagnostic power of that criterion is low. The identification of

schizophrenia, even chronic schizophrenia, with flat affect and emotional blunting rests on a misconception. In the earlier phases of
schizophrenia, episodes of psychosis may generate profound emotional turmoil and even in the more advanced stages of the disease
emotional upheaval is by no means unknown. Affect may be strange,
but it definitely is there.

Schizophrenia and *schizoaffective disorder* are discriminated through
cross-sectional analysis of symptom patterns, the latter diagnosis
being appropriate if schizophrenia and affective disorder occur concurrently. The differential diagnosis is, however, less clear-cut than
it seems. First, major depression may occur in "nuclear schizophrenia" (Elk et al., 1986). Second, schizophrenic episodes can be accompanied by profound despondency and hopelessness. Thirdly, several
components of major depression other than mood lowering are also
observed in schizophrenia per se, particularly anhedonia, psychomotor symptoms, loss of energy, diminished ability to think and concentrate, and suicidal ideation. Actually, no less than six of the nine
symptoms mentioned as indicative for major depression occur in
schizophrenia as well. Since only five out of those nine suffice for
the diagnosis of major depression, the diagnostic decision of "pure"
schizophrenia or schizophrenia concurrent with major depression
(schizoaffective disorder) may in a given case be wholly arbitrary.
And, finally, depression concurrent with or following a schizophrenic episode can be hard to distinguish from (residual) negative
symptoms (Siris et al., 1988).

The DSM-III-R divides schizophreniform disorder into two subtypes, with or without good prognostic features. Four features indicating good prognosis are listed: acute onset of the psychotic
symptoms; confusion, disorientation, or perplexity at the height of
the psychotic episode; good premorbid social and occupational functioning, and absence of blunted or flat affect. However, in a small
but carefully conducted study of a patient sample with good clinical
description at index hospitalization and at follow-up examination,
confusion, disorientation, or perplexity at the height of the psychotic
episode appeared to be the only feature consistently associated with
a favorable outcome (Guldberg et al., 1990). The DSM-III states that
the good-prognosis features were identified from a large descriptive
literature. In truth, that literature is very heterogenous in terms of
methodology and definition of schizophrenia and it has been clearly

demonstrated that prediction of outcome varies with the definition chosen (Kendell et al., 1979).

The demarcation of schizophrenia from adjacent DSM-III-R diagnostic domains is, therefore, far from clear and this calls into question the very usefulness of those diagnostic distinctions. Be this as it may, one thing is clear: It makes no sense to subclassify an entity as long as its boundaries have not been clearly defined.

2.2. Dressed-up Syndromes

Since symptomatological criteria utterly fail to separate the various diagnostic schizophrenia-(like) categories, other criteria are introduced to typify them. Thus, the impression is created that we deal at least with the precursors of disease entities.

The criterion of *duration* is introduced to differentiate schizophrenia from schizophreniform disorder. A duration of six months of the psychosis is the watershed. It makes sense to differentiate psychoses that, despite treatment, take a more chronic course from those that are, with or without treatment, transient. The issue at stake, however, is whether the factor of duration makes schizophrenia better identifiable and better distinguishable from schizophrenia-like psychoses; the answer is, in both cases, in the negative.

The traditional view of schizophrenia as an essentially chronic, deteriorating condition, the one that has been adopted by the DSM-III, has been seriously challenged. As discussed previously, the outcome of schizophrenia tends to be relatively heterogenous even for those samples diagnosed prospectively (Harding & Strauss, 1984; Zubin et al., 1983; Moller et al., 1988). The second reason why duration is of little help in identifying "true" schizophrenia is that a protracted course is by no means specific for schizophrenia. Brief psychotic reaction is comparable with the European concept of reactive or psychogenic psychoses, save for what the prefix indicates. Schizophrenia-like psychoses seemingly unleashed by profound emotional distress are variable as to duration and may not resolve for months or even assume a chronic course (Jauch & Carpenter, 1988a).

The course of delusional disorder is likewise unpredictable. The disorder may quickly remit, take a protracted course, or become intermittent, whereby psychotic episodes are interspersed with remissions of variable duration. The prognosis of schizoaffective

patients may be statistically better than that of those originally diagnosed as schizophrenics, yet in a substantial percentage of cases the
course is unfavorable, leading to personality damage and states of
chronic psychosis (van Praag & Nijo, 1984; Berg et al., 1983; Coryell
& Zimmerman, 1988b; Levitt & Tsuang, 1988; Marneros et al.,
1989).

A second criterion used in the DSM-III-R to individualize
schizophrenia and schizophrenia-like psychoses is the occurrence
of *life events preceding the psychoses*. It is a particularly important
criterion in the delineation of brief reactive psychosis. In that disorder the psychotic symptoms appear shortly after one or more
events with, what I have called, "objective valence" (see Chapter
11), that is what would have been "markedly stressful to almost
anyone in similar circumstances in that person's culture." Precipitants may be typical for that diagnostic category, but the specificity of that criterion is low.

The traditional view that schizophrenia develops insidiously and
"out of the blue" (DSM-III-R, p. 205) is by no means invariably true.
In 14 of a group of 34 patients, cross-sectionally diagnosed as first
or second break "true" schizophrenics, we found that the psychosis
had developed rather abruptly, i.e. in the course of one to six weeks
and subsequent to an objective life event. If relative life events★ were
also taken into account, the number rose to 22. Over time, the correlation between subsequent psychoses and life events may lessen,
but that might be so only at the surface. In the psychotic world,
threatening events could conceivably be enacted of which we are not
cognizant. In patients diagnosed as schizoaffective disorder, life
events preceding psychotic episodes were even more frequent than
in schizophrenia (Table 5:2); in delusional disorders, they are less frequent but by no means negligible.

Prodromal and residual symptoms occupy, furthermore, a prominent
differential diagnostic role in the DSM-III. For the diagnosis of
schizophrenia, it is required that the active psychotic episode be preceded as well as followed by a phase of clear deterioration from a
previous level of social and occupational functioning; the length of
those phases is not specified. Though a break in the process of
growth and development is not uncommon in a subgroup of partic-

---

★See Chapter 11, pages 244–246 for discussion of this concept.

TABLE 5:2
Life Events 1–6 Weeks Prior to the Occurrence of the Psychoses

	N	Number of patients in whom the psychosis developed after life event	
		Absolute Life Events	*Relative Life Events*
Schizophrenia	34	14	8
Schizoaffective psychosis	38	21	7
Delusional disorder	31	14	3
Normals	30	1	4

ularly young schizophrenics, this criterion is neither necessary nor sufficient for the diagnosis of schizophrenia. The same is true for the postpsychotic persistence of personality changes or residual symptoms. In the group of 34 schizophrenics alluded to above, the notorious break in the developmental curve had occurred in a little less than 50 percent of the patients; in the same percentage of patients, resolution of the psychosis was incomplete for at least one year after the acute symptoms had subsided. The two groups overlapped for 75 percent. Though approximately half as common, prodromal and residual symptoms do occur in patients that were and had been diagnosed as schizoaffective disorder and delusional disorder, respectively. Diagnostic specificity of the criterion under discussion is clearly low.

Personality structure has not been given differential diagnostic weight in the DSM-III-R diagnosis of schizophrenia and schizophrenia-like psychoses. Schizoid, schizotypal, and paranoid personality disorders are only some of a range of personality disorders that might accompany schizophrenia. Moreover, a variety of premorbid personality disorders are also discernible in those suffering from the various types of schizophrenia-like psychoses.

2.3. Conclusions

The attempts to accentuate borders between schizophrenia and the various types of schizophrenia-like psychoses by linking each syndromal diagnosis to other than symptomatological criteria have been unsuccessful. These criteria lack specificity, as do the psychopathological symptoms. It seems a hopeless task to subdivide schizophrenia if that concept itself is so poorly demarcated from adjacent diagnosis entities.

3. SUBCLASSIFICATIONS OF SCHIZOPHRENIA: THE POSITIVE/NEGATIVE DICHOTOMY

3.1. Hopes and Disappointments

Out of factoranalytic research of Strauss et al. (1974), a crude symptomatological division of schizophrenia emerged, i.e. a cluster called positive and one designated as negative. The adjective "negative" covers deficiency symptoms such as: apathy, anergia, avolition, and anhedonia. They represent loss of normal psychological functions. The adjective "positive" stands for symptoms like delusions, hallucinations, certain forms of thought disorder, and bizarre behavior. They represent abnormal psychological functions.

At first it seemed that these concepts were helpful in elucidating the nature of schizophrenia. To begin with, Andreasen and Olsen (1982), found a negative correlation between positive and negative schizophrenic symptoms, indicating that these clusters are opposite ends of a continuum. The validity of the positive/negative paradigm was, furthermore, suggested by a number of observations. Negative symptoms seemed to be more often than positive symptoms correlated with ventricular enlargement, impaired cognitive functioning, lower educational achievement, poor premorbid social adjustment, absence of exacerbation in response to central stimulants, poor response to neuroleptic drugs, and poor prognosis (Andreasen, 1982). In the course of time, however, many of these observations proved hard to confirm.

Some authors found no correlations between positive and negative symptoms (Lewine et al., 1983), suggesting that those clusters represent independent dimensions. Others reported a positive correlation (Bilder et al., 1985; Kay, 1991, 1992), an indication that they usually occur side by side. Ventricular enlargement has been a rather consistent finding in computed tomographic (CT) scans of schizophrenic patients. The proportions of patients reported to have enlarged ventricles (2 SDs higher than the mean in a control group) varies however from 3–35 percent (Jernigan, 1986). Studies of sulcal enlargement have also been inconsistent. The CT findings, moreover, are not specific. Ventricular enlargement has been reported in a variety of psychiatric conditions, such as Alzheimer's disease, alcoholism, bipolar depression, delusional depression, and anorexia nervosa (Pfefferbaum et al., 1988a). A relationship of ventricular enlargement with negative symptomatology (e.g. Williams et al., 1986), cognitive impairment (e.g. Golden et al., 1980), and chronicity (Luchins & Meltzer, 1986) was originally reported, but several later studies failed to replicate these findings. Pfefferbaum et al. (1988b), for instance, did not find a correlation between enlargement of ventricles and sulci on the one hand and measures of negative symptoms or neuropsychological impairment on the other. Neither was the cerebral atrophy in schizophrenic patients found to be clearly related to measures of disease severity or chronicity. Other groups reported comparable findings (e.g. Goetz & van Kammen, 1986; Farmer et al., 1987). Doran et al. (1985) found specific frontal atrophy on the CT scan in schizophrenic patients, supporting the hypothesis of hypofrontality in this disorder. Others, however, failed to find evidence of increased frontal atrophy relative to temporal and occipito-parietal atrophy (Pfefferbaum et al., 1988b). Finally, in most CT scan studies in schizophrenia, the factor of alcohol has not been accounted for, whereas recent studies have found significant correlations between lifetime alcohol consumption and ventricular and sulcal volumes (Pfefferbaum et al., 1988a; Turner et al., 1986).

Negative symptoms, moreover, are by no means characteristic of the chronic forms of schizophrenia, but occur in comparable frequency in acute forms of schizophrenia and in acute exacerbations (Rosen et al., 1984). Rather than boding poor outcome, negative symptoms in acute schizophrenia were actually found to presage a more benign course of illness (Kay, 1991a). In both cross–sectional and longitudinal studies, comparably high negative and positive ratings were observed at all phases of the illness, from the acute to the long–term chronic. These results challenge the hypothesis that positive symptoms prevail in early or good-prognosis schizophrenia, while negative symptoms increasingly dominate as the illness advances (Kay, 1991).

The alleged intractability of the negative syndrome has likewise been challenged. Several authors reported that in response to neuroleptics both the positive and negative syndromes significantly improve (e.g. Meltzer et al., 1988; Kay & Singh, 1989).

Angrist et al. (1980) studied the effect of amphetamines on positive and negative schizophrenic symptoms. Based on Crow's (1980) theory that positive symptoms might be related to dopaminergic hyperfunction and negative symptoms to structural abnormalities in the brain, they predicted positive symptoms to increase, negative symptoms to remain unchanged. As a matter of fact, both syndromes increased, though the positive more than the negative.

Major arguments favoring the validity of the positive/negative typology, then, have become questionable. This typology does not seem to predict treatment outcome, long-term prognosis, the presence or absence of structural brain abnormalities, or the occurrence of impaired cognitive functioning.

What remains of the foundations of positive and negative subtypes is worse premorbid adjustment and lower educational achievement in the negative subgroup as compared to the positive. This difference could be due to an earlier beginning of the schizophrenic disorder, or one might assume that the schizophrenic disorder can coexist with a cognitive impairment that might be part of the schizophrenic disorder or might be coincidental. Either way, it is by no means self-evident that these differences constitute valid markers of distinct schizophrenic subtypes.

3.2. Wishful Categorical Thinking

The inclination to descry a variety of discrete and independent behavioral disorders seems irresistible, especially in biological psychiatry. To satisfy that need, one is willing to twist oneself and to put up with remarkable degrees of wishful thinking. As a representative example, let us consider a recent study of Andreasen et al. (1990) reappraising the validity of the concepts of negative and positive schizophrenia. The sample studied consisted of 110 schizophrenic patients, of which 17 were classified as having positive schizophrenia, nine as negative schizophrenia, and 84 as mixed schizophrenia. This distribution alone could raise doubt about the usefulness of the positive/negative typology and the validity of the data based on it. If so many patients do not fit the typological criteria, how valid are the observations that indicate some indeed do? The doubt is deepened if one takes into account that the uneven distribution was obtained despite quite liberal typological definitions.

Positive schizophrenia was diagnosed if one of the following symptoms was present to a marked degree: hallucinations, delusions, formal thought disorder or bizarre or disorganized behavior, while symptoms called negative, i.e.: alogia, affective flattening, avolition-apathy, anhedonia–asociality, and affectional impairment, were not present to a marked degree. In neither case is it made clear what "marked degree" actually denotes.

The definition of negative schizophrenia mirrors the one of positive schizophrenia. Two of the series of five negative symptoms had to be present to a "marked degree" and none of the positive series should "dominate the clinical picture." Mixed schizophrenia is the diagnosis for the remaining patients not meeting criteria for either of the above categories.

Despite the generous degree of definitional flexibility, no more than 25 percent of the patients fitted the positive and negative categories. Apart from that, these diagnostic categories are as heterogenous as they can be. Someone with attentional impairment and affective flattening is as much a negative schizophrenic as one with prominent alogia and avolition. I leave aside the issue that it is apparently assumed that symptoms like affective flattening and attentional impairment are reliable and unequivocably establishable, but indeed they are not.

In order to make the distribution more even, the classification was adjusted so that patients within the mixed group who had at least two prominent negative symptoms were moved to the negative group. Still other classificatory modifications were used, such as raising and lowering the threshold for considering positive and negative symptoms to be present and splitting the mixed group into "high mixed" and "low mixed," dependent on the greater or lesser prominence of the positive and negative symptoms. Even with such artifices, no more of the positive and negative typology was salvaged than the difference in premorbid impairment and educational achievement.

Pitiable data, to be so twisted in order to salvage a theory that eventually appears to be untenable. At last, one year after publication of the study I discussed and more than 10 years after the concepts of positive and negative schizophrenia were introduced, Andreasen reached the conclusion that this two-dimensional model had failed (Arndt et al., 1991).

3.3. Reappraisal of the Positive/Negative Typology

Though seemingly promising initially, the heuristic value of the positive/negative distinction has, so far, turned out to be fairly disappointing. Several reasons can be conceived of to explain this. As is the case with so many dichotomous classifications, many symptoms are hard to place in one or the other domain, such as many of the so-called schizophrenic thought disorders, bizarre behavior, attentional impairment, self-neglect, and several others. Negative symptoms, moreover, are not necessarily primary manifestations of schizophrenia. They might be secondary to such factors as depression, profound anxiety, drug effect, environmental deprivation, or the need to limit stress with which the patient is unable to cope. In many studies of negative symptoms, it is unclear whether this distinction was made, a distinction which is often difficult to make in any event.

Much more important to an understanding of why the positive/ negative symptom paradigm fell short of the initial expectations is that the terms themselves are fraught with theoretical ballast. They came from Hughlings Jackson, who introduced them in neurology. Positive symptoms were defined as products of brain processes that operate in an excessive or distorted fashion, negative symptoms as the manifestation of loss of normal brain functions. When they were applied to behavioral disorders, researchers lost sight of the fact that the terms "positive" and "negative" can be used only in a strictly descriptive fashion and that the neuronal theory behind them, applied to psychiatry, is not even a metaphor, but an ill-based speculation. Symptoms called negative could be related not only to deficient (excitatory) function, but also to overactivity of (inhibitory) function. Conversely, positive symptoms could conceivably be the consequence not only of overactivity or abnormal activity in (excitatory) neuronal systems, but also to underactivity in (inhibitory) systems.

From the beginning, the epithet "negative" carried the connotation of: chronicity, bad prognosis, unfavorable premorbid make-up, and serious brain damage, while the reverse applied to the concept of positive symptoms. Not so much an error as a prejudice, which is scientifically worse. That prejudice is based on crude metaphorical thinking: Behavioral hypofunction refers to neuronal hypofunction, which refers to severe brain damage; behavioral hyper (or abnormal) function connotes neuronal hyper (or abnormal) function, which connotes (possibly transient) brain dysfunction (as opposed to structural and thus, severe and irreversible brain damage). It is this prejudice that has severely biased positive/negative symptoms research from the start and significantly contributed to the disappointing results.

The prejudice originated in the uncritical application of a neurological concept in psychiatry, but was strongly reinforced, one might even say sanctioned, by Crow (1980) when he used the distinction between positive and negative symptoms as a linchpin for a novel nosological dichotomy in schizophrenology. Type 1 schizophrenia, he proposed, is characterized by acute onset, positive symptoms, normal intellectual functions, normal brain structure, good response to neuroleptics, and, supposedly, increased function in dopamine-regulated systems. In type 2 schizophrenia, on the other hand, the onset was insidious, negative symptoms were predominant, intellectual functioning disturbed, the brain morphologically damaged (enlarged ventricles), and the response to neuroleptics likely to be poor. Predominant positive symptoms, then, would forecast good prognosis; negative symptoms, according to this theory, are a bad omen since they persevere and stand for irreversibility (Carpenter et al., 1988).

This simple and hypothetical dichotomy caught on immediately and became very influential. This is surprising because it should have appeared as flawed on mere clinical inspection alone. Kraepelin's hebephrenia, for example, is characterized by both florid psychotic symptoms and a developmental break manifested by inertia and avolition. The frequently simultaneous occurrence of both types of symptoms is a time-honored clinical observation. A substantial number of those patients go into full remission. In chronic forms of schizophrenia, on the other hand, persistent hallucinations and delusions are at least as frequent as persistent "poverty symptoms." As a final example, paranoid schizophrenia is often persistent, though negative symptoms are anything but prominent. Only the irrepressible need for well–defined and delineated disease entities can explain the willingness to accept as straight what in reality seemed crooked from the very beginning.

4. CONCLUSIONS DRAWN FROM THE FAILURE TO SUBCLASSIFY SCHIZOPHRENIA

1. Attempts to distinguish schizophrenia properly from related diagnostic entities have thus so far been futile. It seems that we are dealing with non–entities. Hence, I do still firmly adhere to the conclusion I arrived at in my 1976 paper: For the time being, schizophrenia can best be regarded as an umbrella concept for those behavioral disorders in which psychotic symptoms occur while consciousness is generally clear, but that differ in most other respects. The predominant symptomatology varies widely. The onset of the psychopathological manifestations may be abrupt or insidious. The psychosis may last briefly or for a long(er) time or may take an intermittent course. Remission may be complete or various degrees of personality damage and behavioral alterations may endure. The breakdown is either preceded by emotional or physical adversity, or harmful events are seemingly absent. Schizophrenia may occur among relatives, but sporadic cases are by no means rare. Morphological brain lesions may or may not accompany the psychosis and those lesions might be relatively "mild," i.e. only demonstrable with high tech devices (such as CT scan and MRI), or "crude," i.e. the result of severe brain injury due to such processes as trauma, infection, and tumor. Premorbid adjustment is weak from infancy on, becoming disturbed a variable time prior to the psychosis, or else it has been undisturbed up to the manifestation of the psychosis. Premorbid personality structure is often disturbed, but in a wide variety of ways. All in all, a truly astonishing variability.

2. The concept of positive/negative schizophrenia, contaminated as it was from the beginning with nosological speculations, should be thoroughly purified.

The concept of positive symptoms, as it stands, seems to me useless. It is no more than a hodgepodge of symptoms of an entirely different nature that only through extreme thought–twisting can be brought under the same denominator (excessive or distorted neuronal function) that in itself is a mere speculation.

The concept of negative symptoms seems to possess more internal consistency. To be useful, however, it has first of all to be uncoupled from theoretical speculations. A negative symptom is a deficit symptom, representing reduction of a psychological function, such as reduction in volition, hedonic functioning, motor activity, level of initiative, emotional responsivity, emotional "width," and social relatedness. The term is purely descriptive and should be divested from implications regarding the underlying brain dysfunctions or any a priori judgment about duration, persistence, or prognosis. The common denominator of those phenomena (psychological deficit symptoms), though useful, is probably too broad. Imagine an internist deciding to study in one broad sweep deficiencies in excretion, digestion, circulation, and respiration. The venture would be megalomanic in design and futile in outcome.

Just like the body, the mind is a composite of discrete and separable functional domains, each of which should be studied in its own right as to relationship to disturbed neuronal functioning, prognostic significance, therapeutic responsiveness. The term "negative" brings together a wide variety of psychological deficits. That is taxonomically useful, but in research each deficit has to be taken individually. If, for instance, the sum score of negative symptoms does not seem to correlate with a biological variable, the next step is to analyze whether it might correlate with one of the negative symptoms individually.

3. Let me digress for a moment on this plea for a dimensional analysis of existing psychopathology as a means to further biological research in psychiatry.

The brain governs the entire spectrum of psychological functions. As such, it is fundamentally different from all other organ systems in the body. However complex their physiology may be in terms of "wiring," they are all geared towards a common goal, a final common path such as, for instance, excretion in case of the kidney, circulation in case of the heart, and digestion in case of the intestines. Regulating as it does all domains of the "psychological apparatus," the brain is comparable to the body as a whole, not to any other single organ system.

As much as it is unlikely that one and the same pathological process would underlie dysfunctions in, for instance, excretion, circulation, and digestion, so it is improbable that disturbances in such diverse psychological functions as volition, cognition, and perception could be extrapolated to the same pathophysiological process. It is, of course, conceivable that one singular error of metabolism is responsible for a variety of subordinate brain processes, disregulating ultimately a variety of psychological functions. The likelihood of tracing that alleged underlying process, however, is not great because our ability to delineate valid diagnostic entities is so limited. Ergo, the search for *the* cause of schizophrenia or of one of the schizophrenia-like psychoses is doomed to fail. It seems more logical and productive to follow the reverse route, that is, to dissect a particular syndrome into its component parts, i.e. the psychological dysfunctions, and search for correlations between them and biological dysfunctions. Having elucidated (some of) such correlates, one might be able to construe what the common underlying biological denominator might be and proceed from there with goal-directed efforts towards its elucidation (van Praag et al., 1975, 1987c, 1990b).

5. RESPONSE TO THE CLASSIFICATORY FAILURES: THE FATALISTIC VIEW

1. The failure of attempts to subgroup schizophrenia led to recommendations to abandon them. Weinberger (1987), discussing structural brain lesions as they occur in schizophrenia, noted that in both the postmortem and the CT anatomical studies the distribution of data is normal, not bimodal or polymodal. In other words, there are no segregated clusters of patients with similar pathology, as might be expected if discrete pathogenetic subgroups existed. Instead, what is generally reported is a pathological continuum, analogous to what is found in such brain disorders as Alzheimer's disease. Weinberger, then, suggests that clinical heterogeneity is not caused by qualitatively different pathologies, but by the extent of the pathology. In that case, careful clinical subgrouping would make little sense.

Weinberger's argument would carry considerable weight if indeed a firm relation between brain pathology and schizophrenia had been established, but it has not (Kirch & Weinberger, 1986). The anatomical pathology, predominantly found in the periventricular limbic and diencephalic areas and in the prefrontal cortex, is nonspecific, does not demonstrate a consistent picture, is not found in all cases of schizophrenia, and also occurs in other, unrelated disorders such as Alzheimer's disease. Trauma and tumors can affect the same areas without causing schizophrenic symptomatology. The same reasoning holds for the CT scan findings. They are not found consistently, are not specific, and have been found, for instance, in major depression as well (See Chapter 4). This state of affairs does not at all justify repudiation of subgrouping, but rather encourages the search for subgroups of schizophrenics in which particular neuroanatomical lesions accumulate.

2. Opposition against subgrouping was also voiced by McGorry et al. (1990). Disheartened by the lack of correlation between pathophysiological variables and present-day schizophrenic subcategories, they propose to draw the sampling boundary between psychosis and nonpsychosis, eschewing conventional subdivisions within the psychotic manifestations of the so-called schizophrenic spectrum. This approach, I fear, would really usher in an era of diagnostic chaos and scientific stagnation. Suppose, as an analogy, that because of certain similarities all heart diseases would be equalized and as a group made the target of scientific explorations. There is every reason to believe that the dividend would be close to zero.

"It is doubtful whether there has ever been much value in distinguishing between one variety (of schizophrenia) and the other," laments Kendell (1987, Ch. 53, p. 15) and, for that reason, "contemporary interest is focused primarily on how schizophrenia should be defined rather than on how it should be subdivided." His conclusion is correct and, hence, we are moving firmly ahead in a blind alley.

6. RESPONSE TO THE CLASSIFICATORY FAILURES: RECOMMENDATIONS

Though, admittedly, the yield of the attempts to subdivide schizophrenia has so far been meager, we should not give up. First, because the available data overwhelmingly suggest pathogenetic heterogeneity of schizophrenia. Second, because the heterogeneity hypothesis has received much lip service, but scant, sustained research attention.

Third, because the major current subdivision, distinguishing positive and negative schizophrenia, was flawed from the start by neurological fantasies. Where should we go from here in the search for the nature of the schizophrenias?

The way ahead, I submit, is a stratified one.

6.1. First Research Stratum: Aimed at Identification

The group of schizophrenic patients in which a particular variable, such as a biological function, is to be studied has to be symptomatologically homogenous or at least tending towards homogeneity. This requirement implies rejection of the "choice-principle" as applied in the DSM-III and subsequent editions, permitting different symptom constellations to qualify for the same diagnosis. Syndromal heterogeneity of an experimental group runs counter to the prime prerequisite of medical research: careful delineation and definition of the phenomena in whose origin one is interested.

In addition, the syndromes should be "value-free," that is, symptomatologically defined only, with no nosological strings attached. So far, few if any correlations have been demonstrated between a schizophrenic syndrome and other clinically relevant variables such as: premorbid adjustment, family loading, severity and duration of symptoms, course, biological dysfunctions, and treatment response. These nonsymptomatological variables should therefore be scored on independent axes, that is independent of the syndrome. Actually, their relationship to a particular schizophrenic syndrome should be a prime target of study in the renewed attempts I advocate to develop a meaningful classification of the schizophrenias.

The primordial starting point of schizophrenia research is the carefully defined, "value free" syndrome.

6.2. Second Research Stratum: Aimed at Demarcation

Let us assume that in a subgroup of a syndromally well-defined group of schizophrenic patients a biological dysfunction has been ascertained. The next stratum of research, then, will entail further localization of the dysfunction via the study of contrasting groups. To this end, patients are selected presenting both the syndrome being studied and the biological dysfunction, but contrasting with respect to one nonsymptomatological variable. The prevalence of the biological dysfunction is compared in patients with and without the nonsymptomatological variable. Such a variable could, for instance, be: occurrence or absence of schizophrenia in the family; intact or damaged personality structure; premorbid functioning normal or disturbed; presence or absence of CT scan abnormalities; signs of DA disturbances demonstrable or absent; successful or unsuccessful treatment.

Let us assume that the biological dysfunction occurs preferentially but not exclusively in patients exhibiting the syndrome under study and certain CT scan abnormalities. The next investigational step is then comparison of patients with that syndrome, the biological dysfunction, and CT scan abnormalities, but differing with respect to another variable, for instance the occurrence of schizophrenia in the family. In one investigational group, schizophrenia runs in the family; in the other group, only sporadic cases are included. In this fashion, one continues until the occurrence of the biological lesion has been charted as precisely as possible.

6.3. Third Research Stratum: Aimed at Discrimination

The next layer of examination is discriminative in nature. The question is addressed whether the biological variable ascertained in a particular syndromally defined subgroup of schizophrenics and subsequently further anchored at a number of nonsymptomatological variables is typical for that subgroup or whether it also occurs in other schizophrenic or nonschizophrenic syndromes.

Thus, via comparative studies, the specificity of the biological dysfunction will be further determined.

6.4. Fourth Research Stratum: Aimed at Dimensional Analysis

This stratum differs from the others in terms of its direction. It cuts vertically through the other strata. If, in a symptomatologically homogenous group of schizophrenic patients, a biological dysfunction is found only in a subgroup, the possibility should be entertained that the dysfunction does not correlate with that syndrome as such, but with a psychopathological component of that syndrome, one that might occur, but might be absent as well. If a dimensional correlation were to be made plausible, the research strategy would take a slightly different course from the sequence described in the previous three sections.

In order to determine whether the dimensional correlation holds, the biological function would be studied in schizophrenic and non-schizophrenic patients in whom that particular psychopathological component was definitely present or absent. Next, one would proceed to the demarcation phase and establish whether the correlation increases in power when other nonsymptomatological variables are introduced, such as family loading, CT scan abnormalities, etc. (see Section 6.2). Finally, the discrimination phase is reached in which one would explore to what extent the biological/psychological correlation is indeed specific for this particular psychopathological dimension.

6.5. A Long Way to Go

The research strategy outlined above is quite complicated and time-consuming. I like to believe, however, that it would ultimately provide more meaningful results on the nature of schizophrenic psychoses than to continue the search for the Holy Grail, that is, *the* cause of schizophrenia.

It goes without saying that a research program of this magnitude will exceed by far the possibilities of a single research group and will be contingent on collaborative and coordinated efforts of several groups over a long period of time. The National Institute of Mental Health of the USA and comparable research funding and organizing agencies in other countries could play a seminal role in this regard.

6.6. Charting of the Schizophrenic Terrain

How can one carve out from the vast terrain of schizophrenic psychopathology symptom clusters that rest on more than historical venerability? Since the concept of the schizophrenias has enjoyed so much lip service and so little sustained experimental interest, we have almost to start from scratch. The subtypes of schizophrenia proposed by the DSM-III-R are useless. Except for the paranoid subtype, they lack any empirical substructure to keep them erect.

The distinction between positive and negative schizophrenia, though it fell short of initial expectations, remains a reasonable starting point for further research. The grouping together of deficiency symptoms has a distinct clinical appeal since they frequently occur in concert. The fact that they cluster, however, does by no means imply a common pathogenesis. The cluster of negative symptoms is to be considered as no more than a first classificatory cut and concerted efforts should be made to subdivide it further in a meaningful way. To designate the remaining schizophrenic symptomatology as "positive" is not helpful. The cluster lacks inner consistency and one would be hard pressed to find an appropriate common clinical denominator. "Abnormal psychological functions" is being used as such, but that definition is as revealing as the taxonomic designation "abnormal physical functions" would be for an internist.

6.7. A Provisional Topographical Map

Under the leadership of the late Dr. Stanley Kay, detailed studies of the schizophrenic psychopathology were carried out in our Department over the past eight years (Kay, 1991). To this end, the Positive and Negative Syndrome Scales (PANSS) were developed, a strictly operationalized and standardized instrument that permits a full scope of symptom assessment. The procedure is based on specified information from caretakers, plus a four-phase patient interview that consists of nondirective, semistructured, structured, and directive segments. Patients are then rated on 30 symptoms along a seven-point severity index ("absent" to "extreme"), for which each rating level is individually defined per item. Seven items are summed to yield a positive syndrome score, another seven to yield a negative syndrome score, and an additional 16 items for a general psychopathology score.

A detailed PANSS Manual (Kay et al., 1993) provides a handbook of rating definitions, as well as the norms and percentiles on 240 schizophrenic inpatients; the latter offer an empirical anchor for screening, score interpretation, group comparisons, and evaluation of changes. Videotapes also have been developed to automate and standardize the PANSS training and augment the reliability and comparability across research centers.

The PANSS was used in a psychopathological study of 240 schizophrenic inpatients drawn mainly from a state psychiatric hospital located in the Bronx. All were independently diagnosed as schizophrenics according to DSM-III criteria and those with affective, schizoaffective, organic, or any other diagnosable mental disorders were excluded. An orthogonal principal component analysis of the 30 PANSS symptoms confirmed the presence of independent negative and positive syndromes. However, the negative and positive syndromes were not sufficient to explain the range of symptomatology in schizophrenia (Kay & Sevy, 1991) (Table 5:3). In addition, a symptom cluster was found mainly associated with excitement and impulsivity, as well as a depressive syndrome that included symptoms of depression, anxiety, and guilt feelings. The emergence of a distinct affective component, despite the diagnostic screening out of affective and schizoaffective patients, suggested that this is an integral facet of schizophrenia and one which perhaps does not receive sufficient attention from clinicians, researchers, and theoreticians.

A second important finding was that the positive syndrome was restricted to the items of delusions and hallucinations, while disorganized thinking was part of a separate but weaker cluster of items. These data indicate, Kay (1991, 1992) concluded, that indeed the positive syndrome as conceptualized by Crow (1980) and Andreasen et al. (1982), is a nonunitary construct.

Actually, then, the principal component analysis revealed not four but seven orthogonal factors with eigenvalues >1 that accounted for 64.7 percent of the total variance (Kay & Sevy, 1991). The first four factors were called, respectively, negative, positive, excited, and depressive. These had eigenvalues >2, were clearly distinct from one another, and embraced five or more symptoms each. The other three factors altogether included only five symptoms, and these had high loadings with other components as well. Therefore, the first four were construed as representing the primary components of schizophrenic psychopathology.

Yet, I suggest that the cognitive and paranoid clusters be retained for research purposes. First, because they possess clear face validity, familiar as they are to every clinician. Moreover, paranoid schizophrenia is a time-honored clinical entity and tentative evidence provides it with a measure of individuality. For instance, delusions tend to remain encapsulated, while personality structure and social adjustment often remain relatively intact for a long time. Moreover,

TABLE 5:3
Means, Standard Deviations, and Component Loadings of 30 Schizophrenic
Symptoms (Kay & Sevy, 1991)

COMPONENT/Symptoms	Plotting Code	Mean	(SD)	Equimax rotated component loadings						
				1	2	3	4	5	6	7
NEGATIVE										
Emotional withdrawal	A	3.06	(1.17)	**.80**	★	★	★	★	★	★
Passive/apathetic social withdrawal	B	2.88	(1.29)	**.79**	★	★	★	★	★	★
Lack of spontaneity & flow of conversation	C	2.80	(1.45)	**.76**	★	★	★	★	★	★
Blunted affect	D	3.11	(1.06)	**.71**	★	★	★	★	★	★
Poor rapport	E	2.77	(1.36)	**.71**	★	.22	★	★	★	★
Poor attention	F	2.55	(1.35)	**.68**	★	.24	★	.22	★	★
Active social avoidance	G	2.70	(1.26)	**.56**	★	★	★	★	.45	★
Motor retardation	H	1.93	(1.08)	**.55**	★	★	★	★	★	★
Disturbance of volition	I	2.26	(1.30)	**.51**	★	.24	.31	★	★	★
Mannerisms and posturing	J	1.77	(1.18)	**.38**	★	★	★	.26	★	★
POSITIVE										
Unusual thought content	K	3.54	(1.50)	★	**.84**	★	★	★	★	★
Delusions	L	3.59	(1.59)	★	**.84**	★	.26	★	★	★
Grandiosity	M	2.71	(1.65)	★	**.76**	★	★	★	★	★
Lack of judgment and insight	N	4.21	(1.30)	.32	**.52**	★	★	.36	★	★
Hallucinatory behavior	O	2.75	(1.66)	★	.43	★	.39	.25	★	★
EXCITED										
Excitement	P	2.26	(1.19)	★	★	**.83**	★	★	★	★
Poor impulse control	Q	2.08	(1.15)	★	★	**.71**	★	★	★	★
Tension	R	2.48	(1.17)	.22	★	**.66**	.39	★	★	★
Hostility	S	2.15	(1.18)	★	★	**.61**	★	★	.51	★
Uncooperativeness	T	2.13	(1.27)	.48	★	**.49**	★	★	.38	★
DEPRESSIVE										
Anxiety	U	2.67	(1.19)	★	★	.28	**.71**	★	★	★
Guilt feelings	V	1.87	(1.17)	★	★	★	**.66**	★	.28	★
Depression	W	2.16	(1.25)	★	★	★	**.64**	★	.31	★
Somatic concern/delusions	X	2.54	(1.40)	★	.21	★	**.60**	★	★	★
Preoccupation	Y	2.89	(1.15)	.30	.32	★	**.53**	★	★	.49
COGNITIVE & OTHERS										
Difficulty in abstract thinking	Z	4.14	(1.35)	.52	★	★	★	**.57**	★	★
Disorientation	a	1.96	(1.18)	.51	★	★	★	**.56**	★	★
Conceptual disorganization	b	3.33	(1.49)	.39	.48	★	★	**.52**	★	★
Suspiciousness/persecution	c	3.07	(1.30)	★	.47	★	.23	★	**.61**	★
Stereotyped thinking	d	2.95	(1.27)	.30	.41	.27	.31	★	★	**.45**
Eigenvalue percent				5.68	3.54	2.94	2.92	1.58	1.53	1.25

★Component loadings < .20

decreased platelet MAO activity (Meltzer & Zureich, 1987) and increased noradrenaline concentration in the cerebrospinal fluid (Van Kammen et al., 1989) seem to distinguish it from other schizophrenic syndromes.

The six symptomatological domains mentioned here constitute, I believe, an appropriate starting point for further research into the nature of schizophrenia. In any given study, patients should be selected that exhibit predominantly the symptoms of a particular domain. The studies we referred to above, however, revealed that at least the four major syndromes are statistically independent, which signifies that they are neither directly nor inversely related. This implies that those syndromes are not co-exclusive, but can coexist in the same patient and often do. To fully reveal the psychopathological nature of the group to be studied, the component (syndromal) loadings, therefore, have to be stated.

7. SUMMARY AND CONCLUSIONS

1. In schizophrenia research, it is common to see papers introduced with a profession of support for Bleuler's heterogeneity concept of schizophrenia and then proceed with the order of the day and report studies on schizophrenia without attempts to subdivide. In this chapter, I reviewed the schizophrenia concept from various angles, such as symptomatology, etiology, pathogenesis, course, and treatment outcome, to assess how much sense it makes to continue studying schizophrenia as a coherent whole. The conclusion is reached that the available evidence renders the unitary concept untenable and strongly favors the view of schizophrenia being a blanket term for a series of different diseases. The unitary hypothesis is most likely a dead end and should be abandoned as an improper and unproductive alley in schizophrenia research.

2. The two principle attempts to subdivide or at least subtype schizophrenia are discussed. The one proposed in the DSM-III is largely a theoretical construct devoid of validity, even of face validity. As such, it does not qualify as an adequate psychopathological structure on which to base research.

The distinction between positive and negative schizophrenia is considered as a more useful one, though the initial expectations that this classification would usher in a major breakthrough in schizophrenology have not been fulfilled. Psychological deficiency symptoms tend to cluster and the negative syndrome possesses for clinicians distinct face validity. One should keep in mind, however, that clustering of symptoms in no way implies similarity of pathogenesis. The positive syndrome, on the other hand, is utterly heterogeneous, lacks a common clinical denominator, and is, at best, a very broad rest category.

3. In a series of psychopathological studies conducted in our Department and spearheaded by Dr. Stanley Kay, the presence of independent positive and negative syndromes was confirmed, but it was also demonstrated that these two syndromes were insufficient to explain the range of symptomatology in schizophrenia. In addition to those two, four other clusters were found which were designated as: excited, depressive, paranoid and cognitive. Moreover, it appeared that the positive syndrome was restricted to items of delusions and hallucinations. The positive syndrome as it was conceptualized by Crow (1980) and Andreasen et al. (1982) indeed seems to be a heterogeneous construct.

4. Finally, a stratified strategy for research into the pathogenesis of the schizophrenias is proposed. The first stratum is the search for biological dysfunctions in groups of patients that are symptomatologically similar or at least tend towards symptomatological homogeneity. The "choice-principle" as applied in the DSM-III leads to diagnostic concepts that cover a variety of syndromes and is, as such, useless in psychiatric research. As a tentative map for the phenomenology of schizophrenia, the six syndromes are proposed that resulted from the psychopathological studies of Kay and his coworkers (Kay, 1991).

If a biological dysfunction is identified in some patients in a syndromally defined group of schizophrenic patients, the next step is to demarcate the occurrence of that dysfunction further. To this end, the method of comparing contrasting groups is recommended. Next, the discriminative phase is reached in which the specificity of that particular biological dysfunction for that particular schizophrenic disorder is further examined.

The fourth and last stratum is the one in which dimensional analysis takes place. The question is studied whether the biological dysfunction relates to the schizophrenic syndrome as such or to a particular psychopathological dimension that might or might not be specific for that syndrome. This stratum stands perpendicular to the previous three, in that the question of the syndromal or dimensional relatedness of a biological variable should be raised in every research stratum.

The road ahead as outlined here is long and difficult; it presents no shortcuts and is contingent on collaborative research and research planning in several centers. In stimulating and coordinating such efforts, national research funding and organizing agencies could play a seminal role. This approach seems to be more promising than the continued hunt for the Holy Grail: *the* cause of schizophrenia. May facts finally prevail over fancy.

SECTION II
Nosological Tunnel Vision

−6−

Paradox of Paradoxes
The Unsuitability of the Medical Model for Biological Psychiatry

1. HOW TO SYSTEMATIZE PSYCHOPATHOLOGY FOR BIOLOGICAL PSYCHIATRIC RESEARCH

The aim of biological psychiatry is to first understand the relationship of brain dysfunction and abnormal behavior and then to correct these abnormal behaviors via direct intervention in the brain. Given this aim, what is the most sensible way to systematize abnormal behavior in order to study its biological roots? The current and most obvious conceptual framework is the nosological one. Within that frame of reference, psychiatric disorders are considered to be discrete entities, each with its own typical symptomatology, causation, treatment, and prognosis. Unit of measurement is the disorder itself. The search is for biological markers and, eventually, causes of a disease entity, such as schizophrenia, major depression, or panic disorder. If a biological variable does not significantly correlate with a particular disease entity, it is (dis)qualified as being nonspecific.

The nosological approach has dominated thinking in biological psychiatry from its very beginning in the second part of the 19th century. This comes as no surprise. At that time, nosology was in its heyday in partnership with pathology. Pathology had provided major building blocks for Virchov's attempts to classify physical disorders categorically, and Kraepelin in his conceptualization of mental disorders was deeply influenced by the developments in medicine. It was no more than natural that uncovering the (neuro) pathological roots of the entities delineated by Kraepelin was to become the major focus of biological psychiatric research of the day.

With the renaissance of biological psychiatry in the fifties, nosology retained its predominant position, not due to its inherent logic, but out of sheer habit. The nosological tradition was strong, particularly in European psychiatry, and had been passed on unquestioned from generation to generation of psychiatrists. In the USA, it was the publication of the DSM-III that strongly reinforced a nosological orientation not only biological psychiatry, but in clinical practice as well.

2. NOSOLOGICAL ORGANIZATION OF PSYCHOPATHOLOGY

2.1. The Urge to Botanize

The core idea underlying nosological taxonomy is the classical Kraepelinian assumption that psychiatric disorders can be classified on more axes than symptomatology alone; that a predictable relation exists between syndrome on the one hand, and such variables as duration, severity, concomitant personality disorder on the other, and that, therefore, mental disorders can be divided into discrete entities of which the underlying brain dysfunctions can be meaningfully explored.

Though its position seems almost unassailable, nosological taxonomy is, I would submit, an unreliable partner for biological psychiatric research. It is a siren, who can be held responsible for the fact that though a lot of "biology" has been uncovered in mental disorders most of it seems to be without any (nosological) specificity to speak of. The major reason for the stalemate in which we find ourselves today is that the disease entities that are being explored are, for the most part, pseudoentities. It would be little less than a miracle if a single cause, or even a single marker, would be found identifying such an "entity."

Let me briefly clarify that statement. In terms of psychopathology, many of present-day's nosological entities are anything but sharply defined. Take the schizophrenic disorders as an example (van Praag,

1976; Andreasen, 1989). Kraepelin (1899) distinguished five sub-groups; in terms of symptoms as disparate as anemia and jaundice. Kleist described 21 subforms (see Leonhard, 1960). The DSM-III employs the choice-principle: To qualify for a particular syndromal diagnosis, the presence of *x* out of *y* symptoms suffices, no matter which ones. Hence, the same label covers a multitude of syndromes.

Although the nosological approach assumes predictable relation-ships between the syndromal diagnosis of schizophrenia on the one hand and such variables as severity, treatment response, and concom-itant personality disorder on the other, in fact no clear-cut relation-ships exist. Even within one syndromal cluster, these variables vary (see for instance, Endicott et al., [1982, 1986] and Deutsch & Davis, [1983]). Let us take paranoid schizophrenia as an example. This con-dition may become chronic or it may remit; it may hamper someone's social functioning entirely or the symptoms can be established only in a careful and pointed interview; the premorbid personality may be schizotypal, more paranoid, or with only minimal signs of dis-ordered personality. Neuroleptics may fully eliminate the paranoid symptoms, either rapidly or over a protracted treatment period, or the symptoms may stubbornly resist all pharmacotherapeutic efforts. Considering this variability, it makes little sense to consider schizo-phrenia, or even paranoid schizophrenia, as a single disorder (see Chapters 4 and 5) (van Praag, 1989).

Schizophrenia is in this context only a paradigm. The group of mood disorders provides further examples of quasi-nosological enti-ties. Major depression, melancholic type, is an example. In terms of symptoms, this is a quite rigorously described subtype of depres-sion. It corresponds with the pre-DSM-III concept of endogenous depression, while we named the syndrome subsumed under these headings vital depression. Though clinical lore has it that this type of depression is by definition severe, we demonstrated that in fact it occurs in all shades of severity. Duration is likewise variable, from a few days to several years. The same can be said of the course of the disorder: The frequency of the depressive episodes is variable and unpredictable, recovery from an episode might be complete or only partial. The syndrome seems sometimes "endogenous," i.e. occur-ring "out of the blue," sometimes precipitated by stressful events. Premorbid personality structure might be normal or definitely dis-turbed. For all those reasons we operationalized vital depression on purely symptomatological grounds and suggested that variables such as severity, duration, frequency, and personality structure be scored on independent axes (see Chapter 3).

In the realm of the personality disorders the urge to systematize abnormal behavior categorically has been equally strong, from Freud on up to the DSM-III-R. The DSM-III distinguished 12 such disorders; the DSM-III-R added another two, tentatively, "for further study." By blowing up a particular set of personality traits and designating them as a discrete "disorder," one can extend the list ad infinitum. This is a fruitless exercise. Ample evidence exists that the so-called personality disorders strongly overlap and that categorical distinctions represent little more than rather grotesque stereotypes (see Chapter 9).

The same logic applies to most other entities we distinguish in the psychiatric vernacular. They are, in truth, no more than broad umbrellas for a range of loosely related syndromes that differ in most other respects that are considered clinically relevant. It is unlikely that those entities are being carried by a single pathology and hence they can hardly be considered as an appropriate focus for biological research. The nosological tradition, I dare say, is largely a construct of wishful thinking, not of empirical data. It is kept alive by the ineradicable hope that mental pathology is organized in neat "packages," practically handy and aesthetically pleasing.

2.2. Examples of Nosological Tunnel Vision

A typical example of nosological tunnel vision provided the discussion round the recent report that two markers on chromosome 11 were linked to the occurrence of bipolar disorder (Egeland et al., 1987). To this date, this finding has not been replicated (Detera-Wadleigh et al., 1987; Kelsoe et al., 1989). The failure to replicate was explained by raising methodological issues as well as possible genetic heterogeneity of bipolar disorder (Merikangas et al., 1989; Owen & Mullan, 1990), though in closely inbred populations the latter possibility seems unlikely. The validity of the psychiatric diagnosis was not seriously questioned. However, even bipolar disorder, considered to be one of the most sturdy diagnostic categories in psychiatry, contains a fair amount of psychopathological heterogeneity. For example, a broad range of syndromes extending from mild

hypomania to severe manic psychoses with mood–incongruent delusions all sail under the same diagnostic flag. The same holds for the
range of syndromes in between mild vital (endogenous, major)
depression and severe psychotic melancholia. Moreover, the border
between bipolar disorder on the one hand, and the group of schizoaffective and schizophrenic psychoses on the other is fluid indeed
(Kendell & Brockington, 1980). Apart from these diagnostic deliberations, the question of what is transmitted was ignored. Is it really
a disease that is transmitted, or is it a particular component of the
bipolar syndrome that might occur, but might be absent as well? Or
is it a set of psychological dysfunctions within the personality structure that act as a vulnerability factor for bipolar disorder, but may
or may not be present in a given case?

It has been suggested that progressively wider diagnostic definitions will be a better "fit" for genetic models. In my opinion, this
goes in the wrong direction. The "spectrum–disorder" concept only
accentuates the heterogeneity of the phenotype and diminishes the
chance of finding specific psychopathological variables that are
genetically transmitted.

Psychopharmacology provides another example of the nosological
paradigm acting as an intellectual straitjacket. The concept of the disease entity has always enjoyed primacy throughout this discipline's
40–year history. Drugs are developed that are thought to be effective
in a particular disorder. Patients diagnosed with that disorder are
sought out for clinical studies and other patients are excluded. If the
drug is then found to have therapeutic potential, it is marketed as
a treatment for that disorder and is not supposed to be prescribed
for other conditions. This approach precludes an investigation of
which psychopathological components of the disorder were particularly responsive, nor do we learn what the drug effects may have
been in other behavioral disorders. If the starting point is nosology,
then we will inevitably find nosological indications.

Recently, more or less by accident, we have begun to discover that
the nosological specificity of psychotropic drugs seems to be limited.
Tricyclics (Liebowitz et al., 1988) and MAO inhibitors (Sheehan et
al., 1980), for instance, are effective not only in depression, but also
in panic disorder. Similarly, selective 5-HT uptake inhibitors are beneficial in depression as well as in panic disorder (DenBoer et al., 1987;
Schneider et al., 1990) and in obsessive compulsive disorder (Jenike

et al., 1990). Certain benzodiazepine derivatives exceed the realm of the anxiolytics and may be effective antidepressants as well (Rudorfer & Potter, 1989). Lithium's prophylactic potency is not restricted to classical unipolar and bipolar depressions, but also includes schizoaffective disorders (Bouman et al., 1986). It is moreover an effective aggression–reducing agent (Wickham & Reed, 1987).

In sum, the nosological/categorical fixation severely limits our understanding of how psychotropic drugs work clinically and constitutes a roadblock in the search for innovative psychopharmacological agents.

2.3. Comorbidity: the Parasite of Nosological Classifications

Comorbidity refers to the concurrent presence of independent psychiatric disorders. The same patient meets criteria for more than one disorder. Comorbidity is rampant in psychiatry (e.g. Sanderson et al., 1991). As an example, I mention a few data relating to depression. In four independent studies of major depression, the percentage of comorbid diagnoses amounted to 100 percent (Barlow et al., 1986), 100 percent (de Ruiter et al., 1989), 73 percent (DiNardo & Barlow, 1990) and 65 percent (Sanderson et al., 1990) respectively. For example, social phobia was codiagnosed in 47 percent, 67 percent, 42 percent, and 58 percent of cases and generalized anxiety disorder in 83 percent, 67 percent, 45 percent and 91 percent.

In a group of patients suffering from vital depression (endogenous depression; major depression, melancholic type) we found that 79 percent qualified for additional diagnoses, such as generalized anxiety disorder (58 percent), panic attacks (22 percent), personal depression (neurotic depression; dysthymia)* (30 percent); substance abuse (19 percent); alcoholism (26 percent) and schizophrenia (9 percent).

If one includes the group of personality disorders, the situation grows even more chaotic. Most depressive patients show signs of premorbid personality pathology. In our cohort, it was no less than 69 percent. Most commonly dependent (45 percent) and avoidant personality disorders (37 percent) were diagnosed, but other types of personality disorders were by no means rare, such as "histrionic"

---

*In other words, these were cases of double depression or—the term I do prefer—mixed depression.

(27 percent), borderline (19 percent), paranoid (7 percent), and schizoid (8 percent) personality disorder. Forty-nine patients qualified for more than one personality disorder. In personal depression, the percentage of concomitant personality disorder rose to 80 percent. Sanderson et al. (1991) found a concurrent personality disorder in 50 percent of patients with major depression, 52 percent of dysthymic patients, and 69 percent of patients with double depression.

To face this chaotic situation, the hierarchical principle has been introduced. Psychiatric disorders are rank ordered according to severity whereby the more severe disorder takes precedence over the less severe. It remains unspecified whether the concept of severity refers to individual suffering, to annoyance society has to put up with, or to loss of reality testing. Moreover, there exists hardly any evidence that this principle makes sense—that, for instance, lower ranking disorders disappear automatically when higher ranking disorders have been treated successfully. I qualify the hierarchical principle as a harmful *deus ex machina*. In clinical practice, one cannot with impunity disregard whole domains of pathology. For research, the application of this principle borders on (unintentional) fraud. Variable A, one concludes, relates to disorder B, but one fails to mention that other disorders were concurrently present that could and should have been considered as possible correlates of variable A.

Another approach to handling the problem of comorbidity is to presume the existence of and thus to diagnose several disorders in the same patient. This assumption might be useful in clinical practice, but it is useless for research because of the impossibility of deciding to which of the disorders a particular biological variable relates.

3. SYNDROMAL ORGANIZATION OF PSYCHOPATHOLOGY

Another level of organization of psychopathological phenomena which is preferable to the nosological system for biological research in psychiatry is the syndromal (van Praag & Leijnse, 1965). In this approach a mental disorder is typified by a cluster of symptoms that usually go together. The patient's diagnosis is, for instance, the *syndrome* of major depression, melancholic type, or that of paranoid schizophrenia, or of obsessive-compulsive disorder. Other variables, such as severity, duration, recurrence, prognosis, treatment outcome, and concomitant personality disorder are assessed separately and rated on independent axes. Syndromal typology is a better starting point for biological psychiatry than (current) nosology is. Yet, this system, too, is seriously flawed as far as biological research is concerned. Syndromes rarely occur in isolation. Patients often present (parts of) several syndromes: depression and certain forms of anxiety; schizophrenic syndromes with manifestations of mood disorder; addiction disorder and personality disorder, to mention a few. Practically speaking, it is virtually impossible to determine which syndrome is related to a given biological variable.

4. SYMPTOMATOLOGICAL/DIMENSIONAL/ FUNCTIONAL ORGANIZATION OF PSYCHOPATHOLOGY

4.1. Beyond the Disease Entities and Syndromes

A third level of organization of psychopathological phenomena may be named symptomatological, dimensional, or functional. Though these terms are related, they are not identical or interchangeable. This approach is far removed from the larger psychopathological constructs—nosological entities or syndromes—and instead focuses on smaller components of psychopathology. It searches for correlations between biological variables and individual psychopathological symptoms.

A psychopathological symptom is seldom an all-or-nothing phenomenon, but rather occurs in a wide range of severity and blends almost imperceptibly into normality. Many phenomena familiar from psychopathology do occur in normal individuals as well, such as anxiety, depressed mood, suicidal ideation, perceptual disturbances, and overvalued thoughts bordering on delusions, to mention only a few (e.g. Posey & Losch, 1983). In normal individuals, they are, however, of short duration and surmountable without treatment, nor do they seriously interfere with everyday life. Thus, I prefer the term dimension which captures the gradual transition from outright pathology to normality.

Psychopathological dimensions are rarely specific for a given syndrome or nosological entity. This may, in part, explain the failure to find specific markers of psychiatric disorders. If biological variables were related to psychopathological dimensions, then one would expect them to be nonspecific on a syndromal and nosological level. Dimensional specificity would, in most cases, exclude syndromal or nosological specificity.

Psychopathological symptoms or dimensions are not entities sui generis. They are the behavioral manifestations of an underlying psychological dysfunction. For instance, the phenomenon the patient experiences as a hallucination presupposes a perceptual dysfunction; the thought disorder diagnosed as a delusion is a product of a damaged critical function: The patient is unable to assess thoughts for probability and to screen out those that evidence suggests are highly unlikely; suicidality reflects insufficiently regulated aggression or, more generally, a disordered impulse-control function.

A psychological dysfunction may occur at a certain point in life, transient or lasting, or it may be present during the entire life span. In the first case, it forms a component of a psychopathological syndrome; in the second case, it is part of a disordered personality structure. For example, sadness, pessimism, dependency can be part of a depressive syndrome or of a particular personality disorder.

I consider psychological dysfunctions as *the* elementary units of classification in psychopathology rather than nosological entities or syndromes. Biological psychiatry, however, has not given them serious consideration. That is a glaring omission, since other organizational systems lack precision and reliability and since their application in biological psychiatry has so far yielded little relevant diagnostic information (van Praag et al., 1975, 1987c). In contrast, several lines of evidence indicate that certain biological variables, originally introduced as markers of disease entities, but which turned out to possess disappointingly low diagnostic specificity, relate quite strongly to particular psychopathological dimensions or psychological dysfunctions. Let me summarize a few illustrative examples. (See for a more detailed discussion Chapters 7 and 8.)

4.2. Fruits of the Functional Approach

Low baseline and post-probenecid concentration of the serotonin (5-hydroxytryptamine; 5-HT) metabolite 5-hydroxyindoleacetic acid

(5-HIAA) in cerebral spinal fluid (CSF) was originally observed in depression (van Praag & Korf, 1971a; Asberg et al., 1976; Westenberg & Verhoeven, 1988). This phenomenon—suggesting diminished 5-HT metabolism in the CNS—was observed in approximately 30 percent of cases of depression, irrespective of the syndromal subtype or course of illness, though it was more common in major depression than in dysthymia (van Praag et al., 1973) and in severe than mild depression (Peabody et al., 1987). This 5-HT disturbance is probably state-independent, i.e. it persists after subsidence of the depressive symptoms, but the number of longitudinal studies remains small (van Praag, 1977b; Asberg et al., 1986).

In the meanwhile, Asberg et al. (1976) demonstrated that those depressed patients with low CSF 5-HIAA were more likely to have made suicide attempts than those individuals with normal 5-HIAA levels. The correlation between low CSF 5-HIAA and suicide attempt appeared not to be restricted to depression, but was also demonstrated in other diagnostic categories, in particular, schizophrenia (van Praag, 1983a; Ninan et al., 1984) and personality disorder (Traskman et al., 1981). Finally, low concentration of CSF 5-HIAA was also found in aggressive individuals with a variety of personality disorders (Roy & Linnoila, 1988). The hypothesis, then, seems justified that low CSF 5-HIAA, originally described as a feature of depression, is related to disturbed aggression regulation irrespective of the direction of the aggression and irrespective of the nosological context in which it occurs.

The benefits of relating biological variables to psychopathological dimensions rather than to disease entities may be appreciated in anxiety studies, as well. Challenge tests with m-chlorophenylpiperazine (MCPP)—a postsynaptic $5-HT_1$, $5-HT_2$ and $5-HT_3$ receptor agonist—in panic disorder revealed signs of 5-HT receptor hypersensitivity. MCPP induced anxiety and panic attacks in panic disorder patients, but not in major depressives and normal controls (Kahn et al., 1988a). Moreover, the cortisol response to MCPP was more pronounced in panic disorder than in the other two groups (Kahn et al., 1988b). In obsessive compulsive disorder (OCD), MCPP has been reported to cause a striking exacerbation of anxiety and OCD symptoms (Zohar et al., 1987). Furthermore, preliminary data suggest that the signs of increased postsynaptic 5-HT receptor sensitivity in panic disorders are related to the state of heightened anxiety, not to the panic attacks as such. It seems plausible, then, to conclude that increased anxiety is the psychopathological correlate of the observed 5-HT receptor hypersensitivity, rather than a particular nosological entity.

A third example of the fruitfulness of the dimensional approach derives from the study of dopamine (DA) in depression. Low post-probenecid concentration of the DA metabolite homovanillic acid (HVA) in CSF, suggesting diminished DA metabolism in the CNS, has been found in some depressed patients. This phenomenon was particularly obvious in severely retarded depressives (van Praag & Korf, 1971b; Papeschi & McClure, 1971; Banki, 1977a). Treatment with the DA precursor, L-DOPA in these cases led to improvement of motor functioning and increased initiative, but depressed mood remained (Goodwin et al., 1970; van Praag & Korf, 1975). Since low CSF HVA is also found in Parkinson's disease and in inert schizophrenics (Lindstrom, 1985), it seems justifiable to hypothesize that low CSF HVA relates to diminished drive, not to a particular syndrome or nosological entity.

Some scattered evidence, finally, points to anhedonia as the possible behavioral correlate of the noradrenergic (NA ergic) dysfunctions that have been reported in depression (van Praag et al., 1990). For instance, L-tyrosine (the precursor of both DA and NA), though having no overall therapeutic effect in major depression, melancholic type, seemed to improve anhedonia. This effect is probably NA- not DA-mediated, since L-DOPA, which has a strong effect on DA synthesis and only a slight effect on NA metabolism, failed to improve anhedonia. If confirmed, the functional viewpoint would predict to find a comparable NA ergic dysfunction in other diagnostic categories with disturbed hedonic functioning.

Since the functional approach does not presuppose a hard and fast distinction between normal and abnormal psychological dimensions, it is possible to identify relationships between biological variables and psychological functions in normal populations. For example, in a study of 285 normal volunteers screened for accuracy of smooth pursuit eye movements (SPEM), it was found that low accuracy SPEM, typically found in schizophrenic patients, was, in fact, associated with social isolation, inadequate rapport, eccentricity, and other schizotypal characteristics (Siever et al., 1989). In another study of a nonpsychiatric population, low plasma monoamine oxidase

(MAO) was found to be related to a higher incidence of contact with mental health professionals and more frequent use of alcohol and cigarette smoking. High plasma MAO activity was related to higher levels of anxiety and somatization (Irving et al., 1989).

The functional approach seems to me the only sensible way to handle the problem of comorbidity. One moves beyond nosology, characterizes a particular psychiatric condition according to the component psychological dysfunctions, and examines the possible relationship between psychological and biological dysfunctions. The proof of the pudding is in the eating. Thirty years of biological psychiatric research has contributed little to the diagnosis of psychiatric disorders. Few of the biological dysfunctions that were uncovered possess appreciable diagnostic specificity. Functional analyses of the biological data, on the other hand, yielded meaningful relationships from the very onset.

4.3. For a Functional Psychopathology

This plea for a functional psychopathology does not constitute a rejection of the traditional nosological taxonomy. A categorical diagnostic system, however imprecise the current version may be, is a necessary language for easy professional communication. Nonetheless, research is urgently needed to enhance the informative value of that language. However, the plea does mean that a nosological diagnosis is incomplete and that psychiatry should pursue a *three-tier diagnostic approach*.

The *first* tier is the nosological diagnosis, that is, the broad, general diagnostic framework. Major depression would be an example. The *second* tier of diagnosis includes a detailed description of the syndrome, its severity, duration, and course, each of these variables to be scored independently and on separate axes. Other clinically relevant variables such as etiological factors, premorbid personality structure, and family history are treated in the same way; after careful assessment they, too, are to be scored on independent axes.

The *third* tier comprises the dimensional or functional diagnosis, depicting the dissection of the syndrome into its component parts: the psychological dysfunctions. For example, in the case of major depression, it would entail a detailed depiction of disturbances in mood-, anxiety- and aggression-regulation, in drive and in hedonic functioning, amongst other psychological dysfunctions. I use the word depiction, not description, to indicate that many psychological (dys-)functions are measurable quantitatively and with great precision (that is, if the patient is willing to collaborate with an experimental clinical psychologist). In contrast, the presence of syndromes and nosological entities may be estimated and expressed only in terms such as mild, moderate or severe.

Development of the third diagnostic tier will not only refine the diagnostic process but place the study of psychopathology on a truly scientific footing.

4.4. Functional Psychopharmacology

Another consequence of three-tier diagnosing is a move of psychopharmacology from a nosological to a functional orientation. I foresee that the indication for a particular psychotropic drug will no longer be based primarily on the tier-one diagnosis, for instance schizophrenia or major depression, but rather on the functional disturbances that are the chief manifestations of that illness. For instance, drugs will be prescribed that correct disturbances in perception, cognition, impulse control, mood regulation, etc. These medications will be dispensed simultaneously: a goal-directed, dysfunction-oriented polypharmacy. Three-tier diagnosing would, thus, redeem the maligned concept of polypharmacy. The development of a functional psychopharmacology would be predicated on the development of drugs with great selectivity on the biochemical level. In the field of 5-HT drugs, with representatives influencing specific subpopulations of 5-HT receptors, that process has already begun.

A three-tier diagnostic system with a corresponding functional pharmacology is not a chimera. Cardiology, for one, provides a telling example. In that specialty, stratified diagnosing is the rule. Myocardial infarction, for instance, is a tier-one diagnosis, always to be complemented with a tier-three analysis explicitly stating the functional sequelae, in terms of rhythm, conduction, frequency, etc. Drugs are, then, dispensed on the basis of the tier-three, not the tier-one diagnosis. When multiple functions are disturbed, several drugs will often be administered simultaneously. It is in this direction that I expect to see clinical psychopharmacology develop. It is *the* scientific approach to drug treatment, at least as long as we cannot address the cause(s) of the disease directly.

The tier-three diagnoses would contribute not only to the scientific sophistication of biological psychiatry and psychopharmacology, but equally to the practice of psychotherapy. A detailed analysis of the "psychic apparatus" into its component psychological functions—those that are disordered and those still intact—would provide the psychotherapist with a map to guide his psychological interventions, and would preclude "fishing expeditions" in the realm of the mind that are currently all too common, particularly among psychodynamically oriented psychotherapists.

Another field that will benefit from a functionally oriented psychopathology is that of measurement of abnormal behavior. So far, the presence of a psychiatric syndrome of symptom is expressed as a rough estimate, that is, as mildly, moderately, or severely present, or anywhere in between. Many psychological functions and dysfunctions, however, are measurable in real quantitative terms and with considerable precision and reliability. Functional psychopathology will thus lay the groundwork for a scientifically based psychopathology.

In *conclusion*, functional psychopathology would be to psychiatry what physiology is to medicine: a level of organization of psychopathology fundamental for the understanding of abnormal behavior. Its pragmatic importance for biological psychiatry and psychopharmacology seems obvious, but psychotherapy and psychosocial interventions should profit as well. Functional psychopathology is not an alternative for nosological/categorical classification, but its complement. A three-tier diagnostic system for mental disorders, to be developed in close collaboration with experimental clinical psychologists, seems to me an indispensable precondition for the scientific maturation of psychiatry.

5. SUMMARY

This chapter addresses the question: What is the most productive way to systematize abnormal behavior in order to study its biological roots? Though nosology still occupies the premier position in biological psychiatry, it is, in and by itself, a treacherous beacon. Syndromal organization of psychopathology is likewise seriously flawed. A functional organization of psychopathology is considered the most appropriate framework for biological research and a plea is made for a three-tier diagnostic system of psychiatric disorders. Tier-one comprises the nosological diagnosis, tier-two a description of the syndrome and its etiology, and tier-three a detailed depiction of the component psychological dysfunctions. Development of the third diagnostic tier would bring psychopathology onto a true scientific footing.

Classical nosology has been considered the quintessence of the medical model in psychiatry (Katz & Wetzler, 1991). Psychiatric disorders are viewed as whole entities of which the pathogenesis can be meaningfully explored. The unit of measurement is the disorder itself. If one accepts that definition, then, paradox of paradoxes, the medical model is an unsuitable point of departure for biological psychiatric research.

−7−

Beyond Nosology
A Specimen of Functional Analysis of Biological Data in a Mental Disorder

1. FUNCTIONAL PSYCHOPATHOLOGY: A LOOK BACKWARD

As I have discussed in Chapter 6, biological psychiatry from the very beginning has oriented itself towards nosology, a way of looking at behavioral disorders as distinct, clearly separable entities, each with its own symptomatology, causation, outcome, and treatment. Finding a marker and, eventually, the cause of, for instance, schizophrenia, depression, or panic disorder has been and still is the major goal of biological psychiatric research. The introduction of the DSM-III in 1980 forcefully reinforced biological psychiatry's nosological orientatión.

For many years now I have advocated and pursued another route, marked by what I have called a functional approach to psychopathology (van Praag & Leijnse, 1965; van Praag et al., 1975, 1987c). Most parsimoniously formulated, this concept holds three tenets.

1. The basic units of classification in psychopathology are not syndromes or nosological entities, but psychological dysfunctions, such as disturbances in perception, cognition, memory, information pro-

The research referred to in this chapter was carried out in collaboration with A. Apter, G.M. Asnis, A. Bleich, S.L. Brown, L.C.W. Dols, J.M. Harkavy Friedman, R.S. Kahn, J. Korf, M.L. Korn, R. Plutchik, W.M.A. Verhoeven, and S. Wetzler.

This chapter was adapted from van Praag H.M., Asnis G.M., Kahn R.S., Brown S.L., Korn M., Harkavy Friedman J.M., & Wetzler S. (1990). Monoamines and abnormal behaviour. A multi-aminergic perspective. *British Journal of Psychiatry, 157*:723-734.

cessing, and many others. *They* are the elementary constituents of which psychiatric syndromes are made.

2. Nosological classification of a given psychiatric disorder is the first step in diagnosis. The next step in the diagnostic process is dissection of the syndrome into its component parts, i.e. the psychological dysfunctions and their subsequent measurement.

Examples of functional analysis of categorical diagnoses are provided by medicine. Myocardial infarction is a categorical diagnosis which will be routinely complemented by an analysis of its functional sequelae in terms of, for instance, heartbeat frequency and rhythm, conductance, and output. Treatment is predicated on the functional analysis, not on the nosological diagnosis.

3. In biological psychiatric research, correlations between biological and psychological dysfunctions should be sought.

Functional psychopathology is dimensional in orientation, viewing a given psychiatric disorder as a conglomerate of psychological dysfunctions, most of them nosologically nonspecific and occurring in different severities and in different combinations in the various psychiatric syndromes. The nosological approach is categorical, viewing psychiatric disorders as discrete entities, each with its own causation, symptomatology, and course.

The term "functional" is not identical with "symptomatological." Psychiatric symptoms are the behavioral expression of a psychological dysfunction, not the dysfunction itself. A visual hallucination, for example, is a symptom, a particular perceptual disturbance, the underlying dysfunction. Within the functional framework, the latter is the target of biological research.

We have pursued the functional approach in psychiatry for many years and believe this route to be productive, as the following exposition is meant to illustrate. I restrict myself here to depression, but in other diagnostic categories, such as anxiety disorders and schizophrenia, this approach seems equally fruitful.

2. THE ROLE OF DOPAMINE IN ABNORMAL BEHAVIOR

In the late sixties, we reported the occurrence of dopamine (DA) disturbances in depression, most notably in vital depression (major depression melancholic type, called melancholic depression in this treatise) (van Praag & Korf, 1971b). In some patients, the probenecid-induced accumulation of the major DA metabolite homovanillic acid (HVA) in CSF was decreased, indicating a lowered DA metabolism in the CNS, particularly in the nigro-striatal DA system, the region that is predominantly represented by CSF HVA. Guided by Parkinson's disease with its severe disturbances in motor functioning and profound DA depletion, we searched for correlations between lowered CSF HVA and motor retardation. Comparing groups of depressed patients with and without pronounced motor retardation and lack of initiative, the HVA accumulation after probenecid appeared to be twice as low in the retarded patients as in the nonretarded depressives and in a control group. Similar findings were reported by other investigators (Papeschi & McClure, 1971; Banki, 1977a; Banki et al., 1981).

If lowered DA metabolism in the nigro-striatal system underlies retardation and inertia, increasing DA availability could be expected to exert an activating and energizing effect. L-DOPA was the drug of our choice to boost DA metabolism, since we had demonstrated in humans that it increases DA metabolism substantially, while having little impact on NA metabolism. Moreover, the increase in DA metabolism persists over time (van Praag & Lemus, 1986).

L-DOPA (at an average dose of 260 mg/day) in combination with a peripheral decarboxylase inhibitor was first studied in a group of biochemically undifferentiated melancholically depressed patients and found to be lacking in overall therapeutic effects. Subsequently, we compared the effect of L-DOPA (290 mg/day) and a peripheral decarboxylase inhibitor in melancholic patients with lowered post-probenecid CSF HVA and in melancholic patients with normal HVA response. Motor retardation and inertia were significantly more pronounced in the former group. L-DOPA was shown to improve motor functioning and level of initiative in the low HVA group and to normalize the HVA level. Mood and hedonic functioning were not significantly influenced. Anxiety levels rose slightly, but significantly. In the group with normal HVA response, L-DOPA failed to exhibit therapeutic effects (van Praag & Korf, 1975).

We repeated the latter experiment in a different group of patients, using L-tyrosine instead of L-DOPA (van Praag, 1986b). In contrast to L-DOPA, L-tyrosine, the precursor of the catecholamines (CA) DA and NA, significantly increases CSF MHPG in humans, indicating increased NA metabolism. CSF HVA, on the other hand, rises relatively slightly, suggesting that tyrosine's impact on DA metabolism (in the nigro-striatal system) is less pronounced than that of L-DOPA. Again studying melancholic patients with and without lowered CSF HVA accumulation after probenecid, we observed no therapeutic effect of tyrosine on motor retardation and inertia in either group. Anhedonia improved, but anxiety worsened (see section 4.3), so that total ratings did not change significantly. Normalization of CSF HVA did not occur.

Based on these findings, we hypothesized that diminished DA metabolism in the nigro-striatal system underlies decreased motor activity and lowered level of initiative, irrespective of nosological diagnosis (van Praag et al., 1975). In accordance with this hypothesis are the observations by Lindstrom (1985) that low CSF HVA occurs in schizophrenics with pronounced lassitude and slowness of movement.

When one attempts to link the DA system to the ability to carry out goal-directed behavior, one has to take into account that such behavior is a composite of different components. First, an initial stimulus is needed. This can be an instinctual drive, such as hunger, thirst, or sex; an emotion, such as anger; or a cognitive set (e.g. the realization of having to prepare for a test). Next, the goals to respond appropriately to the stimulus have to be selected, e.g., to find food to satisfy hunger, to display aggressive behavior to reduce anger, or to move to a library and study, in the case of an upcoming test. Subsequently, the behavior to attain these goals has to be initiated and sustained. Finally, signals should be set in operation when the mission has been accomplished so that the behavior can be terminated. The term "drive" is used to indicate an initial stimulus of an instinctual nature. It is also used for the entire process of initiation and completion of goal-directed behavior. For the sake of brevity, we use the term in the latter sense in this chapter.

The sequence leading to goal-directed behavior can be disturbed at any junction. The human data suggest that DA is involved in the mobilization, facilitation, and sustenance of goal-directed behavior. The large pool of animal data available accords with this conclusion (Crow & Deakin, 1985; Freed & Yamamoto, 1985; Ashton, 1987).

3. THE ROLE OF SEROTONIN
IN ABNORMAL BEHAVIOR

3.1. Whither "5-HT Depression"

Disturbances in central serotonin (5-hydroxytryptamine, 5-HT) metabolism were first reported in depression. They were inferred to exist based on the finding of lowered postprobenecid minus baseline levels of 5-hydroxyindole acetic acid (5-HIAA, the major degradation product of 5-HT) in cerebrospinal fluid (CSF) of depressed individuals, indicating diminished 5-HT metabolism in the CNS (van Praag et al., 1970).

Subsequently, disturbances in other systems, indicative of central 5-HT ergic functioning were observed. First, disturbances in platelet 5-HT, such as deviations in 5-HT content and uptake and in the density of imipramine receptors, were reported. Blood platelets have been considered as a model of central 5-HT ergic nerve endings. Furthermore, disturbances in the ratio of the plasma concentration of tryptophan and the so-called competing amino acids were found. This ratio determines the influx of tryptophan into the CNS, and CNS availability of tryptophan, in its turn, is an important determinant of 5-HT synthesis rate. Moreover, several hormonal challenge tests indicated disturbances in 5-HT ergic functioning. Finally, psychopharmacological experiments with indirect 5-HT agonists such as the 5-HT precursor 5-hydroxytryptophan (5-HTP) and the selective 5-HT uptake inhibitors, and 5-HT antagonists, such as parachlorophenylalanine (PCPA) (a 5-HT synthesis inhibitor), suggested that manipulation of central 5-HT can effect mood changes (Brown et al., 1991).

The data most clearly and directly related to central 5-HT metabolism are derived from CSF studies, although these studies are the most cumbersome to conduct. The interrelation between the various 5-HT indicators is insufficiently known. (For review on 5-HT and depression, see e.g. van Praag, 1982c; Goodwin & Post, 1983; Brown et al., 1991).

Initially, depressed patients with and without demonstrable disturbances in central 5-HT seemed indistinguishable in psychopathological terms. In 1971, interpreting the available data at that time, we introduced the concept of biochemical heterogeneity of depression (van Praag & Korf, 1971a). Some forms of depression, we postulated, are linked to disturbances in 5-HT functions; others are not or are to a lesser extent only. The same syndrome, then, could be the ultimate outcome of various pathophysiological processes. As an analogy, we mentioned the anaemia syndrome. Anaemia patients present by and large the same symptoms, but the pathogenesis of the syndrome is heterogeneous, and with that the treatment.

Subsequent studies, however, made the postulate of a separate category of "5-HT depressions" untenable (van Praag & Lemus, 1986). They indicated that increasing 5-HT availability *alone* is not a sufficient antidepressant measure. This argues against the concept of a depression type that is generated predominantly by central 5-HT disturbances, leading to decreased 5-HT availability.

3.2. Contra "5-HT Depression"

First we demonstrated in a double-blind, placebo-controlled, comparative study that 5-HTP is an active antidepressant in hospitalized patients with rather severe forms of melancholic depression, while tryptophan turned out to be no better than placebo (van Praag, 1984). Both 5-HT precursors increase central 5-HT metabolism to an equal extent, as reflected in the probenecid-induced accumulation of 5-HIAA in CSF. They appeared to differ, however, in their effect on catecholamine (CA) metabolites in CSF (reflecting intracerebral metabolism of the mother amines). 5-HTP increases the metabolism of DA as well as of NA, while tryptophan does not (van Praag, 1983b). In high doses (>5g i.v.), tryptophan even lowers DA and NA metabolism, possibly by interfering with the influx of tyrosine, the precursor substance of the CAs, in the CNS (van Praag et al., 1987a).

5-HTP's ability to stimulate CA metabolism is thought to be due to the presence of aromatic amino acid decarboxylase in CA ergic nerve cells. Hence, 5-HTP is converted to 5-HT not only in 5-HT ergic but also in CA ergic neurons. In the latter, 5-HT functions as a false transmitter, as a consequence of which the synthesis rate of CA increases. The net functional effect of the two opposing processes, i.e. false transmitter formation leading to decreased function and increased CA production leading to augmented function, is probably heightened CA ergic activity.

If 5-HTP's therapeutic superiority to tryptophan is related to its combined effects on 5-HT and CA systems, one would expect to raise tryptophan's antidepressant efficacy above the significance level by combining it with a compound capable of increasing CA availability selectively. We showed in humans that tyrosine is presumably such a compound. It increases CA metabolism, while 5-HT metabolism is not measurably changed. Combining tryptophan with tyrosine indeed led to significant antidepressant activity (van Praag, 1986d).

A second observation supports the hypothesis of 5-HTP deriving its therapeutic potential from its dual influence on 5-HT ergic and CA ergic systems. In about 25 percent of patients initially treated successfully with 5-HTP, the response subsided in the second month of treatment (van Praag, 1983b). This phenomenon is paralleled by normalization of CA metabolism (again, as reflected in the CSF concentration of CA metabolites) while the metabolism of 5-HT remained increased. We hypothesized that clinical relapse and normalization of CA metabolism were related. If so, reactivating CA metabolism should restore clinical remission—and, indeed, it did. Adding tyrosine to the 5-HTP regime in the group of relapsers once again led to subsidence of the depression and to a rise of CA metabolism (van Praag & Lemus, 1986).

These data suggest that *combined* augmentation of 5-HT and CA availability in the CNS provides the best conditions for antidepressant activity, and as such, they argue against the existence of a separate diagnostic entity called "5-HT depression." 5-HTP's behavioral effects in monkeys have also been demonstrated to be a function of its influence on 5-HT and CA systems (Raleigh, 1987).

If 5-HT disturbances are not linked to a particular *syndromal subtype of depression*, could it be that they relate to particular *psychopathological dimensions* that may occur in depression, but might be lacking as well, explaining the occurrence of 5-HT disturbances in some, but not other depressions (van Praag et al., 1987c).

This hypothesis seems plausible in the light of recent observations, the dimensions in question being disregulation of aggression and heightened anxiety. The relevant data will now be briefly summarized.

3.3 5-HT and Disturbed Aggression Regulation

In 1976, Asberg et al. confirmed our findings of a subgroup of depressed individuals with low CSF 5-HIAA, and added the important observation that in that subgroup suicide attempters seemed to accumulate. This finding was confirmed by many, though not all investigators. Subsequent studies revealed, moreover, that low CSF 5-HIAA was observed not only in depressed suicide attempters, but likewise in nondepressed, nonpsychotic (e.g. personality disturbed) suicide attempters and in schizophrenic patients who had made suicide attempts because "voices" had ordered them to do so, but who were not suffering from depression, as defined by the DSM-III (van Praag, 1986b).

Lowered concentration of CSF 5-HIAA has also been reported in individuals with increased outward-directed aggression, but belonging to different diagnostic categories (Brown et al., 1979, 1982; Bioulac et al., 1980; Linnoila et al., 1983; Lidberg et al., 1984, 1985; Virkkunen et al., 1987). The biological study of aggression in humans is known to be fraught with methodological difficulties such as the usually short duration of aggressive outbursts and the fact that these explosions are more often than not intertwined with a host of factors, social or toxicological (drugs, alcohol), for which it is hard to control. The fact that all studies published so far on the subject have reported low CSF 5-HIAA seems to indicate that the finding is a robust one that stands out in spite of considerable background noise. Depressed patients with low CSF 5-HIAA show not only an increased rate of suicide attempts but also an increased frequency of signs of outward-directed aggression (van Praag et al., 1986).

Dysregulation of aggression can be a major feature of depression, as evidenced by the greatly increased incidence of both suicidal behavior and signs of outward-directed aggressiveness, but it may also be a subordinate symptom (Plutchik et al., 1989). This could explain the apparent arbitrary occurrence of low CSF 5-HIAA in mood disorders.

Lowering of CSF 5-HIAA reflects diminished 5-HT metabolism in the CSF, which could be a primary condition or a phenomenon secondary to hypersensitivity of postsynaptic 5-HT receptors. Since we found no correlation between 5-HT receptor sensitivity and aggression (Wetzler et al., 1991), diminution of 5-HT metabolism seems to be the most likely hypothesis. If that were to be the case, increase of 5-HT availability in the CNS could be expected to decrease (certain types of) aggression. The available data, though few and preliminary in nature, seem to support this supposition. Lithium and L-tryptophan, both compounds that enhance 5-HT ergic activity, have been reported to reduce aggression (Volovka et al., 1990; Morand et al., 1983). Eltoprazine, a postsynaptic $5-HT_{1A}$ and $5-HT_{1B}$ agonist, strongly and selectively diminishes certain types of aggression in animals (Olivier et al., 1990).

One would expect selective 5-HT uptake inhibitors to possess antiaggressive potential, but no controlled studies to that effect have been conducted. Recently, evidence suggesting just the reverse has been published: Six patients treated with fluoxetine reported a sudden increase in suicidal ideation (Teicher et al., 1990). However, the case for a causal connection is not strong. First, evidence that increase in suicidality is more common with fluoxetine than with other antidepressants is lacking. Second, no reports of increased suicidality with other selective 5-HT uptake inhibitors have been published. One of them, fluvoxamine, has already been marketed for over 10 years.

The facts, then, seem sufficiently robust to carry the hypothesis that the signs of diminished 5-HT metabolism in the CNS, as originally observed in depression, are related to dysregulated aggression, irrespective of the direction it takes and of the nosological context in which it occurs.

3.4. 5-HT and Heightened Anxiety

Anxiety is a second psychopathological dimension occurring in depression, but is by no means specific for that disorder. It also seems to be 5-HT related. Several pieces of evidence point in that direction.

5-HT potentiating drugs, in particular 5-HTP, that increase 5-HT synthesis and the 5-HT uptake inhibitors such as clomipramine, trazadone, fluvoxamine, and fluoxetine were reported to have therapeutic effects in panic disorder (Evans & Moore, 1981; Koczkas et al., 1981; Evans et al., 1986; Kahn et al., 1984, 1987; Den Boer et al., 1987). Even more interesting, the effect of those indirect 5-HT agonists seems to be biphasic, at least in some patients (Kahn &

Westenberg, 1985). An initial phase of increased anxiety, lasting 2–3 weeks is followed by a phase of amelioration in which anxiety and panic attacks diminish. We explained this biphasic effect by postulating a) hypersensitivity of post-synaptic 5-HT receptors and b) relatedness of this phenomenon to the anxiety attacks. Under these circumstances, increasing 5-HT availability would first lead to additional stimulation of an already hyperactive 5-HT system and hence to clinical deterioration. Down regulation of the receptor system due to increased 5-HT availability would eventually lead to amelioration of the anxiety disorder (Kahn et al., 1988c).

Recently, additional evidence favoring this hypothesis was acquired. Panic disorder patients were challenged with m-chlorophenylpiperazine (MCPP), a relatively selective postsynaptic 5-HT receptor agonist. Healthy individuals served as controls. The major findings were twofold. Patients with panic disorder showed a substantial increase in anxiety during the test, in comparison to placebo. In the control group no significant response occurred, on either MCPP or placebo (Kahn et al., 1988b). Moreover, the ACTH and cortisol response to MCPP was augmented in panic disorder patients, again as compared to a) the response to placebo and b) the MCPP response in the control group (Kahn et al., 1988a, 1991a).

Another piece of confirmatory evidence is found in the development of drugs that diminish central 5-HT activity and possess anxiolytic potential. Buspirone is an established anxiolytic. It is a substance with a high affinity for presynaptically located 5-HT1A receptors and probably decreases 5-HT ergic activity (Taylor et al., 1985). Ritanserin is a selective antagonist of postsynaptically located 5-HT2 receptors, of which anxiolytic actions have been reported (Ceulemans et al., 1985). Both drugs seem to be effective in generalized anxiety disorder. In panic disorder, ritanserin has been found to be ineffective (Den Boer & Westenberg, 1990). Recently, selective antagonists of 5-HT3 receptors have been developed which animal experiments have pinpointed as potential anxiolytic agents (Jones et al., 1988). In humans, the various 5-HT receptor systems cannot yet be studied separately and independently.

If, indeed, in (certain) states of increased anxiety (certain) post-synaptic 5-HT receptors are hypersensitive, one would expect a compensatory diminution of central 5-HT synthesis. Diminution of

5-HT synthesis would be reflected in a drop of 5-HIAA concentration in CSF. This has not been observed (Eriksson et al., 1991). In depressed patients, on the other hand, a negative correlation between CSF 5-HIAA and anxiety levels has indeed been established (Banki, 1977b; Rydin et al., 1982; van Praag, 1988b).

The present data do not permit extending the 5-HT hypersensitivity hypothesis beyond panic disorder, but some preliminary data indicate that 5-HT receptor hypersensitivity may be related to increased anxiety in general rather than to panic disorder alone. First, we found a correlation between cortisol response to MCPP and anxiety level as measured one week prior to the test in both panic disorder and major depression, suggesting a relationship between the general state of anxiety and 5-HT receptor hypersensitivity. The relation between CSF 5-HIAA and anxiety in depression, mentioned above, points in the same direction, and so does the finding that suppressors of 5-HT activity like ritanserin and buspirone are effective in generalized anxiety disorder.

3.5. A Dimensional 5-HT Hypothesis

Signs of decreased central 5-HT metabolism, then, seem to correlate not with a particular syndromal depression type but with particular affective disturbances, i.e. increased (auto) aggression and augmented anxiety.

If the psychopathological dimensions of increased aggression and heightened anxiety are both related to disordered 5-HT metabolism, one would expect these dimensions to intercorrelate, and indeed they do. In a recent series of studies on predictors of suicide and violence in groups of psychiatric patients with a diversity of diagnoses, we found trait anxiety to be strongly correlated with both suicide risk and violence risk (Apter et al., 1990).

The data favoring a dimensional 5-HT hypothesis, linking 5-HT disturbances to disordered aggression- and anxiety-regulation across diagnoses, seem fairly convincing. What is the role, one might ask, of disturbed aggression- and anxiety-regulation in the occurrence of depression? Is the role of these dysfunctions subordinate or could they trigger a depression. In the latter case, the concept of a "5-HT related" depression would be a viable one, after all. This subject will be discussed in the next chapter.

4. THE ROLE OF NORADRENALINE IN ABNORMAL BEHAVIOR

4.1. Inside the Pleasure Principle

So far we have discussed NA-ergic involvement in drive- and affect-regulation. Both domains are frequently disturbed in depression (in particular in major depression, melancholic type) but those disturbances are by no means specific for that disorder.

A third major sphere of dysfunction in melancholic depression pertains to the ability to experience pleasure. Normally, much of what we do, perceive, or think, is not emotionally neutral, but is provided with a charge—globally speaking, a positive or a negative one. It generates pleasure or displeasure in whatever way that may be defined. Anhedonia, the inability to experience pleasure, is a typical symptom of melancholic depression. It is one of the few almost pathognomonic symptoms in psychiatry.

Anhedonia is unlike flat affect or emotional blunting as may be observed in schizophrenia. Flat affect pertains to a global inability to experience, or at least to express, emotions; anhedonia indicates the inability to link a particular mental or motor activity with the experiential quality of gratification, a quality that has been "stamped in" when similar activities were carried out in the past. In melancholic depression, the emotional defect is "localized" and there is no global defect in experiencing or expressing emotions. On the contrary, particularly negative emotions such as sadness, guilt, and shame are felt with profound intensity. In very severe cases of melancholic depression, the ability to experience discomfort is also impaired. Mental and physical activities that usually would be experienced as aversive have less capacity to produce this effect. The state of anhedonia is experienced vividly and forms an additional reason for distress. This is not so in the case of emotional blunting.

Behavior is strongly motivated by the attainment of pleasure and the avoidance of discomfort. The decreased ability to experience such modalities will reinforce the state of drive-reduction characteristic for melancholic depression.

In animals, brain systems have been found that code for naturally occurring rewarding and aversive experiences. The so-called reward and punishment systems (Olds & Milner, 1954) are, at least in part, monoaminergically innervated, the former by CA, the latter by 5-HT. DA is thought to be particularly involved in mobilizing and directing goal-directed behaviors. DA neurons constitute a "go-system" or "incentive-system" guiding the organism to areas in the environment associated with reward (Crow, 1973). In addition, DA neurons have been implicated as a substrate for intracranial self-stimulation (Wise, 1982; Mason, 1984).

Though a role for NA in self-stimulation is less well supported than for DA, NA-ergic neurons seem to play a role in what we have called "emotional memory" (van Praag et al., 1988b), i.e. in the consolidation and retrieval of the emotional arousal induced by particular behaviors. Alternatively, NA-ergic tracts constitute the connections between the neural representation of rewards anticipated to be associated with particular behaviors and the DA-ergic incentive system (Crow, 1973, 1977). NA-ergic mechanisms have also been implicated in selecting among a choice of possible behaviors to attain a particular goal, based on experiences of reward or punishment that those behaviors elicited on prior occasions (Robbins et al., 1985; Ashton, 1987). A reward-related role of NA-ergic mechanisms in self-stimulation is supported by experiments with clonidine, an α2-adrenergic agonist. This substance disrupts the rewarding component of brain stimulation in a selective manner, probably via activation of presynaptic α2-receptors, and by doing so curtailing NA-ergic impulse flow (Franklin, 1978; Hunt et al., 1976). The catecholamine synthesis inhibitor α-methyl-p-tyrosine magnifies this effect (Hunt et al., 1976).

4.2. A Noradrenaline Hypothesis of Anhedonia

NA-ergic mechanisms seem to enable the animal to couple the experience of reward or anticipated reward to a particular activity. The hedonic component of the melancholic syndrome can be conceived of as a dysfunction of exactly that coupling mechanism. Situations that used to create pleasure are perceived as usual, but are now devoid of an emotional charge. Stein (1978) was the first to suggest depression to be "a disorder of positive reinforcement or reward function." We do not subscribe to this generalization, but would suggest a more focused version of this hypothesis. The hedonic disturbance in depression is, we submit, related to NA-ergic insufficiency, a transmission defect resulting in inability to couple the reward component to mental or physical activities that used to carry such a charge.

The NA hypothesis of anhedonia fits into the general framework of the classic information-processing theory of human cognition, in which two sets of structures are being postulated, one for storing information, and the other for information transfer from one structure to another. In this model—and we follow here Kihlstrom's (1987) description—information from the environment is transduced into a pattern of neural impulses by the sensory receptors. This pattern is briefly held in the sensory registers, one for each modality, where it is then analyzed by processes known as feature detection and pattern recognition. Information that has been identified as meaningful and relevant to current goals is then transferred to a structure known as primary or short-term memory. Here, the information is subject to further analysis, whereby the perceptual information is combined with information retrieved from secondary or long-term memory. In the primary memory, processes such as judgment, inference, and problem-solving take place. On the basis of an analysis of the meaning of the stimulus input, a response is generated. Finally, a trace of the event is permanently encoded in the secondary memory. It is in the short-term memory, one might assume, that the percepts, i.e., the perceptual information, are linked with the appropriate emotion, i.e., the emotion that was aroused in similar circumstances on previous occasions.

NA metabolism and NA-ergic functions have been studied in depression and in anxiety disorders. In the former, NA-ergic hypofunction has been postulated (Siever, 1989); in the latter, NA-ergic hyperfunction (Redmond & Huang, 1979). The concept of the NA-ergic nature of anhedonia, conceived as a psychopathological dimension, has not been systematically studied and, hence, is largely hypothetical. Some scattered data, however, admittedly at best tentative in nature, are sufficiently intriguing to prompt further investigation.

4.3. Preliminary Studies of the Noradrenaline Hypothesis of Anhedonia

Clozapine. Anhedonia can be pharmacologically induced by neuroleptics. With anticholinergic phenomena and extrapyramidal symptoms, it is one of the more common side effects. The motor symptoms are thought to be related to nigro-striatal DA ergic block-ade. Most neuroleptics also block variably NA-ergic transmission. Conceivably, the latter effect could underlay the hedonic disturb-ances. Drugs that deplete NA stores, such as reserpine, and drugs which reduce NA-ergic function via presynaptic inhibition, such as clonidine, can cause depression and anhedonia.

Clozapine is a so-called atypical neuroleptic, one of a group of compounds with more selective effects on meso-limbic and meso-cortical DA systems than their "typical" counterparts. This could explain why their propensity to elicit motor side effects is lower and their therapeutic potential probably greater. In addition, clozapine has a profound blocking effect not only on 5-HT$_2$ receptors, but like-wise on NA receptors, particularly after acute administration (Burki et al., 1974; Bartholini et al., 1972, 1973; Buus Lassen, 1974).

We studied the effects of 100 mg clozapine administered daily for two weeks to six normal volunteers in a placebo-controlled, double-blind, two-group design. Mood, drive, and hedonic functions were assessed via a structured interview and recorded by a (blind) inter-viewer on a five-point scale. Effects occurred more or less sequen-tially. First, listlessness was reported (after 2–3 days); subsequently, lack of energy; finally, in the second week, lowering of mood (van Praag et al., 1991). The "clozapine-syndrome" resembled that of mild vital depression (major depression, melancholic type). The hedonic deficit elicited by clozapine was significant and in the first few days was "pure" (that is, not combined with other psychological disturbances).

Moreover, we compared clozapine with perphenazine (Trilafon) in acutely psychotic patients without evidence of brain damage. Clozapine augmented the concentration of the NA metabolite 3-methoxy-4-hydroxyphenylglycol (MHPG) in CSF, while per-phenazine did not (van Praag et al., 1976). The reverse proved to be true for the DA metabolite HVA; its concentration rose during per-phenazine, but not after clozapine. These data suggest that clozapine, in contrast to perphenazine, has a blocking effect on postsynaptic NA receptors, conceivably accounting for the hedonic defects observed in the "clozapine syndrome."

Tyrosine. In depressed patients, tyrosine, the precursor of DA and

NA, increases the CSF concentration of HVA and MHPG (van Praag & Lemus, 1986), indicating that tyrosine furthers CA synthesis and metabolism. It has no overall therapeutic effect in depression, but is not devoid of pharmacological activity either. In a preliminary experiment, we found that discrete components of the depressive syndrome did change significantly. This was particularly true for anxiety, which increased, and for hedonic functioning, which improved (van Praag et al., 1991). These preliminary findings suggest that tyrosine exerts a measurable effect on NA availability, while also significantly reducing anhedonia.

Clonidine. Clonidine, in low doses, stimulates presynaptic α2-adrenergic receptors, leading to diminished NA release. Administered to normal test persons, it induced impairment of paired-associate learning (Frith et al., 1985). Sedation is an unlikely explanation because clonidine did not affect other memory functions. It decreased blood pressure, suggesting diminished NA-ergic impulse flow, but this effect could, of course, be totally peripheral.

This finding suggests that NA neurons are involved in coupling of the neural representation of associated stimuli. This is as far as one can go; it does not imply that these neurons are involved in linking an emotional memory trace ("pleasure") with a particular behavior.

Hormonal studies. The growth hormone response to clonidine (supposedly mediated by postsynaptic α2-adrenergic receptors in the hypothalamus) has been shown to be blunted in endogenous depression as compared to neurotic depression (Checkley et al., 1984). The most important symptomatological distinction between the two syndromes is the presence or absence of anhedonia (van Praag, 1962, 1989). Conceivably, the NA-ergic deficit and the hedonic disturbances correlate, but data to this effect are not available.

Another hormonal disturbance observed in major depression is blunting of the plasma cortisol response to desmethylimipramine (DMI), a tricyclic antidepressant and a selective inhibitor of NA uptake (Asnis et al., 1985). Correlating blunted DMI response with items of the SADS (Schedule for Affective Disorders and Schizophrenia, Endicott & Spitzer, 1978) related to anhedonia, we found a significant correlation with "lack of reactivity," not with "loss of interest" and "social withdrawal" (van Praag et al., 1989). The study was a retrospective one and no attempts had been made to specifically delineate the symptom of anhedonia and differentiate it from symptoms that show a certain similarity but which we consider as basically different.

In conclusion, then, the evidence in favor of an NA-ergic deficit underlying anhedonia is scanty and tentative, indeed, but yet sufficiently intriguing to warrant further investigations.

5. A DIMENSIONAL MONOAMINE HYPOTHESIS

We discussed evidence of MA-ergic dysfunctions underlying the major domains of psychological dysfunctioning in melancholic depression: drive, affects, and hedonic functioning. Sufficient evidence seems available to implicate DA in drive reduction and 5-HT in disturbed aggression regulation and heightened anxiety. Tentatively, a link has been proposed between NA-ergic dysfunction and anhedonia (Fig 7:1).

5-HT ergic and DA-ergic systems (Green & Deakin, 1980; Williams & Davies, 1983; Fuenmayor & Bermudez, 1985; Curzon et al., 1985) and 5-HT ergic and NA-ergic systems (Ferron et al., 1982; Reinhard et al., 1983; Manier et al., 1984; Feuerstein & Hertting, 1986; Heal et al., 1986; Asakura et al., 1987; Devau et al., 1987) are strongly mutually intertwined. If the psychological dysfunctions under discussion are linked to MA-ergic dysfunctions, one would expect the psychological dysfunctions 1) to often go in concert and 2) to influence each other's severity. Disorders of drive, mood, and hedonic functioning meet in the melancholic syndrome, but no systematic data are available about their quantitative interaction. Clinical experience, however, suggests the likelihood that such interactions do occur. Anhedonia reinforces lack of drive and will tend to aggravate mood lowering. Mood lowering, in its turn, will negatively impact on drive, while drive reduction will probably act as a mood-lowering force.

Disturbances in drive and in regulation of anxiety and aggression are by no means specific for melancholic depression, but occur likewise in other behavioral and in certain neurological disorders. This could explain the nosological non-specificity of MA disturbances.

MAJOR AREAS OF DYSFUNCTION IN MAJOR DEPRESSION, MELANCHOLIC TYPE (ENDOGENOUS OR VITAL DEPRESSION)

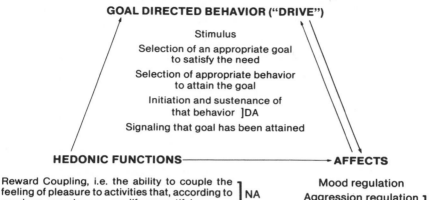

Figure 7:1. Depiction of the major domains of psychological dysfunction in major depression (melancholic type) and the hypothesized MA-ergic dysfunctions underlying these psychological dysfunctions.

Signs of decreased DA metabolism have, for example, been found in retarded depression and in Parkinson's disease; 5-HT disturbances have been reported in depressed suicide attempters but also in suicide attempters with other diagnoses and in individuals with outward directed aggression irrespective of diagnosis. 5-HT disturbances have moreover been implicated in panic disorder, but the odds are that they relate rather to increased anxiety across diagnoses. Anhedonia, on the contrary, seems to be relatively characteristic for melancholic depression. One would expect then the same to be true for the alleged signs of NA ergic hypofunction, but no data are as yet available.

Recently, Cloninger (1986, 1987) advocated the dimensional approach for the biological study of personality disorders. He introduced a system of personality variants based on three dimensions; i.e., novelty seeking, harm avoidance, and reward dependence; traits he additionally linked to particular MA ergic systems. The scheme has elegance but lacks empirical foundation and will be hard to verify. To define and measure psychopathological dimensions such as anhedonia, mood lowering, drive, and anxiety is hard enough; to do the same for delicate distinctions in personality make-up is infinitely more so. To view biological variables occurring in psychiatric disorders from the vantage point of psychopathological dimensions has been demonstrated to be feasible and productive. Whether the same will be true when personality dimensions are substituted for psychopathological dimensions remains to be seen. Considering the present state of psychiatry's diagnostic methodology, I believe that Cloninger went one step too far.

6. FUNCTIONAL PSYCHOPATHOLOGY: A LOOK FORWARD

MA disturbances found in psychiatric disorders look chaotic if viewed from a nosological vantage point, being demonstrable in so many different diagnostic entities. Interpreting them from the functional viewpoint brings order to the apparent chaos. Thus, MA research clearly demonstrates the usefulness of the functional approach in psychopathology. The implications of this approach, however, reach beyond the boundaries of biological psychiatry in several important ways.

First, they reach into the realm of clinical psychopharmacology. Several psychotropic drugs have turned out to be diagnostically nonspecific. Tricyclic antidepressants are efficacious in certain forms of depression *and* in certain anxiety states. The same is true for MAO inhibitors. Clomipramine and the selective 5-HT uptake inhibitors, like fluvoxamine and fluoxetine, are effective antidepressants *and* a useful treatment in obsessive-compulsive disorder. Carbamazepine is an established antiepileptic agent *as well as* an asset in the prophylaxis of episodic mood disorders. Certain benzodiazepines are effective in generalized anxiety disorder and against all components of panic disorder, and also exert a therapeutic effect in depression. These observations are puzzling from a nosological but not from a functional point of view. One could conceive of a particular drug influencing a particular functional system in the brain and, thus, a particular set of psychological dysfunctions, irrespective of diagnosis. The greater the biochemical specificity of a drug, one could argue, the greater the chance it will be nosologically nonspecific, but effective against certain (clusters of) psychological dysfunctions, across diagnoses.

Once correlations between psychological and biological dysfunctions have been established, the next step inevitably will be the search for drugs that can selectively correct the biological dysfunctions. Such drugs would be expected to ameliorate the corresponding psychological dysfunctions, irrespective of nosological diagnosis. Within a nosological frame of reference, treatment is directed towards a particular disorder, within a functional framework, towards the underlying or resulting dysfunctions. In the former approach, treatment is preferably restricted to one drug; in the latter approach, combinations of drugs will be used, contingent on the existing spectrum of dysfunctions. Functional psychopathology will lead to functional psychopharmacology and functional psychopharmacology will inevitably tend to use drugs in combination.

Elsewhere, we have given a (hypothetical) example of transnosological indications of a group of psychotropic drugs, i.e. the selective 5-HT reuptake inhibitors, the first group that seems to possess a high degree of selectivity, at least as far as MAs are concerned (van Praag et al., 1987b). One could object that neuronal systems do not act in isolation, but interact with numerous others. That does not mean, however, that selectivity is illusory and that limiting a drug's primary actions is meaningless. Fluoxetine, for example, is a selective inhibitor of 5-HT uptake with little effect on NA reuptake. Its impact on NA-ergic functioning is not negligible, but certainly much less than that of a drug that primarily inhibits the uptake of both MA, such as amitriptyline. Indeed, perfect selectivity is unattainable, but that goal can certainly be advanced.

Goal-directed, dysfunction-oriented polypharmacy is not a chimera, but a strategy legitimately employed in other medical disciplines. In Chapter 6, I mentioned an example: myocardial infarction. Once this condition has been diagnosed and the cardiac condition functionally analyzed, drugs will be administered to regulate the discrete disturbances in, for instance, rhythm, conduction, frequency, and output. These drugs are often prescribed simultaneously. This, typically, represents goal-directed, dysfunction-oriented multipharmacy.

A second field that will benefit from a functional orientation of psychopathology is that of psychometrics: the measurement of abnormal human behavior. So far, we estimate the presence of a symptom or syndrome in such terms as mild, moderate, and severe. Most psychological dysfunctions, however, are quantitatively measurable with considerable precision, provided the patient is willing and able to participate in the examination. Functional psychopathology could lay the groundwork for a scientifically based psychopathology. Thus, it not only is a productive framework for biological research in psychiatry, but could, in addition, be evolving into a forceful catalyst for psychiatry's ongoing scientific orientation.

I introduced the functional/dimensional approach in psychopathology as a complement of and not as an alternative to the nosological/categorical approach. I still fully subscribe to this standpoint, as much as I do to the view that the exclusive adherence to nosology has not served biological psychiatry well. In fact, it has been a factor stunting its growth.

7. SUMMARY

Classical nosology has been the major cornerstone of biological psychiatric research; finding biological markers and, eventually, causes of disease entities has been the major goal. Another approach, one I have designated as "functional," seems possible, attempting to correlate biological variables with psychological dysfunctions, the latter being considered to be the basic units of classification in psychopathology. I have pursued this route for many years, and based on the resulting findings I formulated the following hypothesis. Signs of diminished DA, 5-HT, and NA metabolism, as have been found in psychiatric disorders, are not disorder-specific, but are rather related to psychopathological dimensions, i.e. hypoactivity/inertia, increased aggression/anxiety, and anhedonia, respectively, independent of the nosological framework in which these dysfunctions occur. As an implication of the functional approach to psychopathology, I foresee a shift from nosological to functional application of psychotropic drugs. Functional psychopharmacology will be dysfunction-oriented and, therefore, inevitably geared towards utilizing drug combinations. This prospect is hailed as progress, both practically and scientifically.

Functional psychopathology, moreover, focusing on disturbed psychological functions rather than on psychiatric symptoms, is a potentially powerful impetus to move the study of mental pathology in a more scientific direction. Functionalism in psychopathology, finally, constitutes a productive matrix to generate innovative hypotheses on the inner structure of mental disorders. The next chapter will provide an illustration of this.

—8—

Is Depression a Mood Disorder?

In the previous chapter, it was demonstrated that the functional view-point is a productive point of departure to interpret biological findings in behavioral disorders. This chapter is complementary in that it aims to show that this viewpoint also provides a fruitful intellectual matrix for provocative, new psychopathological hypotheses.

1. THE THESIS

Is depression a mood disorder? Let me clarify this apparent paradox by rephrasing the question. In depression, is mood regulation primarily disturbed or is it a secondary phenomenon, that is a result of disturbances in other psychological functions? One can rephrase that question in psychopharmacological terms and ask if antidepressants are mood-elevators or if their primary psychopathological target is another psychological domain and mood-elevation is secondary to that. These issues are obviously not only of theoretical but also of practical relevance. The ideal anti-depressant should be geared towards the primary disturbance in depression. If mood-lowering is not that, the search for new antidepressants should be targeted at those psychological dysfunctions that presumably are fundamental.

The thesis I submit holds that in certain types of depression, it is the regulation of aggression and anxiety that is primarily disturbed, not mood-regulation. This is hypothesized to be the case in depression in which the central 5-HT system is disturbed. The nature of these disturbances, however, cannot yet be defined with any degree of precision. I will outline the evidence on which this thesis rests.

2. PSYCHOPATHOLOGICAL EVIDENCE

Katz et al. (1991) studied in detail the behavioral effects of the classical tricyclic antidepressant amitriptyline in the first few weeks of treatment, in particular in patients with major depression. Contrary to clinical lore that claims that weeks may pass before the therapeutic effect of antidepressants becomes noticeable, the initial signs of improvement in the responder group appeared in the first week of treatment.

More importantly, they established that the first psychopathological components to be positively affected were anxiety and hostility. Improvement of mood lagged behind and began to appear only in the second treatment week.

We have obtained comparable results with electroconvulsive therapy applied twice weekly to patients suffering from major depression, melancholic type (Fig. 8:1). The first psychopathological components to be affected were motor retardation, drive reduction, and anxiety, generally in the second week of treatment. Mood-

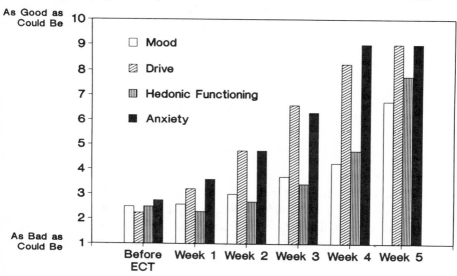

Figure 8:1. Effect of electroconvulsive therapy (ECT), administered twice per week to patients with vital depression (endogenous depression; major depression, melancholic type) on different components of the depressive syndrome.

elevation, again, was a late phenomenon and started to become manifest in most patients only in the third treatment week.

Mood-lowering is a symptom that is not only late to wear off, but also slow to emerge. In a group of patients with major depression, melancholic type (vital or endogenous depression) we found anxiety and irritability to be the most frequent prodromal symptoms (Table 8:1). Only 35 percent of the patients reported that the depressive episode had begun with lowering of mood. "Important others" mentioned irritability and anhedonia most frequently as early signs of imminent depression, while sadness appeared also to them a relatively infrequent early symptom. In a prospective study of recurrent major depression, we found that relapse was heralded in 62 percent of cases by anxiety, in 39 percent by increased aggressivity, in 34 percent by both symptoms together, and in 21 percent by mood-lowering. Fava et al. (1990) also found irritability and anxiety to be the most frequent early signs of depression. In mood disorders, finally, (auto)aggression and anxiety are two features that are highly intercorrelated (Apter et al., 1990, 1991).

In conclusion, hostility and anxiety frequently herald major depression, while mood-lowering is often both late to appear and slow to disappear. These findings suggest that mood-lowering in those cases is a symptom secondary to disturbances in anxiety and aggression regulation.

3. BIOLOGICAL EVIDENCE

3.1. 5-HT Disturbances in Depression

I will restrict my deliberations to the serotonergic system because this system provides the evidence for the thesis outlined above.

Disturbances in central serotonin (5-hydroxytryptamine, 5-HT) have been repeatedly reported in depression (See Chapter 7). Different research strategies have been used, such as the measurement of the major 5-HT metabolite 5-hydroxyindoleacetic acid (5-HIAA) in cerebrospinal fluid (CSF); postmortem study of 5-HT, 5-HIAA and 5-HT receptors in the brain of suicide victims; hormonal challenge tests with various 5-HT agonists such as tryptophan, 5-hydroxytryptophan (5-HTP), and m-chlorophenylpiperazine (MCPP); and the study of

TABLE 8:1

First Manifestations of the Depressions in Patients Diagnosed as Vital (endogenous; melancholic) Depression or Personal* Depression (neurotic; dysthymic) Depression and the Occurrence of These Features in Normal Controls (N in Each Group Is 50)

	VITAL DEPRESSION		PERSONAL DEPRESSION		CONTROLS (N = 50)
	Symptom Pronounced	Symptom Mild or Absent	Symptom Pronounced	Symptom Mild or Absent	
Low Spirits	11	39	42	8	2
Anxiety	41	9	24	26	3
Irritability	38	12	21	29	4
Inability to Enjoy	16	34	7	43	1
Lack of Drive	18	32	11	39	2
Diminished Concentration	21	29	17	33	2
Difficulties Thinking Through	12	38	8	42	1
Fatigue	9	41	29	21	6
Disturbed Sleep	24	28	24	26	3
Diminished Appetite	14	36	6	44	2

*See Chapter 2, Section 2.21 for definition of this concept.

peripheral 5-HT related variables with presumably informative value for central 5-HT, such as 5-HT content of and number of imipramine receptors on blood platelets.

In 1970 we reported decreased accumulation of 5-HIAA in CSF after administration of the transport inhibitor probenecid in depressed patients as compared with a control group (van Praag et al., 1970). This phenomenon suggested diminished 5-HT metabolism in the central nervous system (CNS). Several postmortem studies reported an increased number of 5-HT2 receptors in the frontal cortex of depressed individuals, a phenomenon conceivably secondary to decreased availability of central 5-HT (Arango et al., 1990; Stockmeyer & Meltzer, 1991).

Lowered postprobenecid 5-HIAA accumulation in CSF was found not to be correlated with a particular depressive syndrome, though the phenomenon was more likely to occur in major (vital, endogenous) depression, in severe depression, and in psychotic depression than in dysthymic (personal, neurotic), mild and nonpsychotic depression. To explain the ostensibly capricious occurrence of 5-HT disturbances in depression (since they do not relate to any particular depressive syndrome), we entertained the idea that they do relate to particular components of the depressive syndrome that might be pronounced in a given case, but might be minor or absent in others. The evidence favoring this hypothesis is quite strong and it appears that aggression and anxiety are the psychopathological dimensions that most clearly are related to the 5-HT disturbances in depression.

3.2. 5-HT Disturbances in Depression and Mood-lowering

Surprisingly, we did not find evidence for the involvement of 5-HT ergic systems in mood regulation. Lowering of CSF 5-HIAA in depression appeared not to be related to mood-lowering as recorded by clinicians on a 5-point scale (Fig. 8:2). Moreover, after administration of a low oral dose of MCPP, a 5-HT agonist that binds to all 5-HT receptors, no changes in mood were recorded in patients with major depression or panic disorder, nor in normal controls (Fig. 8:3). Finally, we conducted therapeutic studies with L-tryptophan in depression and used a relatively low oral dose that does not interfere with central catecholamine synthesis (van Praag et al., 1987a). This treatment régime can be considered as one that increases production

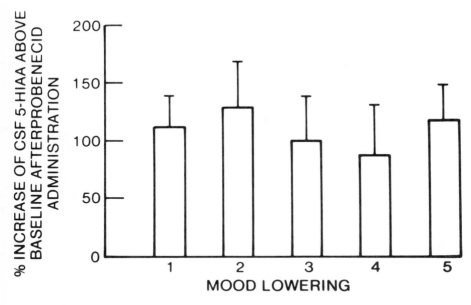

Figure 8:2. Concentration of 5-hydroxyindoleacetic acid (5-HIAA) in cerebrospinal fluid in relation to degree of mood-lowering as assessed by the treating physician on a 5-point scale in untreated patients with vital depression (endogenous depression; major depression, melancholic type).

and release of 5-HT in the brain in a highly selective matter. Yet no change of mood could be registered (Fig. 8:4).

The evidence so far argues against mood-lowering as a major behavioral correlate of the 5-HT disturbances in depression.

3.3. 5-HT Disturbances in Depression and Anxiety

Anxiety is almost ubiquitous in depression. We demonstrated that in depressive patients the CSF 5-HIAA level is strongly and inversely correlated with the degree of anxiety (van Praag, 1988b). If indeed, we reasoned, the 5-HT disturbances in depression relate to anxiety, one would expect a selective postsynaptic 5-HT agonist, like MCPP, to influence anxiety levels. The direction of the change is not a priori predictable. Low CSF 5-HIAA reflects lowered 5-HT metabolism in the CNS, a phenomenon that might be related to a primary 5-HT

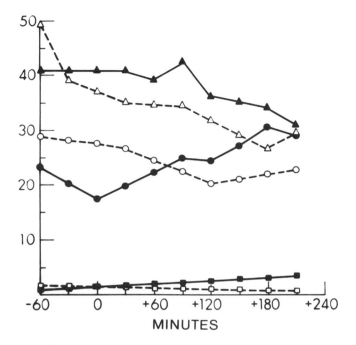

Figure 8:3. Effect of low oral dose on m-chlorphenylpiperazine (MCPP) (0.25 mg/kg) (solid symbols) or placebo (open symbols) on mood in patients with major depression (○) or panic disorder (△) and in normal controls (□) (Kahn et al., 1988b). The mood state was measured with the Profile of Mood Scale (McNair et al., 1990).

ergic *hypo*function or, alternatively, could be compensatory to a primary *hyper*functioning of the 5-HT ergic system.

We studied two 5-HT agonists: first, the postsynaptic 5-HT agonist MCPP. We used a single, low oral dose (0.25 mg/kg) and found it to have anxiogenic properties, but only in patients with increased propensity to generate anxiety, that is in patients with panic disorder (Kahn et al., 1988b). Using the 5-HT releaser fenfluramine as a challenger, Targum (1991) confirmed our findings. Used in higher oral doses and after intravenous administration, MCPP also provokes anxiety in patients with other diagnoses, as well as in normal controls (Charney et al., 1987; Kahn et al., 1990; Kalus et al., 1992).

In panic disorder, MCPP induced not only anxiety but also a greater than normal release of ACTH and cortisol (Kahn et al., 1988a). Both the anxiogenic and the hormonal responses to MCPP

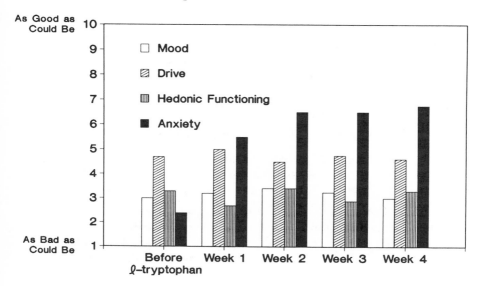

Figure 8:4. Effect of L-tryptophan administered orally for 4 weeks in a dose of 3 g/day to patients with vital depression (endogenous depression; major depression, melancholic type) on different components of the depression syndrome.

could be abolished by 5-HT antagonists and hence are probably mediated via the 5-HT ergic system (Kahn et al., 1990). Based on these data, we hypothesized the existence of hypersensitivity of post-synaptic 5-HT receptors in (some) panic disorder patients (Kahn et al., 1988a,b, 1991). The data do not allow for a specification of the receptor type involved. Signs of 5-HT receptor hypersensitivity have also been observed in another anxiety disorder, obsessive compulsive disorder (Zohar et al., 1987). In generalized anxiety disorders, this issue has not yet been studied.

We also studied the effect of the indirect 5-HT agonist, L-tryptophan in low oral doses in depression. As mentioned before, mood level was not influenced, but anxiety level was. In the course of 1–2 weeks, a gradual decrease of anxiety set in, conceivably due to downregulation of the allegedly hypersensitive 5-HT receptors (Fig 8:4).

In conclusion, a fair amount of evidence points to the anxiety component of the depressive syndrome as the behavioral correlate of the lowered 5-HIAA level in CSF. It remains to be clarified whether in those cases low CSF 5-HIAA reflects hyper- or hypoactivity in the 5-HT ergic systems. Hyperactivity, however, seems to be the most likely of the two propositions, since in panic disorder, a more or less "pure" anxiety disorder, hypersensitivity of 5-HT receptors has been observed.

3.4. 5-HT Disturbances in Depression and Aggression

In 1976, Asberg et al. confirmed our finding of the existence of a subgroup of depressed patients with lowered CSF 5-HIAA and added the important observation that patients with low CSF 5-HIAA show a greater likelihood of having made suicide attempts than those with normal CSF 5-HIAA. Later it was observed that low CSF 5-HIAA also predicted increased subsequent suicide risk (Asberg et al., 1986; Roy et al., 1989). The correlation between low CSF 5-HIAA and suicide attempt was confirmed with remarkable consistency, though not by all investigators. Moreover, it was demonstrated that this correlation extends to other diagnoses (Asberg et al., 1987). In other words, the relation between 5-HT and suicide cuts through diagnostic categories. Low CSF 5-HIAA relates to the strength of the suicidal intent, not to the lethality of the attempt (Plutchik et al., 1989). Lowering of CSF 5-HIAA, moreover, is particularly apparent in recent suicide attempts (van Praag, 1986a).

It has also been reported that low CSF 5-HIAA correlates with outwardly directed aggression. With remarkable consistency, low CSF 5-HIAA has been observed in a variety of personality disorders with high irritability and manifest hostile and assaultive behavior (Coccaro, 1989). On a psychopathological level, the co-occurrence of suicidal and assaultive behavior has been reported repeatedly (Plutchik et al., 1989; Apter et al., 1990).

Thus, the hypothesis seems justified that low CSF 5-HIAA (suggesting decreased 5-HT metabolism) correlates with disturbed aggression regulation, independently of the nosological context in which the aggression occurs and of the direction the aggression takes.

The available data do not allow a judgment as to the question of whether low CSF 5-HIAA in aggression disorders reflects a decrease or an increase in 5-HT ergic functioning. Increased numbers of 5-HT2 receptors have been found in the frontal cortex of suicide victims (Arango et al., 1990; Stockmeyer & Meltzer, 1991) and also on blood platelets in patients suffering from depression (Arora & Meltzer, 1989), in particular in those exhibiting suicidal tendencies (Pandey et al., 1990). The results of hormonal challenge tests with 5-HT agonists, on the other hand, have so far been contradictory. Both indications of increased (Meltzer et al., 1984) and decreased (Coccaro et al., 1989) 5-HT receptor sensitivity have been reported in states with increased (auto)aggression. The challengers used in these studies, however, i.e. 5-hydroxytryptophan and fenfluramine, are not 5-HT selective, but also increase catecholamine availability, making attribution of the results to the functional state of the 5-HT receptor system problematic.

We used the more selective postsynaptic 5-HT agonist MCPP to study 5-HT receptor sensitivity in states of increased (auto)aggression and were unable to demonstrate a correlation between 5-HT receptor sensitivity and levels of (auto)aggression (Wetzler et al., 1991). One has to interpret these data with caution, however, because we studied depressed and panic disorder patients, with levels of outwardly directed aggression remaining within normal limits. Thus, these experiments have to be repeated in individuals with abnormal levels of hostility. In addition, one has to take into account that MCPP, though binding to all 5-HT receptors, has in the human brain a preference, that is nanomolar affinity, for the $5-HT_{1C}$ and $5-HT_3$ receptors (Glennon et al., 1989). It is conceivable that other 5-HT receptor systems are involved in the regulation of aggressive impulses and that these are not sufficiently affected by MCPP.

Finally, the negativity of the MCPP data could be related to heterogeneity of aggressive behaviors. They could differ in patho-physiological substrate and also in psychopathological expression. Psychopathological heterogeneity could manifest itself in such variables as: underlying emotion; intent, goal, effect of the aggressive behavior, and the way it presents itself. By pooling all aggressive behaviors, one might obscure particular biological dys-functions.

In conclusion, then, a variety of data suggest that low levels of CSF 5-HIAA in depression are related to the aggression component of that condition. Aggression dysregulation can be a prominent but also a subordinate symptom in depression and is, of course, by no means specific for depression. The same is true for increased anxiety. This could explain the seemingly capricious occurrence of 5-HT disturbances in depression and the fact that they are not specific for mood disorders but occur in other diagnostic categories as well.

3.5. Biological Evidence: Conclusion

The available evidence thus indicates that the 5-HT disturbances observed in depression are not related to a particular syndrome as such, but rather to certain components of the syndrome, most notably to heightened anxiety and dysregulated aggression. No correlation was found between the 5-HT disturbances and lowering of mood.

Is this an argument supporting the thesis that in certain types of depression disruption of anxiety and aggression regulation are the core symptoms and mood-lowering a derivative feature? Indeed it is, provided one can make plausible that the 5-HT disturbances constitute a fundamental aspect of the pathogenesis of these depressions. I shall advance the evidence suggesting that this, indeed, seems to be the case.

Low CSF 5-HIAA in depression is a trait-related, not a state-related, variable (van Praag, 1977b; Traskman et al., 1981; Asberg et al., 1987). In most patients with low CSF 5-HIAA at index admission, the concentration remains low after remission, though less marked than in the symptomatic phase (Fig 8:5). From a psychopathological vantage point, depression is in essence a recurrent disorder. Many patients, moreover, show considerable sub-depressive rest-pathology in between the depressive episodes. That the biological and psychopathological sets of data are related is suggested by the observation that chronic treatment of recurrent depression with L-5-HTP, an intervention raising 5-HT availability in the brain, reduced the relapse rate significantly (van Praag & de Haan, 1979, 1980), in particular in patients with low CSF 5-HIAA. Lithium, moreover, amongst many other actions, facilitates 5-HT ergic transmission and it is conceivable that this action contributes to its prophylactic effect in recurrent depression (Goodwin & Jamison, 1990).

I entertain the hypothesis that the enduring nature of the 5-HT disturbances represents a biological precondition for the relapse tendency of what could be called the group of "5-HT related depres-

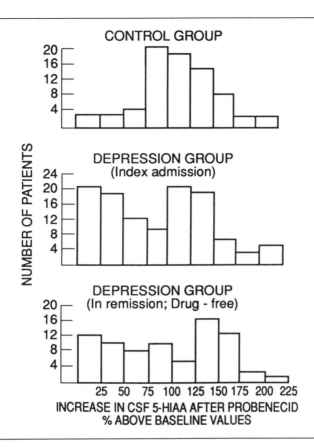

Figure 8:5. Increase of CSF 5-HIAA concentration after probenecid in patients suffering from vital depression (endogenous depression; major depression, melancholic type) and in a non–psychiatric control group. The columns indicate the number of patients showing the increase in concentration given at the bottom of the column. As compared to the control group, there is a significant increase in individuals with low CSF 5-HIAA in the depression group at the time of the index admission. After remission this number is still significantly increased.

sions." As such, these disturbances constitute an integral part of that condition's pathogenesis. Since the 5-HT disturbances found in depression seem to be related to aggression and anxiety, one can infer that regulatory instability of these behavioral systems lay at the root of the appearance and reappearance of the depression.

4. PSYCHOPHARMACOLOGICAL EVIDENCE

If the 5-HT disturbances that might be observed in depression indeed underlie disordered anxiety and aggression regulation and if these psychopathological features constitute the core pathology of "5-HT-related depression," the following two hypotheses seem warranted.

Hypothesis 1. Anxiety disorders and aggression disorders can be effectively treated with 5-HT selective drugs.

Hypothesis 2. 5-HT selective drugs effective in anxiety and aggression disorders will have a therapeutic impact on depression, as well, at least in those cases with pronounced anxiety and aggression pathology.

Selective 5-HT influencing drugs certainly play a role in the treatment of anxiety disorders. The partial 5-HT_{1A} agonist buspirone and related compounds are effective anxiolytics, both in animals (Wieland & Lucki, 1990) and in humans (Cohn et al., 1986; Robinson et al., 1989) and the selective 5-HT uptake inhibitors show therapeutic efficacy in panic disorder and obsessive compulsive disorder (Freeman, 1988; Den Boer et al., 1987; Den Boer & Westenberg, 1988; Perse et al., 1987). In terms of their effect on depression: selective 5-HT uptake inhibitors are established antidepressants. 8-hydroxy-2-(di-n-propylamino)-tetralin (8-OH-DPAT), a potent 5-HT_{1A} agonist, reverses in animals learned helplessness behavior (Gonzalez-Heydrich & Peroutka, 1990). This behavior is regarded as an animal model of depression, and the inference can be drawn that 5-HT_{1A} agonists are potential antidepressants. Preliminary evidence suggests that buspirone indeed combines anxiolytic and antidepressant properties (Robinson et al., 1989; Rodgers & Cooper, 1991). Selective antagonists of 5-HT_2 (Ceulemans et al., 1985) and 5-HT_3 receptors (Costall et al., 1988) hold promise as anxiolytics, but about their antidepressant potential data are lacking.

About the efficacy of 5-HT influencing drugs in aggression disorders, much less is known. Actually, there exists no taxonomic infrastructure to study these behavioral states. Psychiatry does not recognize a class of "aggression disorders" or "impulse control disorders." Even as a psychopathological dimension, increased aggression has been poorly studied. In psychiatric patients, aggression is generally treated as a homogeneous concept and is not further differentiated. This in spite of the fact that aggressive behaviors in animals are clearly heterogeneous in such respects as expression form, function, and underlying pathophysiology. This seriously hampers the study of human aggression and its treatment. Drugs have been developed that selectively diminish particular aggressive behaviors in animals. An example of these so-called serenics is eltoprazine, a selective postsynaptic $5-HT_{1A}$ and $_{1B}$ receptor agonist (Olivier et al., 1990). Its study in humans is hampered by the lack of an established classification system of aggression disorders.

Nevertheless, a few data can be advanced on the effect of 5-HT selective drugs on human aggression. Lithium is an effective antiaggressive drug and at the same time it enhances 5-HT ergic activity (Wickham & Reed, 1987). We do not know, however, whether the biological and psychological actions indeed intercorrelate. Another 5-HT potentiating drug, L-tryptophan, has been shown in two studies to exercise a moderate antiaggressive effect (Morand et al., 1983; Volavka et al., 1990). It is unknown whether this effect is a direct one or a derivative of its sedative potential. The possible antiaggressive qualities of selective 5-HT uptake inhibitors have not yet been studied, but that would certainly make sense (van Praag, 1991b). Teicher et al. (1990) recently reported about depressed patients in whom suicidal preoccupation increased rather than decreased during fluoxetine treatment. It is unlikely, however, that the drug can be blamed for this phenomenon (Brewerton, 1991; Beasley et al., 1991). In the framework of my hypothesis, a selective antiaggressive drug like eltoprazine would be expected to exert an overall antidepressant effect in "5-HT related depression" with pronounced anxiety and aggression.

As to the antidepressant effect of antiaggressive drugs, lithium has a definite, though moderate antidepressant potential (Goodwin & Jamison, 1990). Tryptophan, reportedly, has antidepressant effects in mild, outpatient depressives, though in more severe hospitalized depression we failed to establish an antidepressant response (van Praag & Lemus, 1986).

In conclusion, then, anxiety disorders can indeed be treated via interference with the 5-HT system and 5-HT influencing anxiolytics exert beneficial effects in depression, as well. The data on 5-HT drugs and human aggression are so far few, but they do suggest that global increase of 5-HT ergic activity may lead to attenuation of aggression and that these aggression-reducing compounds might, in addition, exert antidepressant activity. A new class of psychotropic agents is in development, the so-called "serenics," that in animals selectively reduces certain types of aggression and, moreover, increases activity in particular 5-HT ergic systems. Their effect in humans is not yet known. I would predict that, apart from reducing aggression, such serenics would exert a global antidepressant effect in "5-HT related depression."

The preliminary conclusion seems permitted that decrease of anxiety and aggression can be obtained with drugs selectively influencing the 5-HT system and that these drugs seem to exert therapeutic effects in depression, as well.

Phrases like "5-HT influencing drugs and their impact on 5-HT disturbances in certain behavioral states" are unduly unfocused, but we can do no better as yet. The exact nature of the 5-HT disturbances observed in certain psychiatric conditions is unknown and so is the way 5-HT drugs influence the 5-HT ergic system in humans.

5. CONCLUSIONS

1. Depression is a syndrome composed of a multitude of psychopathological dimensions, of which mood-lowering is generally considered to be the major one. It is the validity of this supposition that is being questioned. The thesis is submitted that in certain types of depression (possibly those in which 5-HT ergic functioning is disturbed) dysregulation of anxiety and aggression are the key symptoms, with mood-lowering being a subsidiary. The supporting evidence follows:

Psychopathological evidence. In a significant number of depressed patients, hostility and anxiety are among the first symptoms to appear and the first to disappear with antidepressant treatment, while mood-lowering is a symptom late to appear and slow to go. In depressive syndromes, anxiety is highly intercorrelated with both inward and outward aggression.

Biological evidence. 5-HT disturbances that might occur in depression carry a trait-character and their treatment leads to reduced relapse rate. Hence, these disturbances probably constitute an integral component of the pathogenesis of the disorder. The 5-HT disturbances in depression correlate with heightened anxiety and increased aggression. Inferentially, then, one may conclude that instability of aggression and anxiety regulation are core psychopathological elements in this type of depression.

Psychopharmacological evidence. Several anxiety disorders can be successfully treated with drugs with a selective influence on the 5-HT system. These drugs are likewise therapeutically active in certain types of depression that can, as of yet, not be further specified. The preliminary data available on antiaggressive drugs point in the same direction. Thus, selective attenuation of anxiety and aggression apparently might lead to amelioration of the depressive condition.

2. The exact nature of the 5-HT disorders in depression is unknown and so is the way they are therapeutically influenced by selective 5-HT drugs. To elucidate these processes, PET scanning and SPECT might be helpful as well as challenge tests with 5-HT agonists and antagonists highly selective for particular 5-HT receptor subsystems. Such drugs are now available, but, regrettably, their release for human research presents almost insurmountable difficulties.

3. I submitted the thesis that a certain category of depression cannot be considered as primary mood disorder, but rather as a primary anxiety and/or aggressive disorder, as a theory for further discussion and research. This issue should be capable, I would hope, of exciting not just the inhabitants of intellectual ivory towers. In this respect, an analogy may be helpful. In pneumonia, persistent cough can be a most troublesome feature. Yet, it is a secondary symptom and treating it would not change the course of the pneumonia. If mood-lowering in certain types of depression would indeed be a subordinate symptom, its treatment could be considered as a true "symptomatic treatment." Certainly, I do not want to suggest that mood-lowering is, as it were, the mere "cough" of depression. I do want to make the point that study of the relative "weight" of the various psychopathological components of depression is a basic exercise in furthering our understanding of the nature of that condition and could greatly facilitate the goal-directed search for new, inno-

vative drugs to treat it. The advent of drugs with high selectivity both in terms of working mechanism and psychopathological effect has made this research feasible.

6. SUMMARY

Mood-lowering is generally considered to be the key symptom of depression. This supposition is put to the test and the hypothesis is advanced that in certain types of depression, possibly those in which 5-HT disturbances are prominent, disordered anxiety and aggression regulation are the primordial symptoms, with mood-lowering being a corollary. Further study of this hypothesis is important in furthering our understanding of the nature of depression, a type of information which in its turn could greatly benefit the goal-directed search for innovative, new antidepressant drugs.

Functionalism in psychopathology can open up new insights in classical diagnostic concepts. *Quod erat demonstrandum.*

—9—

"Make-Believes" in Psychiatry

1. INTRODUCTION

The strong emphasis placed on categorical classification of psychiatric disorders over the past two decades ushered in an era of nosological explorers reporting with a certain regularity on new diagnostic discoveries. Some of those are founded in symptoms, for instance the chronic fatigue syndrome; some are based on course, like seasonal affective disorder; others find their origin in etiological considerations, such as the children–of–holocaust–survivor–syndrome, while a construct like panic disorder is based on a composite of criteria. The DSM-I contained 106 psychiatric diagnoses, the DSM-II: 182; in the DSM-III the number of disorders had grown to 265 and in the DSM-III-R a total of 292 diagnostic categories was reached (Frances et al., 1990).

As a harbinger of what we can expect in the DSM-IV: we heard at the annual convention of the American Psychiatric Association in 1991 mixed anxiety depression seriously discussed as a possible new diagnostic category in the DSM-IV. Since anxiety is an integral component of most depressive syndromes, while most anxiety states are mixed with depressive features, that diagnosis would make as much sense as the delineation of a sore throat-congested nose disorder as distinct from a sore throat and congested nose. This is categorical bigotry of a sort that flourished in the pre-Kraepelinean era, when a marked symptom was readily inflated into a disorder often carrying the name of that symptom.

The temptation to discover new diagnostic entities is particularly strong in the realm of personality disorders. The DSM-III has opted for a categorical rather than a dimensional approach. Personality disorders are named after a more or less conspicuous

167

personality trait such as shyness in social relations, narcissism, or the tendency to act out in socially unacceptable ways. Since personality is a delicate composite of countless discrete traits, the categorical approach permits in principle an unlimited expansion of the domain of personality disorders. Someone aiming high in life, for example, could be diagnosed as suffering from an ambitious personality disorder; one unduly concerned and preoccupied with the way he or she is perceived by others, as having a shame personality disorder, and an individual who, to succeed in life, is excessively in need of encouragement from others, as afflicted with an insecurity personality disorder. This is not just a possibility in principle, but a reality. For the DSM-IV, such new categories as depressive, sadistic, and self-defeating personality disorder are being considered.

I will discuss in this chapter a few of these new categorical acquisitions. Some of them were included in the DSM-III, some were not but attracted a fair amount of scholarly attention. This chapter is an anthology, not a review. The examples given are mere paradigms of a willingness in modern psychiatry to accept shadow for substance, to uncritically take constructions of our own making for "disorders," to accept them as entities determined by their intrinsic nature. The natural step then is to study the origins, the treatment, the prognosis of these "disorders." Thus, the emperor is gradually dressed up in nonexistent clothes, as he was in Anderson's fairy tale.

2. CHRONIC FATIGUE SYNDROME

2.1. Signs and Symptoms

Chronic fatigue, severe enough to interfere with one's work and personal life, occurs without doubt. The question to be raised here is whether it is a mere symptom or may also occur as a distinct disorder. Many think it can and have described a novel entity designated as chronic fatigue syndrome (CFS). The Center for Disease Control in Atlanta sanctioned that view by providing the disorder with a "working case definition" (Holmes et al., 1988). The view is strongly endorsed by self-help groups (and there are at least 400 of those in the USA alone, as well as four national organizations (Newsweek,

November 12, 1990)). They consider CFS to be a true disease, probably caused by a virus (Wessely, 1990).

Does CFS present itself as a recognizable syndrome? The core symptom, of course, is pervasive mental and physical fatigue, particularly after physical or mental exercise. With effort, the sufferer may be able to pull himself together, but afterwards he will experience profound fatigue that may last from hours to weeks. I note in this connection that chronic fatigue occurs quite frequently in the general population. A Danish population study showed that in a stratified sample of 1,050 40-year olds, 41 percent of the women and 25 percent of the men felt tired at present (Norrelund & Holnagel, cited by Kennedy, 1988).

Fatigue is a common symptom among patients who seek care from primary care physicians. According to Manu et al. (1988), this complaint is responsible in the USA for 4 percent of office visits to internists and 2.6 percent of visits to general and family practitioners. Well over 10 million office visits annually result from this problem, with three of four such visits devoted to evaluation of chronic fatigue. In the ambulatory practice of internal medicine, fatigue is responsible for more visits than high blood pressure, abdominal pain, back pain, and shortness of breath. In family practice, fatigue is a more common complaint than "cold," headache, pain in the chest, allergic skin reactions, and high blood pressure. The average cost for evaluation of fatigue in family practice, including physician charges, was $100 in 1984, producing a one-billion dollar annual expenditure (Manu et al., 1988).

In the initial reports on CFS, a diversity of neurological signs were reported (Ramsay, 1986), but these findings have not been confirmed (Archer, 1987). No abnormal signs were found in muscles or nerves and dynamic muscle function is normal in the great majority of patients (Stokes et al., 1988; Wessely & Powell, 1989). It should be kept in mind, however, that for physical work it has been demonstrated that fatigue to breaking point occurs long before the nerve–muscle unit is incapable of further performance. This may be seen as establishing the primacy of the CNS in mediating fatigue (Kennedy, 1988).

In the description of the CFS, fatigue and increased fatiguability can be accompanied by a bewildering array of symptoms involving almost all organ systems. Examples are: persistent diarrhea, a variety of cardiovascular symptoms, night sweats, lymph–node swelling, bladder infection, vision problems, concentration and memory disturbances, acne, loss of hair, and many others. They seem to vary from patient to patient and no particular pattern is evident from the literature.

The working definition proposed by the Center for Disease Control (Holmes et al., 1988) applies the "choice-principle": to qualify for the diagnosis of CFS, x out of a much larger list of y symptoms have to be present. The choice-principle, however, is a classificatory misfit. It leads to diagnostic chaos as long as other diagnostic anchor points such as etiology, pathogenesis, course, or treatment response are lacking. Moreover, the list of symptoms in this definition heavily tilts towards an infectious explanation, a theory for which little evidence exists. Manu et al. (1988) reported that of 135 consecutive patients who had attended a fatigue clinic, with at least a six-month history of debilitating fatigue, 95 percent failed to meet the criteria of the Center for Disease Control.

The same can be said of a definition proposed by Hickie et al. (1990). Apart from persistent and disabling fatigue for more than six months, the choice of symptoms and signs is an arbitrary one with an unwarranted emphasis on infectious/immunological criteria, while the application of the "choice-principle" guarantees that a variety of syndromes sail under the same flag.

Just as the symptomatological presentation of the CFS is variable, so is its course. The symptoms may lift or linger for years. A treatment is not available.

In conclusion, then, the symptom pattern of the so-called CFS does not present any consistency. To grant this conglomerate of symptoms the status of a syndrome makes as much or as little sense as to recognize, for instance, a chronic cough syndrome.

2.2. Etiology

2.2.1. *Viruses*

Typical for the discussion of the possible etiology of CFS is, first of all, the insistence that it is an organic disorder and, second, that infectious/immunological factors are involved. This view is held by many authors and is most strongly defended by those afflicted. Illustrative in this respect are the synonyms for CFS, such as myalgic encephalomyelitis, postviral fatigue, pseudomyasthenia, chronic Epstein–Barr virus syndrome, and fibromyalgia. The more neutral name, CFS, is severely criticized by patient organizations. "Instead of affirming the infectious nature of the illness, it reinforces its psychiatric nature . . . the implications feed right into the alternative healing misinformation mill" (Radford, 1988). CFS is supposed to have an external cause, beyond the patient's control. Psychological determinants apparently are seen as a denial of the reality of a disease, as close to malingering.

It is, indeed, an old clinical observation that chronic fatigue and lack of energy may occur in the aftermath of virus infections, in particular, mononucleosis infectiosa, influenza, and hepatitis infectiosa. Such infections are, so we learned in medical school, often followed by what was called a prolonged convalescence. Imboden et al. (1961), however, demonstrated that this phenomenon occurs almost exclusively in "psychologically vulnerable" persons. In many patients with CFS, moreover, evidence of such virus infections is lacking. Several other viruses have been implicated in CFS, most notably the Epstein–Barr virus (EBV). An association was reported between high titers of antibodies to this virus and CSF (Straus et al., 1985; Jones et al., 1985). However, these findings were not substantiated. Gold et al. (1990), for instance, failed to demonstrate significant differences in the prevalence of active EBV infection between a CFS group and a control group. Similarly, no correlation was found between EBV antibody titers and the severity of the symptoms or their clinical course over time. The human herpes virus 6 has likewise been proposed and rejected as a possible cause. Recently, de Freitas (in Palca, 1990) has suggested infections with HTLV-II, a human retrovirus of the same general category that includes the AIDS virus, as a possible cause for CFS. Other virologists, however, looked for retroviruses in CFS patients and failed to find them (Palca, 1990). The antiviral drug acyclovir did not ameliorate CFS (Straus et al., 1988).

This, of course, does not exclude the possibility that infections with those or other viruses could play an etiological role in some CFS patients. Chronic production of cytokines, such as interferon, which is released by lymphocytes in response to viral infections, may account for the morbidity reported by these patients. Cytokines are soluble products of lymphocytes that may precipitate fatigue and neuropsychiatric symptoms in humans (e.g. Hickie et al., 1990; Denicoff et al., 1987; McDonald et al., 1987). Evidence is lacking, however, that viruses are in a major way involved in the causation of CFS.

2.2.2. *Relation to Depression*

Depression and fatigue. Fatigue, interfering with activities of daily living and personal relationships, is a prominent symptom of depression, particularly of vital depression.

The syndromes of vital depression and its counterpart, personal depression, resemble the syndromes described under the headings of endogenous and neurotic depression. I preferred the terms "vital" and "personal" for two major reasons. First, endogenous depression is supposed to occur out of the blue, while neurotic depression is thought to be the nadir of a neurotic development. In reality, these syndromes are etiologically nonspecific, i.e. they may be provoked by biological, environmental, and psychological stressors, or may occur ideopathically, that is without apparent cause. Second, the concept of endogenous depression carries the connotation of being severe, that of neurotic depression of being milder. However, we demonstrated that those syndromes occur in all degrees of severity, from mild to very severe. I preferred the terms "vital" and "personal" because they are neutral, devoid of implications regarding etiology or severity.

Vital and personal depression bear only a vague resemblance to the DSM-III-R concepts of major depression and dysthymia. Each of these DSM-III diagnoses includes a medley of syndromes, while vital and personal depression are carefully defined. Second, the DSM-III concepts are linked to the factor of severity: major depression being severe, dysthymia mild, at least milder than major depression. Vital and personal depression are, as noted, defined independently of the factor severity.

Recognizing that vital and personal depressions are prototypes and that many depressions do not meet the definition, we named the interjacent syndromes mixed depression. For a more detailed exposition of the concepts of vital and personal depression, see Chapter 3.

We found that fatigue is much more pronounced, or at least more emphasized, in mild than in severe vital depression, probably because in the latter group fatigue is overshadowed by such symptoms as anhedonia and motor inhibition (Table 9:1). Though common in vital

TABLE 9:1

Symptoms Reported to be Most Incapacitating and Distressing in a Group of 50 Patients with Severe Vital Depression (Hamilton>18) and 50 Patients with Mild Vital Depression (Hamilton<18)

	Number of Patients Reporting the Symptoms			
	Severe Depression		Mild Depression	
	Symptom Pronounced	Symptom Mild or Absent	Symptom Pronounced	Symptom Mild or Absent
Low Spirits	45	5	11	39
Anxiety	23	27	31	19
Irritability	9	41	33	17
Inability to Enjoy	28	22	31	19
Lack of Drive	16	34	37	13
Diminished Concentration	12	38	35	15
Difficulty Thinking Through	24	26	33	17
Fatigue	9	41	37	13
Disturbed Sleep	29	21	27	23
Diminished Appetite	31	19	21	29

depression, fatigue is by no means rare in personal depression, particularly if accompanied by pronounced personality dysfunctions. In those patients, mood-lowering and personality pathology are strongly intertwined, though it is often hard to decide what came first, the neurotic lifestyle causing sorrow or the recurring depressions causing personality deformations. It is clear, however, that both components mutually reinforce each other strongly.

The description of personality disorders in the DSM-III is deficient in that the psychological consequences of personality malfunctioning are disregarded; yet, it is those that constitute essential ingredients of the "neurotic condition." Anger frequently occurs, stemming from interpersonal and intrapersonal conflicts; sorrow, intermittently or as a chronic experiential undercurrent, is the inevitable consequence of disappointing relationships and incomplete self-realization; anxiety is the escort of feelings of loneliness, alienation, and lack of self-confidence. Fatigue, too, belongs in the list of psychological sequelae of personality disorders. The unceasing preoccupation with seemingly insolvable conflicts is apparently exhausting.

TABLE 9:2
Frequency of Persistent Fatigue in a Variety of Psychiatric Disorders

	N*	Severe Fatigue**	Mild Fatigue***	Fatigue No Prominent Symptom
Vital Depression****	40	19	12	9
Personal Depression****	40	10	14	16
Personality Disorders	40	9	17	14
Anxiety Disorders (Generalized Anxiety Disorder and Panic Disorder)	40	7	21	12
Schizophrenia	40	3	5	32
Normal Controls	40	2	6	32

*Randomly selected from a larger cohort
**Fatigue interfering with daily life
***Fatigue not clearly interfering with daily life
****For definition of this concept see p. 172 and in Chapter 3.

In support of this reasoning, we found fatigue to be common not only in personal depression but also in generalized anxiety disorder and in nondepressed personality disorders, particularly in those characterized as character neurosis★ (Table 9:2). The relation between fatigue and intrapsychic tension is well known to normal individuals as well. When one is confronted with feelings of sustained anxiety or anger that one is unable to neutralize, fatigue up to exhaustion may readily appear. Unfortunately, the possibility of personality pathology as determinant of incapacitating fatigue is entirely ignored in the literature on CFS.

CFS and depression. The psychiatric status of CFS has been and still is subject of ongoing controversy. Its relation to depression is especially contested. Similar discussions took place some 100 years ago when it was fashionable to diagnose neurasthenia, which in fact is a close diagnostic relative of CFS (Wessely, 1990). The views vary from depressive symptoms being absent in CFS (Bell & Bell, 1988) to being a major cause of these patients' fatigue (Manu et al., 1988). Systematic studies leave little doubt that depressive illness frequently coexists with CFS. In several series, 50–70 percent of patients with

---

★The concept of character neurosis is discussed in Chapter 3, Section 2.52.

CFS had psychiatric diagnoses, the majority of which were affective disorder (Manu et al., 1988; Kruesi et al., 1989; Hickie et al., 1990), anxiety ranking second (Hickey et al., 1990). Hypochondriasis or somatization disorder seems to be an appropriate diagnosis in only a minority of CFS patients (Manu et al., 1988; Wessely & Powell, 1989). Figures on lifetime prevalence rate for (major) depression in CFS patients vary from as high as 67 percent (Taerk et al., 1987) to 12.5% (Hickie et al., 1990). The latter figure is lower than the rate found in the general population in the Epidemiological Catchment Area Survey (Robins et al., 1984).

Another controversy is whether depression in CFS is a reaction to the fatigue or rather its major determinant. The study of Hickie et al. (1990) speaks in favor of the former hypothesis. If CFS is a form of depressive disorder, they reasoned, a similar pattern of current symptoms and past psychiatric disorders would be expected to emerge in depression and in CFS. The findings did not support that proposition. The study of Wessely and Powell (1989), on the other hand, provides tentative evidence for the possibility that depression is a major determinant of the fatigue. They compared CFS patients with two control groups: one suffering from major depression, the other from peripheral fatiguing neuromuscular disorders. There was no difference in subjective complaints of physical fatigue between all groups. Mental fatigue and fatiguability was equally common in CFS and depressed patients, but occurred only in those neuromuscular patients who also suffered from psychiatric disorders. Overall, the CFS patients more closely resembled the affective than the neuromuscular patients. Attribution of symptoms to physical rather than to psychological causes was the principal difference between matched CFS and depressed patients.

This debate derives its emotional charge from the view that depression preceding CFS could be the cause of that disorder, while depression following it would reduce the importance of the affective pathology to that of a mere corollary. That view, however, is deceptive. Depression, in particular vital depression, can be precipitated by physical or psychological injuries, but subsequently becomes autonomous, that is independent of the precipitants. The depression persists after the physical stressor has been eliminated or the psychological stressor has been removed or alleviated. The depression, "secondary" in origin, has become "primary" and in need of treatment in its own right. Depression secondary to chronic fatigue is not necessarily an epiphenomenon; untreated it could be expected to intensify the fatigue.

In conclusion, psychiatric disorders, particularly depression, often accompany CFS. The depression might precede the CFS or follow it, but the relative frequency of these two sequences is not known. Be this as it may, there is as yet no evidence that CFS is "merely" a depression variant, a form of "masked depression."

2.2.3. *Other Alleged Etiologies*

Many other etiologies have been suggested to explain CFS, such as overexertion; overstressing of the immune system; pollution with tobacco, gasoline, or other allergens; severe allergy; autointoxication with poisonous compounds produced in the colon and leaking into the bloodstream. Supportive evidence is lacking and, for the time being, these theories can be best referred to fantasy land.

2.3. Conclusion

Having reviewed the available data, I see a clear conclusion: Chronic incapacitating fatigue constitutes a symptom, not a syndrome or a disorder. It is a component of many physical and psychological diseases (Schwartz, 1988), but in some cases the cause of the fatigue remains elusive. Patients suffering from chronic fatigue are ill served by nosological certification of a CFS. This easy but meaningless label could easily replace careful diagnosis and prevent appropriate treatment.

3. SEASONAL AFFECTIVE DISORDERS (WINTER DEPRESSION)

3.1. Origin of the Concept

3.1.1. *The Concept*

Winter depression was conceptualized as a distinct diagnostic entity by Rosenthal et al. (1984) and defined according to symptoms, course and treatment (Rosenthal et al., 1984; Wehr & Rosenthal, 1989):

1. The syndrome was thought to have distinctive features, including overeating with weight gain, carbohydrate craving, and oversleeping. Some authors also emphasized fatigue and general lack of energy (Blehar & Lewy, 1990) and prominent anxiety (Teicher & Glod, 1990).

2. The syndrome is supposedly triggered by light deficiency occurring, as it does, in the fall or winter and disappearing in the spring. In the latter season, the patient would remit or, more frequently, switch into a (hypo)manic episode.

3. This depressive condition would regularly recur on an annual basis and,

4. respond to a novel treatment: phototherapy, that is exposure to bright white light (2500 Lux) for 3–4 hours per day, on a daily basis for at least one week.

Wehr et al. (1987) described a counterpart of winter depression, showing the reverse picture: occurring regularly in spring or summer, disappearing or switch into (hypo)mania in the fall, and presenting the "typical endogenous" symptoms of decreased appetite, weight loss, and insomnia. It was named summer depression. It has so far received much less attention than winter depression. Though the term seasonal affective disorder (SAD) in principle pertains to all depressions with seasonal periodicity, it is generally used interchangeably with winter depression.

The concept of winter depression caught on immediately and is presently identified as one of the fastest growing areas of biomedical research (Garfield, 1988). In recognition of that development, Wehr and Rosenthal (1989) note, the DSM-III-R has included the category of seasonal subtypes of affective disorder. Since winter depression did not quite get the DSM-III hallmark as a disorder, I have not included it in Section 5, below.

3.1.2. *Foundations of the Concept*

The original data (Rosenthal et al., 1984) were not as neat as the concise definition of the disorder would suggest. Winter, the time of onset, extended from September to January; spring, the time of resolution, extended from January to May. Some patients experienced (anticipatory?) anxiety as early as July or August. Although depressions occurred predominantly in the winter, brief depressive episodes "associated with either poor weather or stressful life events" had also occurred at other times of the year. On follow-up of the 29 patients participating in the initial study, it was found that 11 of them failed to become depressed in the next fall or winter. Though 27 patients were reported to meet RDC diagnostic criteria for bipolar I or II affective disorder, no data are provided on whether or not the (hypo)manic episodes occurred predictably in the spring subsequent to the depressive episode.

In terms of symptomatology, a substantial minority did not report increased appetite (10) or weight increase (7); though sleeping was reported to be increased by 28 patients, 26 noted that sleep was interrupted and not refreshing. Only 11 of the original 29 patients underwent phototherapy and all of them experienced antidepressant effects. The magnitude of the response rate suggests that a placebo effect is not to be excluded.

A more important consideration and one that seriously relativizes the significance of the initial data is the way they were collected. The patients included in this study were self-referred following a newspaper article in the Washington Post of June 12, 1981 written by the investigators and describing in some detail the syndrome they were looking for and the proposed treatment. This method is flawed. First, a coherent syndrome could have been induced by suggestion. Second, there might have been a strong incentive to report the symptoms as indicated in the newspaper article, since the NIMH offers treatment free of charge. Moreover, light therapy was introduced as a probable "major breakthrough in the treatment of a devastating disorder that often strikes the most attractive and creative people." This recommendation might have served as a powerful placebo.

At the end of their landmark paper, Rosenthal et al. (1984) proposed a new diagnostic entity: seasonal affective disorder. The initial data, it seems to me, did not justify that proposition.

3.1.3. *Conceptualization in the DSM-III-R*

The DSM-III-R included seasonal affective disorder as a subtype of affective disorder. The DSM definition is, on the one hand, a thinned version of the Rosenthal concept; on the other hand, it seems to be overly restrictive. Atypical vegetative symptoms are not being required. The season of onset is not specified; as a result, other forms of seasonal affective disorder, such as summer depression, will be

grouped together with winter depression. The definition is restrictive in that onset and remission of the depression should occur in a
particular 60-day period of the year and in that there be at least a 3–1
ratio between seasonal and any nonseasonal depressive episodes that
might occur. These criteria are wholly arbitrary. No one has demonstrated that winter depression regularly occurs in a narrow, 60-day
window, nor shown what the ratio to nonseasonal episodes amounts
to in typical cases of winter depression.

The DSM guidelines are not helpful for research directed towards
elucidation of the concept of winter depression.

3.1.4. *Points for Discussion*

The issue I want to raise is not that of seasonality of mood disorders. That concept rests on time-honored observations, from
antiquity on (Wehr & Rosenthal, 1989; Wehr, 1989). In medical
school I learned that depression, particularly vital (endogenous)
depression, might preferentially occur in spring and autumn. Many
textbooks at the time mentioned that phenomenon (e.g. Kraines,
1957) and several studies had confirmed it (e.g. Slater, 1938;
Leuthold, 1940; Eastwood & Peacocke, 1976). Peaks for suicide were
also reported to occur in late spring and autumn (Swinscow, 1951;
Meares et al., 1981; Eastwood & Stiasny, 1978; Parker & Walter,
1982), though these data have not been uniformly confirmed (e.g.
Zung & Green, 1974). Wehr and Rosenthal (1989) reviewed eight
studies that had examined month of onset of depressive episodes.
The study comprised altogether 4,667 episodes in approximately
2400 patients; in each study, a spring peak and an autumn peak were
demonstrated.

Seasonality of depressive episodes is *not* the point for discussion
here; the legitimacy of winter depression as a distinct diagnostic
entity *is*. Is it an entity in its own right of which features such as
etiology, epidemiology, and treatment can be rightfully studied, or
do we deal with a pseudo-entity and are we, in researching it, chas-
ing shadows? Let me specify the issues.

Is the *symptomatology* of depressions with autumn onset ("winter
depression") typically "atypical" or rather variable? Phrased differently, is autumn onset characteristic for atypical depression or do various depression types show autumn preference?

Is the *course* of depressions with autumn onset predictable, in that they recur yearly or at least regularly at the same time of year and do they remit spontaneously or switch into (hypo)mania in springtime?

Is *light treatment* in depression with autumn onset effective and, if so, is this effect specific, in that non-seasonal depression does not respond well and phototherapy exceeds the response rate of antidepressants?

Since this is not a review of SAD, but another exposition to demonstrate the inflationary trend in present-day psychiatric taxonomy, I will restrict myself here to the concept of winter depression.

3.2. Symptomatology

3.2.1. *Data from the Literature*

Winter depression is claimed to be characterized by "atypical" symptoms, a view that seems to be open to easy verification. If this is correct, one would expect that patients with recurrent winter depression would show predominantly atypical symptoms, in contrast to nonseasonal depressions. If the reverse would also be true, that is, if in a mixed group of typical and atypical depressives the latter would report predominantly winter onset, the thesis would be strengthened, though it could survive the absence of such evidence.

Surprisingly, one searches the literature largely in vain for such evidence. The study of Rosenthal et al. (1984) used media recruitment for the study of winter depression. Confirmatory evidence collected in Great Britain (Thompson & Isaacs, 1988), Japan (Takahashi et al., 1991) and Switzerland (Wirz-Justice et al., 1986) used the same method, one that is, as we have noted, unfit to verify the thesis. Most studies of general outpatient populations found that winter onset does by no means predict "atypicality." Thase (1986) reported that in the depressed outpatients he studied, the majority of those with winter onset did not show atypical features. Moreover, atypical vegetative symptoms were also observed in nonseasonal depression. In a study by Garvey et al. (1988), the only significant difference in symptom profile between patients with seasonal and nonseasonal depression was carbohydrate craving occurring more frequently in the former group. Bick (1986) described four cases of severe seasonal affective disorder; only two of them reported hypersomnia and a

TABLE 9:3
Depression-Type and Time of Onset

	N	Time of Onset					
		Autumn/Winter Number Percent		Spring/Summer Number Percent		Non-Seasonal Number Percent	
Vital Depression*	128	24	19	13	10	91	71
Personal Depression*	89	7	8	5	6	77	86
Mixed Depression*	76	5	7	8	10	63	83

*For description of these syndromes, see Chapter 3.

slight increase of appetite, though not specifically craving for carbohydrates. The other two reported anorexia and terminal insomnia during depressive episodes.

3.2.2. *Our Data*

Our own data do not indicate a linkage between atypicality and winter onset of depression. They were collected between 1958–1966, long before the concept of winter depression was introduced and are thus unbiased either way. We had at our disposal relevant data of 128 patients with vital depression, 89 patients with personal depression, and 76 diagnosed as mixed depression (Tables 9:3 and 9:4).* Of that cohort, 54 percent was hospitalized and the remaining 46 percent was treated in an outpatient setting.

Vital depression. In the group of vital depression, 24 patients (19 percent) had suffered at least three depressive episodes with autumn/winter onset in three separate years. At the index episode, eight reported hypersomnia and/or overeating (33 percent) and six of them indicated that previous episodes had also been characterized by atypical symptoms. Five of the eight patients with atypical symptoms reported both symptoms, the other three one symptom. Apparently, atypical vegetative symptoms do not always occur in tandem. Sixteen of the 24 patients (66 percent) with winter depression reported

*Best-fitting diagnoses in present-day terminology: major depression, melancholic type, dysthymic depression, and double depression. See also Chapter 3.

TABLE 9:4
Time of Onset of Depression and Vegetative Symptoms

| | | Vegetative Symptoms | | | |
| | | Typical | | Atypical | |
	N	Number	Percent	Number	Percent
Vital Depression	128				
Winter Onset	24	16	66	8	33
Summer Onset	13	9	70	4	30
Non-Seasonal	91	71	78	20	22

decreased sleep and food intake. In all patients, these symptoms occurred together.

Thirteen of the 128 patients with vital depression (10 percent) reported regular depressive episodes in the spring (March–June) and had had at least three spring episodes in separate years. Four of them (30 percent) manifested atypical symptoms, the remaining atypical vegetative features.

In 91 of the 128 patients with vital depression (71 percent), no seasonal periodicity was found. Atypical symptoms were present in 20 of them (22 percent), in the others sleep and food intake were decreased. The presence of atypical symptoms thus appeared to be independent of the factor of seasonality. Severity was not related to seasonality, either. The average severity of the depression was the same in the seasonal and nonseasonal groups.

Personal and mixed depression. In the group diagnosed as personal depression, regular depressive episodes in the autumn or spring (at least three in separate years) were rare, but not absent and did occur in seven (8 percent) and five (6 percent) patients respectively. The percentages were similar in the group of mixed depressions (7 percent and 10 percent). In some cases, psychological factors could have triggered an episode such as the dislike of resuming work after vacation or reluctance to go on vacation due to marital discord. Hypersomnia as well as insomnia occurred in this group conjointly with overeating, as well as with decreased food intake. Particular symptom combinations were unrelated to time of onset of the depression. We did not inquire specifically for carbohydrate craving in any of the groups.

3.2.3. *Conclusion*

The occurrence of atypical vegetative symptoms, particularly overeating and hypersomnia, in patients with vital depression seems somewhat more frequent in winter depression than in nonseasonal depression, but is by no means typical for winter depression. Atypical symptoms do occur frequently in nonseasonal depression and typical vegetative symptoms (insomnia and anorexia) are by no means rare in winter depression. In personal and mixed depressions, seasonal onset was rare but not absent. In these groups, too, seasonality was not correlated with a particular symptom cluster.

3.3. Course

The definition of winter depression includes the notion that it ends spontaneously the next spring/summer or, more frequently, switches then into a (hypo)manic state. Rosenthal et al. (1984) diagnosed 27 of 29 patients with winter depression as bipolars; Wirz-Justice et al. (1986) too, reported a percentage close to 100% (21/22) and in the group studied by Thompson and Isaacs (1988) the percentage of bipolars amounted to 71 percent. All three studies recruited patients via the media and made the diagnosis of bipolar depression retrospectively. Following up their patients into the next spring/summer Rosenthal et al. (1984), however, found that none of them showed signs of (hypo)mania. Several other studies failed to find a high percentage of bipolars among patients with winter depression (Yerevanian et al., 1986; White et al., 1990; Takahashi et al., 1991). Our data indicate the same. Of the 24 patients with vital depression and winter occurrence and 13 with the same diagnosis and summer occurrence, only four (7 percent) and one (8 percent) respectively were diagnosed as bipolars.

Wehr and Rosenthal (1989) emphasize that winter depression tends to recur regularly on an annual basis. That is not our experience. Only three of the 24 patients with vital/winter depression reported at least three episodes in three consecutive years. Moreover, 12 of them also had experienced depressive episodes with nonseasonal onset.

More important, one searches the literature in vain for systematic prospective data substantiating that indeed winter depression lifts spontaneously the following spring. Our data do not suggest this maxim to be true. All 24 patients with vital/winter depression were treated with antidepressants, either a tricyclic or a monoamine oxidase inhibitor. The following spring, 11 had fully remitted, that is had returned to the premorbid level. The remaining 12 had only partially improved and were still on antidepressants. Unless one assumes that antidepressants had worsened their condition, this finding is hard to reconcile with the notion of spontaneous improvement in spring time. No more than two patients developed manic symptoms while on antidepressants.

These data indicate that seasonal onset of depression does not necessarily imply seasonal remission, that winter onset often occurs irregularly rather than annually, and that winter onset does by no means exclude nonseasonal episodes.

3.4. Treatment

3.4.1. *Efficacy of Phototherapy in Winter Depression*

A virtual consensus seems to exist that exposure to bright light has therapeutic value in winter depression, in particular if administered in the morning (Rosenthal et al., 1988; Blehar & Rosenthal, 1989; Blehar & Lewy, 1990). In the given context, three questions are relevant. First, has the therapeutic efficacy of phototherapy been convincingly demonstrated? Second, is light therapy specific for winter depression? If so, it would support the notion of winter depression as a distinct diagnostic entity. If, on the contrary, light therapy would be effective in nonseasonal depression as well, this treatment modality could be discarded as a validator of a diagnostic category of winter depression. Third, is the effect of antidepressants in winter depression different from that in nonseasonal depression? If that were so, it would strengthen the case for diagnostic autonomy of winter depression. Since the therapeutic specificity of antidepressants is relatively low, equivalence of the two therapeutic modalities would, however, not be incompatible with that hypothesis.

In a review of 14 studies on phototherapy in winter depression, Terman et al. (1989) calculated the improvement rates for morning light, morning plus evening light, evening light, and midday light to be 53, 51, 38 and 32 percent respectively. Studies using brief exposure to bright light (one hour or less) and dim light were used as controls and produced 31 and 11 percent improvement, respectively. Among patients with mild winter depression (Hamilton Depression Score 10–16), 67 percent remitted; in patients with more severe depressions (Hamilton Scale >16), this percentage was 40. These figures are similar to those in patients with mild or more severe major depression treated for 3–6 weeks with placebo (Brown, 1988, 1990).

The evidence for therapeutic efficacy of phototherapy in winter depression is thus not convincing. The strongest argument so far is that morning bright light is more effective than bright light applied in the evening (53 and 38 percent remission rate, respectively) (Brown, 1990). The evidence supporting therapeutic efficacy of light therapy in winter depression is further weakened by the absence of adequately controlled studies, simply because no proper placebo is available. An adequate placebo would be an inert light indistinguishable in appearance from the active treatment. Until the time we know the therapeutic ingredients of bright light, no such placebo will be available (Brown, 1990). The controls used so far, such as light of different intensity or color, and light administered for a shorter duration or at a different period of the day, are insufficient. The patient cannot be prevented from knowing the way he is treated and we do not know whether the "placebo" is indeed inert. Since media publicity has hammered the therapeutic power of light therapy in winter depression so firmly into the public mind, we need a true placebo before light can be authenticated as a genuine treatment modality.

All in all, it has not been excluded that the therapeutic effect of light therapy in winter depression is due to the expectation of patient and doctor regarding its efficacy.

3.4.2. *Efficacy of Phototherapy in Nonseasonal Depression*

The effect of bright light in the various types of nonseasonal depression has received scant attention. Kripke et al. (1989) carried out a number of controlled studies in which dim red light was used as a control treatment. Bright light treatment led to significant improvement in major depression, this in contrast to dim red light, though this response was, according to Blehar and Lewy (1990), less than in winter depression. The exposure was short (1–2 hours) and

applied at various periods of the day, while in winter depression optimal results have been obtained with 4–5 hour exposure in the morning. To enable the study of the specificity of phototherapy, the treatment regime in nonseasonal depression should be similar to that in
winter depression. Volz et al. (1990) found light therapy effective in
patients with nonseasonal major depression, but bright light (2500
lux) was as effective as dim light (50 lux), strongly suggesting the
possibility of a placebo effect. Mackert et al. (1991) reported similar
results, but the decrease in depressive symptoms was not significant.

Several uncontrolled studies also reported positive results in nonseasonal depression (Lewy et al., 1983; Dietzel et al., 1986; Heim,
1988; Peter et al., 1986). Two other uncontrolled studies reached
opposite conclusions. Yerevanian et al. (1986) found nonseasonal
depressives not responsive to bright light treatment, while winter
depression was. The former group, however, was more severely
depressed than the latter. Stinson and Thompson (1990) reported that
13 out of 30 patients with winter depression experienced a remission
during phototherapy and in seven of those the outcome was "fully
satisfactory." Three patients with nonseasonal depression did not
respond. Severity of the depression in the two groups is not
mentioned.

The effect of light therapy in diagnostic categories other than
depression has hardly been studied. Recently, Kanofsky et al. (1991)
reported a patient with seasonal panic disorder who responded well
to light therapy.

Though the available data do not permit much of a conclusion,
they do not seem to suggest that phototherapy is a specific treatment
for winter depression.

3.4.3. *Antidepressants in Winter Depression*

Studies specifically looking at the effect of antidepressants in winter depression are very few. Thase (1986, 1989) reported that a combination of pharmacotherapy and interpersonal psychotherapy was
as effective in seasonal as in nonseasonal depression. Wehr and
Rosenthal (1989) noted that their clinical experience "led them to
believe that patients with seasonal affective disorders can be treated
successfully with conventional antidepressant drugs and that drugs
and phototherapy appear to be synergistic in their effects."

Our own data, as stated, collected long before the conceptualiza-

TABLE 9:5

Efficacy of Antidepressants in Seasonal and Nonseasonal Depression

| | | Response Rate (In Percent) | | | |
| | | Full Remission | | Partial Remission | |
	Number	Tricyclic	MAOI	Tricyclic	MAOI
Winter Depression	24	33	29	30	35
Summer Depression	13	29	26	28	24
Non-Seasonal Depression	91	38	35	30	28

tion of winter depression as a distinct entity, point in the same direction. Twenty-four depressed patients with regular winter onset and 13 with summer onset (out of a group of 128 patients with vital depression; see section 3.2.2.) were treated with either an MAO inhibitor (iproniazid or isocarboxazide) or a tricyclic antidepressant (imipramine). The response rate was the same in seasonal and nonseasonal depression (Table 9:5). The response rate in the patients with atypical vegetative symptoms (overeating and oversleeping) was lower than in those with typical symptoms (decreased food intake and insomnia), though this difference did not reach statistical significance.

Based on the hypothesis that winter depression is related to disturbances in serotonergic functioning, this condition has been treated with serotonin agonists.

Tryptophan and evening light were found to be equally effective in winter depression and both better than placebo (McGrath et al., 1990). The effect of L-tryptophan is, however, controversial, but most studies found it to be no better than a placebo (van Praag & Lemus, 1986). In a placebo-controlled study, the serotonin releaser fenfluramine was shown to exert therapeutic effects in winter depression (O'Rourke et al., 1989). The effect of fenfluramine in nonseasonal depression has not been studied systematically. Comparative studies of phototherapy and antidepressants are not available.

Again, though the data base is exceedingly small, the available information does not suggest that seasonal and nonseasonal depression respond in different ways to antidepressants.

3.4.4. *Conclusion*

The efficacy of bright light has not been demonstrated beyond reasonable doubt; the question of the specificity of light treatment in winter depression has not been satisfactorily answered and whether seasonal and nonseasonal depression respond differently to antidepressants is still an open question. Obviously, the factor of treatment does not yet provide much support for the concept of winter depression as a distinct diagnostic entity.

3.5. Epilogue

The available data do not support the concept of winter depression being a distinct and discrete diagnostic entity. Its symptomatology is variable and so is its course, while the efficacy and specificity of phototherapy for this disorder have still to be demonstrated.

The data available so far suggest that seasonability is not a characteristic of any particular depression type, but constitutes a feature that may occur in a variety of depression types. It seems indicated, therefore, to study seasonality as a dimension of depression rather than as a marker of a (probably imaginary) diagnostic entity in its own right. In this way, we may hope to gain some insight into the fascinating question of how seasonal variables might act as triggers or as vulnerability factors for depression.

4. CHILDREN-OF-HOLOCAUST-SURVIVOR-SYNDROME

4.1. Validity Concerns

Reports published over the past few decades have suggested a profound pathogenic influence on the children of Holocaust survivors due to the concentration camp experiences of their parents. Before a "children-of-Holocaust-survivor-syndrome" can be considered as a valid diagnostic concept, the following questions should have been answered in the affirmative.

First, does a more or less well-defined Holocaust-survivor-syndrome exist? Without evidence for that, it is hard to conceive of specific psychological effects of survivors on their children (Epstein, 1979) and even grandchildren as has been proposed by Sigal et al. (1988).

Second, can psychopathology encountered in Holocaust survivors generally be traced back to psychological or physical trauma endured in the concentration camps rather than to preexisting personality dysfunctions or to postwar experiences such as having immigrated to a new country? If enduring psychopathological effects of the Holocaust have not been demonstrated beyond reasonable doubt, it would make little sense to postulate their transgenerational effect.

Third, is the occurrence of psychopathology in children of Holocaust survivors indeed increased? If not, a general transgenerational pathogenic effect of the Holocaust seems improbable, though this would, of course, not exclude the possibility that in individual cases traumatization of children due to Holocaust scars of their parents might have occurred.

Finally, have individuals from the second generation who fail to cope with life been raised by survivors afflicted with Holocaust related psychopathology? Transgenerational damage presupposes injuries of the parental generation.

The data base on the psychiatric consequences of the Holocaust consists predominantly of case histories viewed from a psychoanalytic perspective. Controlled studies are scarce and often concern clinic populations, making it hazardous to extrapolate conclusions to the general population of Holocaust survivors. To assess possible enduring pathogenic effects of the Holocaust experiences, one has to study randomly selected samples from the survivor population and to compare them with comparable control groups who were spared that ordeal. In trying to reach a conclusion, I will restrict myself to that type of study.

4.2. The Holocaust-Survivor-Syndrome

A psychiatric syndrome that they considered to occur frequently in Holocaust survivors was described by Krystal (1968) and Niederland (1968). It includes a great variety of symptoms, such as: fatigue and lack of energy; restlessness; chronic anxiety and depression; mistrust of others; social withdrawal and diminished responsiveness to the external world (psychic numbness); sleep disturbances with recurrent nightmares reviving the traumatic camp experiences; inability to verbalize the traumatic events; repressed mourning and survival guilt.

Is the "survivor syndrome" a valid diagnostic entity? Chronic depression and anxiety do occur frequently in the general population. The Epidemiologic Catchment Area Study reported a lifetime prevalence rate of 9.5 percent for affective disorders and of 10.9 percent for anxiety disorders (Robins et al., 1984). The question is not whether anxiety and depressive symptoms occur in Holocaust survivors, but whether those symptoms are overrepresented in that group. This has not been demonstrated.

In certain respects, the survivor syndrome resembles post-traumatic stress disorder: psychic numbness, sleep disturbances with vivid nightmares reliving the trauma, guilt feelings about surviving when others were killed (survival guilt), mood-lowering, and anxiety, are seen in both. A major difference, however, is that in post-traumatic stress disorder, symptoms usually begin immediately or shortly after the traumatic experiences, while in Holocaust survivors the symptoms are often described to occur years after the period of incarceration, rendering the postulate of a causal relationship more difficult to establish.

Matussek (1975) evaluated a group of 245 survivors approximately 15 years after confinement. All of them had submitted claims for indemnification from the German government on grounds that they had incurred physical or psychological harm due to the concentration camp experiences. He concluded that no specific concentration camp syndrome exists and that effects of exposure to degrading and frightening circumstances could be manifested in a number of different ways. He also pointed to a positive relation between healthy family life before the incarceration and successful coping with adverse war experiences after liberation.

One might conclude, therefore, that the available evidence does not support the notion that concentration camp experiences can give rise to a particular syndrome that can rightfully claim a name of its own.

4.3. The Holocaust Experiences as a Pathogenic Factor

Have concentration camp experiences been identified as an enduring pathogenic factor in their own right? Case studies do not suffice to prove this point. They might suggest that in a given case the Holocaust experience has been a major etiological factor in an irreversible disruption of the personality structure. They are, however, not generalizable. Comparison of mentally ill Holocaust survivors with mentally ill patients who did not go through this experience provides information on the specificity of the survivor syndrome and of the pathogenic weight of the Holocaust experience relative to other traumatic influences.

To assess whether the Holocaust experiences can be considered as a general pathogenic factor, one has to conduct community studies in which random samples from the survivor population are compared with matched samples from the general population. The survivor group should tend towards homogeneity in terms of such factors as age when incarcerated and duration of the incarceration, as well as in terms of type of concentration camp in which one was incarcerated. Not every concentration camp was an extermination camp; the experience of Jews was entirely different from that of gentile inmates, even in the same concentration camp; hiding was not comparable with incarceration. Not a few studies ignored these dimensions, making the conclusions utterly unreliable. In such community study, furthermore, allowance has to be made for such factors as social and psychological background of the members of both groups and of their postwar experiences.

In the given context, I will confine my discussion to controlled community studies. They are few in number and often wanting in methodological sophistication. Consequently, the conclusions they permit are tentative. Leon et al. (1981) compared 52 survivors of the Holocaust with a control group of 29 persons of similar European background who had immigrated to the USA between 1937 and 1939. The survivors had been in concentration camps, ghettos, or hiding. The psychological adjustment of both groups appeared to be within the normal range. Survival guilt was not demonstrated and cultural rather than specific survivor influences were noted in the present attitudes and behaviors of the survivors. A degree of selection could not be ruled out since only 52.7 percent of the survivors contacted agreed to participate and of those 74.3 percent completed and returned the questionnaires.

Other community studies did find differences in mental health status between Holocaust survivors and controls. Eaton et al. (1982) compared 135 survivors now living in Canada with 133 Jewish controls that had immigrated to that country before the war. In the mental health survey, the Langner Index was used, containing questions relating mostly to mood, anxiety, and somatic functioning. The survivor group reported mild psychiatric symptoms more frequently than the controls, though the differences were small. In the survivor group, 50 percent reported four or more symptoms, while in the control group 33 percent (including somatic symptoms) did so. The survivor group was heterogeneous with respect to war experiences, comprising individuals who had been concentration camp or labor camp inmates, had been in hiding, or had joined the resistance.

In another community health survey (Levav & Abramson, 1984), conducted in Jerusalem, 300 former concentration camp inmates were identified and compared with European Jews without camp experiences. A set of eight questions derived from the Cornell Medical Index and mainly pertaining to mood status and anxiety was used as an index for emotional distress. Concentration camp survivors had higher mean scores and rates for emotional distress than the control group. Yet the differences were again not very impressive and 45 percent of the men and 30 percent of the women survivors had none of the symptoms investigated. Finally, Antonovsky et al. (1971) studied Israeli women of central European origin, aged 45–54, of whom 77 had survived Jewish concentration camps and 200 had immigrated to Israel before the war. They were interviewed for 1.5 hours and a resulting list of 168 items was scored. The survivor group as a whole was less adapted to the climacteric period than the controls, though 40 percent of them were considered to be well adjusted. Differences were particularly found in overall menopausal symptoms, in emotional symptoms, and in the Worries Scale. On the other hand, no differences existed in role satisfaction in family and nonfamily roles and in the "family pleasure-worry balance." An uncontrolled factor was widowhood: 30 percent of the survivors group had been widowed versus only 9 percent in the control group.

None of these studies provided data on prewar psychological functioning of the cohorts studied or on postwar events. Length of imprisonment and age of exposure are also not accounted for.

Though the data base is small and not flawless, it seems probable that Holocaust survivors as a group suffer slightly more from mild psychological symptoms than controls, but no evidence exists that those have a general negative impact on their coping abilities and lifestyle (Sigal & Weinfeld, 1989). In individual cases, the Holocaust experience may have exercised a mentally debilitating influence, but the available data do not permit generalization of this observation. After the war, survivors as a group seemed to have maintained themselves remarkably well. They proved able to cope with the consequences of prolonged victimization and recovered as befit true survivors.

4.4. Transgenerational Holocaust Effects

4.4.1. *Psychopathology*

In the sixties and seventies, many case reports were published claiming "secondary traumatization" (Rosenheck & Nathan, 1985) of children of Holocaust survivors. Most of these studies were grounded in clinical impressions, and relied heavily on psychoanalytic interpretations. The preconceived notion was that psychological damage *must* have been inflicted by Holocaust survivors upon those children and evidence was searched to confirm that viewpoint (Solkoff, 1981).

As the most important problem areas of survivor children, impulse control was emphasized, particularly in the area of aggression and dependency, leading to difficulty with individuation and separation and to an inclination to seek nurturance, help, and emotional comfort from others. Survivor children would evidence symptoms of depression, psychosomatic symptoms, sexual dysfunctions, combativeness, and distrust. High parental expectations would lead to feelings of guilt and shame in their children and to frequent academic failure.

The reason most commonly proposed for psychopathology in the second generation is an excessive degree of mutual affective involvement, an enmeshment, or an excessive affective distance or disengagement of parents and children (Sigal & Weinfeld, 1987). The first condition would lead to overprotection and unrealistic demands being placed on the children to provide the parents with a justification for their camp-suffering and ultimate survival. In the second condition, possibly the more serious one, the relationship between parents and child is defined as detached, numb, and with an incapacity of the parents to relate warmly to their offspring. Those parents, often mistrusting the outside world, would transfer that attitude to their children, rendering them vulnerable for criticism, impatient, and inimical. The parents are described as confronting their children and not tolerating need for care. The children, in turn, were found to be bound to their parents by guilt or by unexpressed anger (Sigal & Weinfeld, 1987). In short, a direct connection was postulated between psychological Holocaust scares of the parents and maladaptive behavior in their offspring.

The data supporting this notion are far from convincing. On the contrary, the available evidence suggests that the psychological adjustment of children of Holocaust survivors, taken as a group, falls within the normal range. Leon et al. (1981), in the study mentioned in section 3.4.3, compared not only survivors with a comparable control group, but also their children. Questionnaires were used to measure the children's perception of parental attitudes as well as their mental health status. The authors did not find the children's personality indelibly injured by their parents' experiences. On the contrary, in terms of psychological adjustment, the group of survivor children was not different from that of a control group. Other investigators came to similar conclusions. Rustin (cited by Solkoff, 1981), for example, compared 77 late adolescent children of Holocaust survivors with an equal number of matched controls, that is with Jewish adolescents from second- or third-generation immigrants. No evidence was found that effects of traumatic experiences of the parents had generated psychopathology in their offspring.

The possible transgenerational effects of immigration were explored in another general population study in which 25 children of Holocaust survivors who had immigrated to the USA were compared with 25 children of other immigrants and 25 children of American-born parents, matched on age and educational level (Weiss et al., 1986). The latter two groups consisted predominantly of non-Jews. The general mental health of the survivor children was found to be not different from that of children of other immigrants. Also, in terms of such factors as anomie, guilt, and alienation, both groups were comparable. The data were suggestive of an immigration effect common to the children of all immigrants, irrespective of their war experiences.

Several other studies of nonclinical subjects reported no significant differences in terms of the rate of psychopathological symptoms between children of Holocaust survivors and matched controls (Gay & Schulman, 1978; Zlotogorski, 1985; Last & Klein, 1984; Rose & Garske, 1987). Sigal and Weinfeld (1989) did not find evidence that children of Holocaust survivors have greater difficulty in communicating with their parents or separating from them than did comparison groups. Nor did they have greater difficulty with the control of aggression or show more signs of anxiety, depression, phobias, low self-esteem, or psychosomatic complaints. Some reported positive effects from being raised by Holocaust survivors, primarily in the area of Jewish identification, but also in the field of general mental health.

4.4.2. Personality

In terms of personality characteristics of children of Holocaust survivors, the data are few and equivocal. Comparing 76 Israeli adolescents, all offspring of at least one parent who was a Holocaust survivor, with 76 matched controls, Last (1988) reported that the former group showed "deficiencies in assertiveness and active coping abilities and a marked urge to resist a sense of basic inferiority." These personality characteristics were more pronounced the more severe the Holocaust traumatization of the parent had been. The mental health status of both groups as measured by the MMPI was similar. Since reliable measurement of personality traits in adolescents is no easy problem, not to speak of assessment of the degree of Holocaust traumatization, this study needs replication before the results can be accepted. In support of certain personality characteristics of second-generation Holocaust survivors, Solomon et al. (1988) found that after the 1982 Lebanon War, children of Holocaust survivors had higher rates of post-traumatic stress disorder (PTSD) than control subjects. All subjects were deemed physically and psychologically healthy before the War. Nadler et al. (1985) found that Israeli children of survivors were more likely to internalize aggressive feelings than control subjects.

In a study comparing matched groups of children of Holocaust survivors, children of Eastern European immigrants, Jewish controls, and non-Jewish controls, Rose and Garske (1987) found no difference in measures of adjustment or maladjustment. They reported indications that Holocaust survivors are handicapped when their children begin to face issues of separation and independence. For survivor children, separations from parents were often abrupt, final, and never fully resolved. However, in none of the three last-mentioned studies was specific knowledge obtained of the mental and physical status of the subject's parents. Hence, it would be premature to relate the difference between survivor children and controls simply to the war experiences of the parents.

4.4.3. *Family Studies*

What about the relational characteristics of survivor families? Sigal and Weinfeld (1987) compared 242 children of Holocaust survivors, 76 children of other Jewish immigrants, and 209 children of native-born Jews. Those samples represented 75.9 percent, 62.6 percent, and 46.3 percent of those originally contacted. One extensive questionnaire dealing with a variety of areas pertinent to personal, marital, and social functioning was utilized to examine the samples. Their findings did not support the viewpoint that children of Holocaust survivors remain enmeshed with their families or alienated from them. Self-report data, the authors admit, have their limitations and do not yield the rich material of a clinical interview. Yet, the list of variables explored was broad and would probably have yielded positive results if the Holocaust experience as a rule were to have led to pathological family interactions. Keinan et al. (1988) compared 47 adult second-generation Holocaust survivors with 46 adult controls and found that the groups did not differ in emotional stability and self-perception. The survivor children perceived their parents as more tense, but also as more attractive. The overall intactness of family relations in Holocaust survivors families was confirmed in several studies (Weiss,1988; Keller, 1988; Gross, 1988), but not all (Leventhal & Ontell, 1989).

4.4.4. *Conclusion*

In sum, then, controlled studies of nonclinical populations of second generation Holocaust survivors failed to reveal evidence of excess psychopathology or of pathological family relations in their parental homes. Some studies found problems with aggression regulation and separation/individuation in survivor children, but since the psychological antecedents of their parents remained unexplored, it would be unwarranted to relate those traits simply to the war experiences of their parents.

4.5. Double Victimization

Far be it from me to suggest that the German concentration camps and, in particular, the extermination camps have not left deep scars in those who survived them or did not profoundly influence their attitude towards life and their fellow man. Being a Holocaust survivor myself, I have no disposition to downplay the existential depth of that ordeal. What I do say is that those devastating experiences have not been shown to have exerted a general and enduring devastating influence on the integrity of the personality structure. Many Holocaust survivors have managed to rebuild themselves and their lives productively. One would do them a great injustice to generalize from case studies and selected clinical populations and to consider the survivor group as a whole as irreversibly traumatized, potentially impaired, psychologically unfit for parenthood, and basically responsible for the mental misery that might befall and, according to some authors, will inevitably befall their offspring. If we did so, survivors would be twice victimized. We psychiatrists have made comparable mistakes in the past by identifying an imaginary "schizophrenogenic" mother as crucial in the etiology of schizophrenia and, an intellectual, cold, obsessional parental ambiance as responsible for infantile autism. Such irresponsible speculations have plunged many families into deep sorrow for which there was no solace.

The survivor group grows progressively smaller. Soon there will be no one left to speak on their behalf. Let it therefore again be clearly stated: the Holocaust has wrecked few, not many. Save the survivor from psychiatric labeling. In general, he or she has been the living demonstration of the power of the mind to withstand unspeakable violations of its integrity and of the ability of a victim to refuse to be victimized.

5. DSM-III SANCTIONED DIAGNOSTIC INNOVATIONS

The foregoing exposition provides by no means an exhaustive list of diagnostic make-believes in psychiatry. I merely discussed paradigms of ill-grounded and prematurely introduced "disorders." As such, they are typical exponents of psychiatry's preoccupation with nosological classification, a mind set that was ushered in by the revival of biological psychiatry in the fifties and that was strongly reinforced by the publication of the DSM-III in 1980. The basic message I wished to convey is that studying the determinants and characteristics of such "entities" is as meaningful as probing the foundation of a castle in the sky.

Though accepted by many clinicians as valid psychiatric entities, none of them is included as such in the third edition of the DSM. Similar questions, however, can be raised about the identity of some diagnostic innovations or reconceptualizations that did receive the official DSM-III stamp of approval. Multiple personality disorder is an example of a new diagnostic construct; panic disorder exemplifies one that was reconstructed. The section of personality disorders as a whole raises the issue of whether it faithfully captures the domain of personality dysfunctions or rather is a product of wishful thinking of minds driven by an apparently irresistible need to organize the world of psychiatry into clear-cut, well-marked, and mutually exclusive diagnostic alternatives.

5.1. Panic Disorder

5.1.1. *Borders and Border Issues*

The syndrome presently called panic disorder was previously known under such names as hyperventilation syndrome and neurocirculatory asthenia. In the DSM-III, it was clearly defined and tied together by the following anchorpoints: (1) Occurrence of discrete periods of fear or discomfort, of (2) great intensity and (3) rapid onset, (4) lasting usually minutes, more rarely hours, (5) associated with a variety of autonomic symptoms, and (6) occurring unexpectedly, that is spontaneously and without clear provocation.

Is this syndrome as it presents itself in the real clinical world indeed so neatly packaged? I believe it definitely is not. By way of illustration, I want to discuss one border issue, that of generalized anxiety disorder (GAD). Is panic disorder a diagnosis in its own right or rather a severe form of GAD? This is not a mere "academic" question, but one with immediate relevance for research into the biology and treatment of these anxiety disorders.

A key feature of GAD as described in the DSM-III is the chronic occurrence of anxiety associated with particular life circumstances and accompanied by a multitude of autonomic symptoms. The intensity of the anxiety is not indicated in the DSM-III definition. Thus, variables that differentiate between GAD and panic disorder are chronicity versus periodicity, and precipitated versus spontaneous occurrence. Those criteria, however, have limited validity, referring as they do to a minority of (perhaps) prototypical patients.

Most, if not all, patients with panic disorder complain of interepisodic anxiety accompanied by autonomic symptoms. This has been interpreted as anticipatory anxiety, that is as fear for the next attack (Klein, 1980). This is not necessarily the way this condition is viewed by the patients. Eighteen of a group of 31 patients diagnosed as panic disorder (or, at the time, rather as hyperventilation syndrome) indicated to me that the chronic anxiety was primary, and not a byproduct of imminent attacks. The acute (but more often subacute) exacerbations were felt to be often precipitated by psychological events, evoking negative feelings such as frustration, anger, disappointment, and disparagement. "I become panicky when I realize what a misfit I am and how unable to change my life around" is a remark by one of those patients capturing a situation that careful interviewing frequently reveals. In other words, interepisodic anxiety can be primary rather than anticipatory, while quite frequently panic attacks seem psychologically provoked. The alarm in these cases is, to use Barlow's (1988) terms, true and not false.

In another group of 25 panic disorder (hyperventilation) patients we studied, 19 showed signs of ego-syntonic personality pathology.* Fourteen of them identified relative life events occurring in the 24 hours prior to the attacks as instrumental in their occurrence. The power of psychological stress to induce severe anxiety attacks is also clear from a study we did on psychopathology in the two weeks preceding suicide attempt. As expected, depression was very common (van Praag, 1982) but anxiety was also common, not infrequently assuming panic proportions (Table 9:6). Klein (1980) reported the precipitation of panic disorder by loss or separation from a significant other, but this is by no means the only type of panicogenic event. Other authors also found that all kinds of stressors might pro-

*See for this concept Chapter 3, Section 2.5.2.

TABLE 9:6
Anxiety (Attacks) in the Two Weeks Preceding a Suicide Attempt in 100
Consecutive Patients Hospitalized After a Suicide Attempt and in Two
Control Groups

	Number of Patients		
	N	Chronic Anxiety	"Bursts" of Anxiety
Suicide Attempters	100	38	33
Depression (anxiety in two weeks before hospitalization)	79	41	5
Normals (anxiety in two weeks before interview)	54	2	–

voke panic attacks and that uncued panic attacks are relatively rare
(Aronson, 1987; Gelder, 1986; Raskin et al., 1982). Not surprisingly,
then, a majority of patients with panic disorder have comorbid personality disorder, mostly diagnosed as avoidant and dependent
(Reich & Noyes, 1988; Wetzler et al., 1990).

The severity of panic attacks, moreover, may vary considerably
in the same patient and quite often they do not reach full panic intensity. It may be typical in this disorder that the anxiety reaches its peak
in a couple of minutes, but in close to 60 percent of our patients anxiety developed more gradually in the course of 30–60 minutes. In
GAD, on the other hand, the anxiety is by no means constant and
low grade. Periods with anxiety alternate with anxiety-free periods,
with the duration of those periods varying from a few hours to days
or weeks in a row. We demonstrated that the same is true for dysthymia.★ The duration of the depressive episodes varies widely and
they alternate with symptom-free or symptom-reduced intervals
that likewise vary in duration. In fact, periods of generalized anxiety
and dysthymia often coincide and their intensities vary concurrently.
In those cases, anxiety, mood-lowering, and ego-syntonic personality dysfunction are inextricably intertwined. Disappointment,
emptiness, loneliness, unrelatedness, meaninglessness, and similar
feelings and thoughts provoke depression and anxiety, mood states
that in turn intensify the state of despair. In short, the differential
diagnosis of panic disorder with interepisodic ("anticipatory") anx-

★See Chapter 3, Section 4.2.

iety and GAD with occasional exacerbations may be difficult to a degree that the decision becomes frankly arbitrary.

5.1.2. *Non-Symptomatological Validators of Panic Disorder as a Discrete Diagnostic Entity*

Other lines of evidence have been proposed to justify the division of the classical concept of anxiety neurosis into panic disorder and GAD. Family and twin studies suggest that in panic disorder genetic loading is heavier than in GAD (Crowe et al., 1983; Torgersen, 1983). Family studies in this field, however, are fraught with inaccuracies. Acknowledging that in a given case the differential diagnosis of panic disorder and GAD can be difficult, indeed, what certainty has one that that distinction has been reliably made retrospectively, in relatives from whom data were generally collected with self-rating questionnaires or via interviews conducted by assistants with little psychiatric experience?

Psychopharmacological data have, furthermore, been posited as evidence for the independent diagnostic position of panic disorder. This disorder would respond to antidepressants, not so much to benzodiazepines, and the reverse would be true for GAD (Klein, 1964). This axiom, however, has been challenged. Benzodiazepines with a triazalo moiety are surely effective in panic disorder (Kahn & van Praag, 1992), but other benzodiazepines such as clonazepam and diazepam are effective also provided high enough doses are being used (Noyes et al., 1984; Herman et al., 1987; Dunner et al., 1986). On the other hand, some evidence suggests that antidepressants are efficacious not only in panic disorder, but in GAD also (Kahn et al., 1986; Johnstone et al., 1980). Imipramine and alprazolam, finally, have been found to be effective against *all* components of panic disorder, that is number of spontaneous and situational panic attacks, phobias, and duration and intensity of anticipatory anxiety (Rosenberg et al., 1991). Thus, the psychopharmacological arguments are not at all strong.

Finally, the results of *provocation tests* are cited to support the case of panic disorder's independent status. Panic disorder patients, so runs the argument, respond to intravenous sodium lactate and 5 percent carbon dioxide (CO_2) inhalation with panic attacks. How specific, one might ask, is this effect? We know that both interventions lead to anxiety of variable intensity in almost all normal individuals;

that no more than 50 percent of panic patients respond with panic attacks and that quite often the induced attacks do not show the typical crescendo pattern with sudden intense anxiety of short duration (Sanderson & Wetzler, 1990; Shear & Fyer, 1988). We do not know whether both tests identify the same patient population, nor whether responses to those challengers in GAD are fundamentally different from those in panic disorder. About the diagnostic specificity of other panicogenic agents, such as caffeine, yohimbine, and M-chlorophenylpiperazine (MCPP), even less is known. And, finally, in many cases it is hard to determine whether physical symptoms came first, provoking anxiety, or whether the psychological and physical symptoms appeared independently. Even in naturally occurring panic attacks, one is often hard pressed to answer that question. It thus seems premature to regard the response to anxiogenics as validating the panic disorder concept.

5.1.3. *Premature Closure on Diagnostic Issues*

Do I question the occurrence of episodes of intense anxiety accompanied by autonomous symptoms? Of course not. The issue I do want to raise is twofold. First, does that syndrome constitute a separate diagnostic entity or is it a subtype of GAD? Second, is the autonomic dysregulation the key disturbance, with anxiety as a consequence; are the autonomic symptoms secondary to the anxiety; or do both conditions occur? In the latter case, we should distinguish between panic attacks as a distinct disorder, as an exacerbation of GAD, and as a consequence of episodic autonomic dysregulation. I have an (unverified) leaning towards that viewpoint, but that is beside the point. The point is that one should study these issues and not ignore them in a premature search for the characteristics of a monolytic concept named panic disorder.

Do we then have to suspend research in panic disorder until all validity issues have been resolved? This is not what I suggest. My viewpoint is that, for the time being, anxiety attacks should be the object of study without nosological strings attached. First order of priority should be the study of their diagnostic status, with two prime questions in mind. First, do they qualify for a separate diagnostic position and, second, is the anxiety attack a primary phenomenon or is episodic autonomic dysregulation the underlying disturbance? In the meanwhile, such issues as the biology of anxiety attacks, their proper treatment, their epidemiology, and many others could be properly studied.

To pretend that we are taxonomically further advanced than we are can only retard scientific progress.

5.2. Multiple Personality Disorder

5.2.1. *Alternate Personalities*

More or less sudden changes in the way a personality functions are a common occurrence in mental disorders. The diagnostic context in which those alterations appear varies widely. A DSM-III axis I diagnosis may be the primary condition. An acute depressive episode (and those may occur from one day to the next), for instance, may change someone from a cheerful, productive, socially adjusted individual into a cheerless, inactive, withdrawn wreck; conversely, a hypomanic episode can turn "a quiet retiring spinster into a flamboyant, promiscuous bar habituée" (actually an example given in the DSM-III-R of multiple personality disorder (MPD)). A psychotic breakdown may bring about a sudden and passing change in personality functioning. The same might happen in temporal lobe epilepsy, generally accompanied by a change in consciousness. Organic brain disorder may be the underlying cause of a sudden personality change, a vivid example being the often abrupt outburst of irritation and aggression in patients with multi-infarct dementia.

An axis II diagnosis might also generate sudden changes in the way one perceives, relates, and reacts to the environment. The hysterical, or to use the DSM-III terminology, histrionic personality provides classical examples. Amiability and charm can momentarily make way for venom and anger, flirtation for rejection, elation for despair. In the hysterical domain, various forms of splitting and regression of the personality can be observed, generally triggered by psychological stressors or subtle interpersonal cues with negative connotation for the person in question. Examples are the fugue, pseudodementia, amnesia, twilight states, trances, and puerilism, the latter being a condition in which the patient behaves and speaks as the child he or she once was (see, for example, Mayer-Gross et al., 1955).

The borderline personality, characterized by instability of mood, impulsivity, and persistent identity disturbances, is par excellence prone to sudden, unexpected changes in personality functioning. In impulse control disorder, abrupt changes in personality can be striking. The condition is characterized by discrete episodes of loss of control of aggressive impulses resulting in serious aggressive acts, grossly out of proportion to precipitating events. In between the "attacks," such individuals may behave in a well adjusted way and may even be perceived as "sweet" and "charming" by those who know them.

The Dr. Jekyll and Mr. Hyde antithesis has always appealed to the imagination. The act of transformation, from a well adjusted, conformistic individual into a Robin Hood, an Al Capone, a Mata Hari, a Bonnie, a Clyde, nourishes a need for romantic escapism.

5.2.2. *Alternate Personalities as a Separate Disorder*

The occurrence of alternate personality states in one individual was hardly recognized as a separate disorder until the publication of the DSM-III in 1980. I quote from Fahy's (1988) review on MPD that it is Mitchill (1816) who is usually credited with the first description of a case that presently would carry the diagnosis of MPD. It concerned a young woman who fell without forewarning into a profound sleep which continued several hours beyond the ordinary term and who after awakening had "lost every trait of acquired knowledge . . . and had to learn everything again." After a few months, another "fit of somnolence invaded her" and on rousing from it she found herself restored to the premorbid level and amnestic for her previous state. The manifestations of what Mitchill called a "double character" continued to show until her death.

Sporadic cases of alternate personalities as a diagnosis by itself were published since. Taylor and Martin (1944) identified 28 cases in the literature between 1874 and 1900. After the second world war, several biographical accounts of patients with multiple personalities appeared that received wide attention (e.g. Thigpen & Cleckly, 1954; Schreiber, 1973; Hanksworth & Schwarz, 1977). Yet, until 1980, only 200 cases had been reported in the world literature (Greaves, 1980; Boor, 1982) and the diagnosis was by no means generally accepted; it was even heavily criticized (e.g. Ellenberger, 1970). In many textbooks it was not mentioned at all or was subsumed under the heading of Hysteria, for instance, in the text by Mayer–Gross et al. (1955).

Then, in 1980, without much ado, the state of alternate personalities appeared as a full-fledged *disorder* in the third edition of the DSM. Since that time, many thousands of cases have been diagnosed (Ross et al., 1989a), predominantly in the USA. Just one British case had appeared in the literature over the past 15 years (Fahy, 1988). A small number of clinicians are responsible for the increased number of reports (Orne et al., 1984).

5.2.3. *Multiple Personality Disorder as Defined in the DSM-III-R*

The requirements for the diagnosis of MPD stipulated by the DSM-III-R are few and multi-interpretable. Only two psychopathological features are mandated: the existence within the person of two or more distinct personalities of which at least two recurrently take full control of the person's behavior. The terms "personality," "distinct," and "full control" remain unspecified and the interrater reliability for the detection of these criteria has not been systematically assessed (Fahy, 1988). Surprisingly, the DSM-III has been criticized for being overly restrictive, thus excluding patients with so-called incomplete forms of the disorder (Bliss, 1983). Lo and behold, the DSM-III-R has taken these incomplete forms into account by classifying them as "dissociative reactions not otherwise specified." They are defined as cases in which there is more than one personality state capable of assuming executive control of the individual, or cases in which a second personality never assumes complete executive control. This is an example of a loose play with words unsupported by any empirical data. One would like modern psychiatry to be shielded from this type of esoteric construction.

The general description of MPD in the DSM-III-R does not make us much wiser. Everything seems possible and nothing is required. The transition from one personality to the other may be sudden or gradual; consciousness may be intact, lowered, or changed; sometimes, the alternates are aware of the existence of others, sometimes they are not; amnesia might ensue after a particular personality state, but the individual might also be aware of the personality change; the different personalities may or may not converse with each other, and, if these internal conversations do occur, they must be differentiated (as stipulated in the DSM-III) from delusions and hallucinations, but it is not indicated how; psychological triggers can be involved in the personality transformation or might be absent; the duration of the various personality states is not specified. I pass by absurdities such as the statements that the number of personalities in any one case may vary from two to over 100 (realistically, to distinguish reliably between such numbers of personality states within one individual would be a superhuman achievement) and that the different personalities may have different eyeglasses and different responses to the same medication, a contention created out of the realm of lore and imagination, lacking any empirical foundation.

5.2.4. *Multiple Personality Disorder and Concomitant Psychopathology*

The DSM-III-R definition recognizes that many other mental disorders may coexist with MPD. It follows here the results of a number of detailed studies of the clinical phenomenology of MPD. Putnam et al. (1986), Ross et al. (1989a), and Coons et al. (1988) reported indirect data derived from a questionnaire circulated among clinicians with a known interest in MPD seeking information about their MPD patients. The great majority of patients reported by Putnam et al. (1986) presented a rich diversity of symptoms such as depression, anxiety, visual and auditory hallucinations, and a variety of hysterical symptoms, such as psychogenic amnesia, fugues, and conversion symptoms. No less than 60 percent of that cohort had reported suicidal behavior, 34 percent self-mutilation, six percent homicidal behavior, and 20 percent of the patients had admitted to sexual assault. Substance abuse was present in 50 percent and 50 percent reported at least one somatic symptom.

The data collected by Coons et al. (1988) are comparable with those of Putnam et al. (1986). Amnesia (100 percent), depression (88 percent), sexual dysfunction (84 percent) and auditory hallucinations (72 percent) were the most common symptoms. Only seven patients of the 50 studied did not meet the criteria for a personality disorder, while 20 qualified for one diagnosis, nine for two diagnoses and 13 for three diagnoses. The diagnoses included borderline personality (56 percent), dependent personality (26 percent), histrionic personality (22 percent), compulsive personality (16 percent), avoidant personality (14 percent), antisocial personality (12 percent), paranoid personality (eight percent) and passive-aggressive personality (four percent).

Ross et al. (1989a) found that in a cohort of 236 patients with MPD, affective disorder had been diagnosed in 64 percent of them, anxiety disorder in 44 percent, schizophrenia in 41 percent, substance abuse in 31 percent, eating disorder in 16 percent and personality disorder in 57 percent. The respondents reported that 72 percent of their patients had attempted suicide, with 2.1 percent actually dying. Voices arguing in the head was found in 72 percent of patients and voices commenting on the patient's actions in 66 percent. Twelve percent of them had been convicted of a crime, 19 percent had worked as a prostitute, and 12 percent had been in jail. Several other authors have reported that many patients with MPD (up to 70 percent) do meet criteria for borderline personality disorder (Horevitz & Braun, 1983; Ross et al., 1989b).

Ross et al. (1990) examined 102 MPD patients with a structured interview in four different centers. Most of them had other concurrent psychiatric diagnoses, such as major depression (91.2 percent), borderline personality disorder (63.7 percent) and somatization disorder (60.8 percent). Substance abuse was common (50 percent) and suicidal behavior was found in 92 percent of the subjects. They see the bewildering variety of symptoms that may accompany MPD not as invalidating its autonomous status but, surprisingly, as an indication that "MPD has a stable consistent set of features." Imagine an internist who, having established that coughs are generally accompanied by a vast array of other symptoms in varying combinations and from different diagnostic domains, would have concluded that a cough disorder exists which has a consistent set of features. Such a contention would not have contributed much to progress in the realm of respiratory disorders.

Putnam (1987) states that MPD should be considered as a superordinate diagnosis superseding all others. The only justification they provide is that working with the alternates can provide a therapeutic device that cannot be utilized in the "unified" individual, a contention that is not backed up by any controlled outcome study. We are back to the traditional psychiatric adage: I think this, thus it is true.

In the DSM-III-R two explanations are offered for the co-occurrence of MPD with a broad array of other psychopathological symptoms. The latter might be features associated with MPD or represent disorders coexisting with MPD. A third and rather obvious interpretation, namely that MPD can be a symptom of a variety of underlying axis I and axis II diagnoses, is not even considered.

5.2.5. *Symptom-Independent Validation of the Diagnosis Multiple Personality Disorder*

Are there any other observations that could validate the conception of MPD as a separate disorder. *Traumatic childhood experiences*, particularly physical and/or sexual abuse, are said to be common in MPD patients; the DSM–III–R claims this to be true in nearly all cases. The relevant data base, however, is not convincing. The information was mostly obtained from self-reports of patients, a source that can be notoriously biased and was not independently verified. None of the studies was controlled.

It is furthermore claimed that MPD has a tendency to *run in families*. With respect to this view, too, the data base is fragile at best. In the study of Ross et al. (1989a), for instance, most respondents did not report the occurrence of MPD in relatives, while some were reporting it to be common, suggesting that much of the information could be flawed. Moreover, in a diagnosis with such a high level of psychiatric morbidity, it is very hard to unravel what it actually is that runs in the family, especially when the study is based on self-reports of patients.

Finally, *physiological measures* have been searched for to validate the diagnosis MPD. Several techniques have been utilized, such as EEG (e.g. Coons et al., 1982), visual evoked responses (e.g. Putnam et al., 1986), skin potential (e.g. Bahnson & Smith, 1975), and cerebral blood flow patterns (e.g. Mathews et al., 1985), but often the studies cover only one or two cases. Several types of functional changes have been reported, but evidence is lacking that they are specific for any one of the various personality states. It seems more likely that they are due to alterations in the arousal level of the subjects. In a study of 30 MPD patients, Coons et al. (1988) found the EEG to be normal in the majority of patients.

5.2.6. *Conclusion*

It is hard to reach any other conclusion than that the case for the diagnosis of MPD is weak indeed (see also, Fahy, 1988 Fahy, et al., 1989). It seems to be a phenomenon, a symptom, rather than a disorder, a symptom that may occur in a wide variety of psychiatric disorders and most notably in the realm of hysterical and borderline personality disorders. The view that MPD should supersede all other diagnoses is based on nothing else but the unsubstantiated assertion that alternate personalities, as such, constitute a treatable condition.

Clinically, MPD seems a risky concept in that it could easily divert attention from the concomitant and probably underlying psychiatric disorder and personality pathology. In view of the present state of our knowledge, it seems apparent that it would be utterly misguided to pursue scientific studies of alternate personalities as a distinct and separate disorder.

Conceptualizing a new disorder is not just an entertaining and noncommittal pastime. Once created, it starts to live a life of its own, possibly a dangerous life, at that. Psychiatrists are liable for failure to diagnose it. MPD is a telling case in point. MPD cases, Hardy et al. (1988) point out, may be a high risk for malpractice litigations in the future. "One can easily imagine," they note, "a patient with sociopathic tendencies rationalizing that because his previous therapist 'hurt' him by failing to diagnose MPD, the therapist deserves to be sued." We seem to have created a true sorcerer's apprentice, a neophyte turning against us.

5.3. Personality Disorders

5.3.1. *Character Assassins*

In the introduction to this chapter, I mentioned the group of personality disorders as particularly prone to proliferation of make-believes. I dare go one significant step further and entertain the idea that the very premise of categorical classification of personality disorder rests on wishful thinking.

The Commedia dell'Arte, a 16th–18th century Italian theater form, used characterological stereotypes, among them Scaramouche, a braggart soldier, a coward, and a liar; Pulcinella, an unscrupulous, coarse quipster; Harlequin, amoral, witty, shrewd, but unsuccessful in matters of love; and the doctor, generally called Graziano, presented as a lustful, garrulous, and boastful old man (Fuccila, 1990). Those were transparent characters, behaving straightforwardly and predictably.

In real life, such characters are rare. Personalities consist of complicated networks of more or less stable, enduring psychological functions, called traits. They are of a bewildering diversity and might operate in a parallel fashion, synergistically, or antagonistically, or they might be engaged in any kind of interjacent interaction. Some traits might be overdeveloped, some might seem atrophic; some are socially effective, some ineffective; some operate within the limits of the norm, some appear to be aberrant; some are maladaptive, some favor social integration. Though the number of individual personality traits seems finite, it is large enough to identify an all but infinite number of personality types.

Personality traits, moreover, show a continuous distribution, with no point of rarity marking a cutoff point for normality. Abnormality of a personality trait is defined by the psychological or biological damage it might inflict on the carrier and those associated with him. The same can be said of such physical variables as blood pressure and plasma cholesterol. Their cutoff points are not defined in absolute terms, but are determined by prognostic implications: values above a certain level predict diminished life expectancy and we learned, meanwhile, why that is so. Personality dysfunctions, however, are much harder to measure and so far their prognostic implications are hardly specified. The distinction between personality type and personality disorder, therefore, is anything but clear.

The thesis that the multiplicity of pictorial expression could be meaningfully understood by subdividing painters into a few prototypes—a Rembrandt-type, a Gaugain-type, a Picasso-type, and a few more would be rejected out of hand, I imagine, by many if not all experts. The assumption that the multiformity of personality structures can be subdivided into a handful of "types" and "disorders" (the most relentless among the character reductionists even going so far as to shrink the complexity of the personality into dualities such as Type A and Type B (Friedman & Rosenman, 1959) and introverted and extroverted personalities (Eysenk, 1947)) has been accepted with little criticism by successive generations of psychiatrists. I find that rather embarrassing.

5.3.2. *Character Deformation*

The third edition of the DSM, having chosen for the categorical approach, distinguishes 11 personality disorders which can be subdivided into three clusters: eccentric, dramatic, and anxious (Zimmerman & Coryell, 1990). An additional two personality disorders (called sadistic and self-defeating) are added, but "need further study." Boundaries between the various disorders are fuzzy, particularly within one cluster where the overlap of symptoms is considerable (Pfohl et al., 1986; Reich, 1990). Clearly, membership in a particular category is not an all-or-none occurrence, but rather a matter of degree, with the transition from normal to abnormal being indistinct. Many criteria, moreover, are not clear-cut, but require inferential judgment. In the DSM-III-R (in contrast to the DSM-III), all categories are polythetically defined. The presence of all defining features is not required (as in so-called monothetic definitions), but only a specified minimum number. Thus, various combinations of criteria are considered to be equivalent and consequently, a particular diagnostic grouping includes a variety of different personality structures.

In actual practice, few patients show all the required characteristics of a particular personality disorder and many show features of several. Due to this, large numbers of patients are considered to suffer from more than one personality disorder or receive the diagnosis of personality disorder not otherwise specified (Morey, 1988), a diagnosis which has an informative value approaching zero. In a series of 41 patients I studied, only six met criteria for one personality disorder, four met criteria for more than one, and the remainder was considered to be "mixed," showing features of several personality disorders without meeting the full criteria for any one. Serious doubt about the validity of these diagnostic concepts is thus in order. If a patient is found to be unduly dependent, insecure, suspicious, and emotionally unstable, then *that* pattern, rendered in some quantified manner, should be the diagnosis, rather than "personality disorder not otherwise specified" or the statement that the patient suffers from (incomplete) dependent personality disorder, (mild) paranoid personality disorder, and (subclinical) borderline personality disorder.

It is often contended that clinicians have an insurmountable preference to think categorically and would refuse to use dimensional systems. I am not so sure that this is true. This preference is undeniable, but it could be acquired rather than innate. If teachers of psychiatry would start to convey the message that present-day taxonomy of personality disorders distorts clinical realities, provides pseudo-certainty, and has no demonstrated usefulness in programming therapeutic interventions, and if, in addition, experimental psychologists and research psychiatrists would guide the practitioner in the use of dimensional assessment devices, I like to believe that a switch in mind set could be reached. The two latest DSM editions are steering the practitioner in a wrong direction.

For research purposes, the categorical approach to personality disorders seems disastrous, particularly for biological research. One could appropriately study the biological underpinnings and determinants of defined and accessible, enduring and relatively stable psychological (dys)functions. To fancy that there exists such a thing as the biology of, for instance, avoidant personality disorder—taking into account the overlap with other personality disorders, the impossibility to define its borders with normality, the heterogeneity of the concept, the ambiguity of many of its features—is stretching the imagination beyond the limits of credibility.

5.3.3. *The Moral of the Story*

It has been argued that the dimensional approach to personality disorders is impractical because of the divergence of opinion as to what dimensions should be studied and what the basic building blocks of the personality really are. This argument is hard to counter, but I can see it merely as yet another reason to grant the conceptualization of a detailed, dimensional taxonomy of personality disorders the highest research priority in psychiatry. Until 1980, a standardized, operationalized classification system for psychiatric disorder seemed an unattainable, almost messianic ideal. This has been shown not to be the case. The DSM-III task force produced a detailed taxonomy that was almost universally accepted in the psychiatric world. The same strategy could and, I think, should be followed to hammer out a dimensional system for the diagnosis of personality disorders. Using the consensus opinion as a method, a task force should draw up a draft taxonomy that subsequently is subjected to systematic study of its utility and validity. There is no a priori reason to assume that the charge of this task force will turn out to be less achievable than that of its DSM-III counterpart.

6. CLOSING

Psychiatry is susceptible to make-believes and the diagnostic make-believes are not the only ones. Etiological examples abound. The schizophrenogenic mother is an example—she was held responsible for the development of schizophrenia in her offspring— and the idea of the infamous, icy, intellectual parents, thought to be at the root of infantile autism, is another. There also is the theory that homosexual tendencies are involved in the development of paranoid pathology, as well as the alleged linkage between traumatization in particular developmental stages and particular personality deformities. Many more examples could be cited. Therapeutic make-believes are equally abundant. The proliferation of psychotherapies in the sixties and seventies was unbridled and countless people were subjected to interventions with unproved efficacy and unknown harmfulness. Megavitamin therapy was embraced as a treatment for schizophrenia before it was found to be a placebo. All sorts of activities that are performed with psychiatric patients are called "treatments" and those carrying them out are "therapists," though little evidence exists that these activities have an enduring beneficial effect on psychopathology.

The vulnerability of our profession to self-deception springs from the lack of a scientific tradition and the resulting proneness to belief-systems. For many years, psychiatrists exhibited little tendency to verify, fascinated as they were with theories, willing to heap one hypothesis on top of the other and eager to believe that time would grant the underlying layer the dignity of truth. Psychiatrists were more intellectual aesthetes than empirical investigators.

Fortunately, over the past few decades this attitude has begun to change in favor of a more investigative orientation. Paradoxically, the ongoing scientific restructuring of psychiatry still carries a flurry of diagnostic make-believes in its wake. The modern eagerness to uncover systematically the origins of mental pathology feeds the inclination to configurate well-defined and manageable diagnostic packages as an easy target to focus research efforts on. This zest fosters diagnostic illusions that can only lead us back to the diagnostic morass out of which we are trying so hard to pull away. The legendary Baron von Muenchhausen managed to pull himself up by his own bootstraps out of the morass. This was, it seems, a once-only feat, and there is little reason to believe that we psychiatrists could repeat it.

PART III
(Re-) Minding Our Business

−10−

Biological Psychiatry Audited

1. PROCEDURE

What impact has biological psychiatry had on the field of psychiatry as a whole? I will contrast the state of the art in psychiatry today with that of almost 35 years ago, a time span determined by the start of my residency training. Personal experience is clearly advantageous for a retrospective.

First, I will discuss the contributions, next the unfulfilled hopes, and finally some undesirable side effects of the biological revolution.

2. CONTRIBUTIONS

2.1. A New Cornerstone for Psychiatry

Biological psychiatry has provided the mother discipline with a third cornerstone, i.e. neurobiology, the other two being psychology and medical sociology. Is this a valid statement? Is the amassed neuroscientific knowledge indeed of such importance to psychiatry as to justify the qualification of cornerstone or do we only pretend so in order not to sound antiquated? The former appraisal seems to be right, a viewpoint I will support with four examples.

1. Clinical psychopharmacology has developed into a mature science, providing the mother discipline with information on the clinical action of psychotropic drugs and on their working mechanism.

217

These data, in their turn, generated new ideas for drug development and brain and behavior research.

I mention one example by way of illustration. In the late fifties and early sixties, animal experiments had made clear that the classical antidepressants increase the availability of monoamines in the brain; one of them was serotonin (5-hydroxytryptamine; 5-HT). These data prompted clinical research into the relation between 5-HT and depression (van Praag, 1982c; Zis & Goodwin, 1982). Findings indicative of such a relation initiated the search for and eventually the development of drugs that increase central 5-HT in a selective manner, most notably, the selective 5-HT reuptake inhibitors (Lemberger et al., 1985). Continued explorations indicated the likelihood of 5-HT being involved not so much in depression per se, as in certain components of the syndrome, i.e. anxiety and dyscontrol of aggression (see Chapter 7). These data, in their turn, generated the hypothesis that compounds capable of potentiating 5-HT are not true antidepressants, but are indicated in states of heightened anxiety/aggression, irrespective of (nosological) diagnosis (van Praag et al., 1987b).

This concept of transnosological indication of psychotropic drugs has a significance reaching far beyond the borders of psychopharmacology and well into the broader realm of psychiatric diagnosis and taxonomy (see Chapters 6 and 7).

2. The search for novel psychotropics seems on the verge of being revolutionized. Two developments are particularly relevant. First, the discovery in the central nervous system (CNS) of specific recognition sites for foreign compounds with psychotropic activity, leading to the search for their natural ligands. In the case of the opiate receptors, this had led to the discovery of the family of the endorphins (Akil et al., 1984). In other cases, such as the imipramine and benzodiazepine receptors, the search is still ongoing (Segonzac et al., 1985; Costa & Guidotti, 1985). The concept of "natural psychotropics" emerges, one that has not yet led to therapeutic breakthroughs, but has provided drug research with a new conceptual framework that is unlikely to become a dead end.

The neuropeptides are a second major impetus for drug development. Many of them have profound effects on components of the behavioral repertoire such as memory, attention, and mood. This holds for animals and there is no evidence that humans are different. Again, no therapeutic breakthroughs yet, but it would be extraordinary if naturally occurring and behavioral active peptides would eventually not find applications in psychiatry. Bringing them in sufficient quantities in the CNS might be a major stumbling block, but it is one that is technical in nature and, as such, bound to be overcome.

3. Progress in molecular genetics has been staggering, but the question here is: Will psychiatry benefit? It seems likely that it will. Only a few years ago, a single gene responsible for Huntington's disease was discovered (Guesella et al., 1983). In Alzheimer's disease, another neuropsychiatric disorder (though closer to the psychiatric pole in the neurological–psychiatric dimension), a gene is being searched for. In the subtype in which the disease seems to be passed on through the generations, a gene defect has been found on chromosome 21 (St. George-Hyslop et al., 1987), close to the amyloid precursor protein and possibly responsible for the excess amyloid production.

Unqualified psychiatric diseases are now being targeted for genetic exploration, bipolar disorder being an example. Starting point was a study of suicide and depression among the Amish in Pennsylvania, a secluded religious group of farmers, all descendants of around 50 couples from Germany who arrived in the USA some 250 years ago. Among them, several pedigrees were found with a high density of manic-depressive disorder. Those families provided compelling evidence that the disorder is carried by a dominant gene with incomplete penetrance (Egeland & Hoffstetter, 1983). Tentative evidence suggested the gene to be located on chromosome 11 (Egeland et al., 1987). This observation has not been confirmed, but that is possibly more related to inaccuracies of psychiatric diagnoses than to flaws in the genetic methodology (see also Chapter 6). Psychiatric genetics is exquisitely sensitive to diagnostic inconsistencies; thus, its development is contingent on a system that generates valid and reliable diagnoses.

4. The brain imaging techniques have opened up exciting vistas on brain structure and functioning. Positron emission tomography (PET) seems to be the most promising technique for psychiatry, though admittedly the payoffs so far have been modest, probably because of the tracer that has been most frequently used, deoxyglucose. This is not a particularly revealing tool. Glucose is the brain's universal fuel. The finding of diagnosis–specific changes in regional glucose utilization would have been surprising, just as surprising as it would have been some 25 odd years ago (when these

measurements were in fashion) to find changes in overall metabolic rate of the body with nosological specificity. Presently, however, much more specific paradigms of brain functioning can be visualized, e.g. certain monoamine-related receptors (Andreasen, 1988). These developments are highly promising and warrant the prediction that PET will become a powerful tool in studying the action mechanism of psychotropic drugs, as well as the pathophysiological underpinnings of behavior disorders. SPECT, morever, once considered to be the "poor man's PET," now successfully competes with PET scanning and is much less expensive.

It can be said, then, that over the past 30 years biology has established itself firmly as one of the basic disciplines of psychiatry.

2.2. Taxonomy

In 1958, no psychiatric taxonomy was available; it might be more accurate to say that as many taxonomies existed as there were psychiatric textbooks. Diagnostic confusion was the order of the day. Psychiatrists of analytic persuasion tended to derogate classification altogether.

The advent of biological psychiatry and psychopharmacology generated a different atmosphere. Symptoms regained their respectability, since they were the very targets of psychotropic drugs. Clusters of individual symptoms (syndromes) seemed to show sufficient internal consistency to be definable and to serve as units of classification in a taxonomy acceptable to the profession at large. At least that was the way we felt and the reason why in the early sixties we proposed a classification of depressions based on strict operational definitions of a set of syndromes (van Praag et al., 1965; van Praag and Leijnse, 1964, 1965). This approach was later adopted and extended in the development of the Feighner Criteria (Feighner et al., 1972) and the Research Diagnostic Criteria (Spitzer et al., 1977), reaching its pinnacle in 1980 when the DSM-III was published. The DSM-III is not an ideal system by any means and awaits a much more rigorous validation than that on which it rests now, i.e. expert opinions. However, for all its flaws, it provided psychiatry for the first time with a comprehensive, detailed multidimensional taxonomy and thus laid the groundwork for a science of psychiatry.

2.3. Assessment

It is also true that when I started my residency training there were few methods available to measure abnormal human behavior in a standardized, reproducible way. Today, psychiatry can boast of a plethora of such methods, for which biological psychiatry, in no small measure, deserves the credit. The study of biological markers of psychiatric disorders, as well as the behavioral effects of drugs over time, forced psychiatrists to take not only diagnosis seriously but also the methodology to assess, to measure, and to register the component parts of diagnoses. Rating scales and the like proliferated. In the early sixties, it occurred to us that one could conceive of an alternative approach, i.e. standardization of *the* instrument of psychiatric evaluation—the psychiatric interview. In this vein, the Vital Syndrome Interview came into being, an instrument to recognize vital (endogenous; major) depression and the first standardized, structured interview to be introduced in clinical psychiatry (van Praag et al., 1965). The method was adopted and applied in a far more elaborate way in the Schedule for Affective Disorders and Schizophrenia (SADS interview) (Endicott & Spitzer, 1978) and the Present State Examination (Wing et al., 1974) both now being widely used in psychiatric research as diagnostic and follow-up instruments.

Psychometric methods allow psychiatrists to register in a standardized and reproducible way what they observe. After taxonomy, assessment devices constitute the second prerequisite for psychiatry's ongoing maturation as a science.

2.4. Pharmacotherapy

The fourth contribution of biological psychiatry to its progenitor is the psychotropic drugs. I refrain from discussing them. They revolutionized psychiatric treatment, particularly that of depression, schizophrenia, and anxiety states. They came with a price tag, i.e. side effects, but the credit balance, the therapeutic benefit, is definitely positive.

Yet, psychotropic drugs do not and will not replace psychological interventions. Drugs are suited to normalize brain dysfunctions underlying abnormal behavior (the *pathogenesis* of the disorder), but they are powerless insofar as psychological factors are concerned that might have contributed to the disruption of brain functions (those factors form part of the *etiology* of the disorder). The latter can be tackled only with psychological means. Optimal psychiatric treatment will address both pathogenesis and etiology of the disorder. Addressing only the pathogenesis and leaving etiology alone is like braking with your foot on the accelerator. It will almost irrevocably lead to relapse. In cases where psychological factors have contributed to the mental pathology (and those constitute the bulk of psychiatric patients), psychotropic drugs are part of the treatment plan—frequently an important part, but no more than that.

2.5. Return of the Lost Son

In 1958, psychiatry was in large measure detached from the rest of medicine. The concepts used by psychosomatic medicine were too restricted and the psychoanalytic language was too arcane to be taken seriously by mainstream medicine. In the sixties, Western Europe generated forces of considerable strength attempting to sever all ties between psychiatry and the medical disciplines and to promote the social sciences as psychiatry's home port (van Praag, 1978b). Biological psychiatry played an important role in preventing this disaster by providing the profession with a language, an attitude, an identity that enabled its practitioners to communicate with other medical specialists. Communication fostered collaboration. Neuropsychiatry and medical-psychiatric programs were established (Caine & Joynt, 1986). By no means in sufficient numbers, but the trend seems irreversible. Psychosomatic medicine lost its esoteric character and, under a new name, behavior medicine, strengthened its medical credibility (McKegney & Schwartz, 1986). The experimental triple board program implemented in six centers in the USA, in which residents are trained in pediatrics, psychiatry, and child psychiatry, is a bold attempt to transcend traditional medical borders and create innovative and, hopefully, useful medical hybrids. Psychiatry today is regaining its position within the family of medicine.

In summary, biological psychiatry has provided psychiatry not only with a new basic science and with new treatment modalities, but also with the tools, the methodology, and the mentality to operate within the confines of an empirical science, the only framework in which a medical discipline can survive. Psychiatry is on its way to become a scientific discipline; in no small measure, biological psychiatry has facilitated that process.

3. DISAPPOINTMENTS

3.1. The Same Wine in the Old Bottles

On the other hand, it must be acknowledged that some of the original expectations have remained unfulfilled and that the biological revolution has also generated undesirable side effects.

Today, we rely largely on the same drugs discovered some 25–30 years ago and their immediate offspring. Only a few new therapeutic principles have been added. Carbamazepine (Tegretol) comes to mind, as well as the recognition that some antidepressant drugs are useful in panic disorder and obsessive compulsive disorder. The new neuroleptic clozapine and the selective 5-HT uptake inhibitors, such as fluoxamine and fluoxetine, are assets, but they are not novel, introduced as they were in the seventies. According to many clinicians, the output of new therapeutic principles has been fairly meager.

That might be so, but there are some exciting possibilities on the horizon. The work of de Wied et al. (1978), for example, suggesting certain endorphin fragments to be natural antipsychotics, certainly qualifies. Although the clinical data so far are admittedly controversial (Verhoeven et al., 1986), this lead is too intriguing to be abandoned prematurely. The work of Zukin and collaborators (Javitt & Zukin, 1991) demonstrating specific binding sites in the brain for the hallucinogen phencyclidine (PCP) seems of comparable importance. It was followed by the discovery that the PCP binding site is part of the NMDA receptor complex. NMDA (N-methyl-D-aspartate) belongs to the group of the excitatory aminoacids. It was, moreover, established that PCP acts as an NMDA antagonist and that the effects of PCP are antagonized by NMDA agonists. These findings gave rise to the hypothesis that an imbalance of the PCP/NMDA receptor complex, leading to overactivity in the PCP system or underactivity in the NMDA system, might be involved in the pathogenesis of psychotic phenomena. This formulation is paving the way for novel approaches to the development of antipsychotic drugs (Meltzer, 1991).

The recognition, finally, that the 5-HT receptor system is heterogeneous has led to the development of agonists and antagonists highly selective for particular 5-HT receptor subpopulations. One therapeutic offshoot of that research line is the 5-HT_{1A} receptor agonists, such as buspirone recently introduced as an anxiolytic. There is, moreover, reason to believe that clozapine owes its unique therapeutic profile at least partly to its 5-HT_2 and 5-HT_{1C} receptor-inhibiting properties. Possibly, then, inhibition of particular 5-HT circuits could add to the antipsychotic potential of dopamine receptor blockade. The recent proliferation of 5-HT selective drugs is likely to generate therapeutic principles in a wide array of psychiatric disorders, such as the anxiety states, mood, aggression, and appetite disorders, as well as the schizophrenias.

The dark cloud of stagnation seems to have a broad silver lining.

3.2. Biological Markers Within Sight?

In the discussion of contributions of biological psychiatry to the mother discipline, I did not mention the biological studies in psychiatric disorders. This does not, of course, mean that I denigrate that work. It does express the view that so far it has resulted in few, if any, findings with practical/diagnostic value. The hope of finding objective signs (markers) of psychiatric diseases for which psychiatrists had been longing for so long has not yet been fulfilled. Non-suppression of cortisol after dexamethasone, blunted thyroid-stimulating hormone (TSH) response after thyrotropin-releasing hormone (TRH), low CSF concentration of 5-hydroxyindoleacetic acid (5-HIAA), low platelet monoamine oxidase (MAO), to mention only the most obvious examples, have been introduced as diagnostic procedures, but have all turned out to be of low specificity and to occur crossdiagnostically.

Is that reason for disappointment? For nosologists it is; for "functionalists" like myself, it is not. As I argued in Chapter 6, I consider psychological dysfunctions to be *the* elementary units of classification in psychopathology, not syndromes or the alleged Kraepelinian disease entities. Those dysfunctions constitute the building blocks of which syndromes and disease entities are made. It is conceivable that biological dysfunctions, as they might occur in psychiatric disorders, relate in a specific way not to syndromes or nosological entities, but to (clusters of) psychological dysfunctions. Because a particular psychological dysfunction is seldom specific for a given syndrome or nosological entity—occurring rather across diagnoses—this would explain the crossdiagnostic occurrence of most biological "markers." This viewpoint has demonstrated its usefulness for biological psychiatry, as explained in Chapters 7 and 8.

The syndromal and functional viewpoints do not relate in an opposing way, but are, rather, complementary. Dissection of psychiatric syndromes in their component psychological dysfunctions should be the next phase in the evolving process of diagnostic sophistication. Since many psychological (dys)functions are measurable in a quantitative sense, this approach could become a powerful impetus toward scientific maturation of psychiatry. In boosting that process, the nonspecificity of biological markers could eventually turn out to be a real blessing in disguise.

3.3. Estimation Versus Measurement

The methodology of measuring abnormal behavior did not really progress; rather, the methodology did improve, but the advances are barely used in biological psychiatry. By and large, we still use the same techniques as we did some 20–25 years ago; we do not measure, but make crude estimates. Is a particular syndrome present or absent and, if present, to a mild, moderate or severe degree? Are we in a stalemate? Not really. At least two avenues open up ahead of us. First, there is the ethological approach in which a behavioral syndrome is dissected in its component parts and the components measured in such terms as frequency, severity, and sequence. The concept of human ethology has been with us for at least 20 years, but we have so far failed to give it real substance. The second avenue is that of experimental psychology, providing the methodology to measure discrete psychological (dys)functions quantitatively. Experimental psychologists are, so to say, our neighbors. We psychiatrists, however, failed to invite and to engage them.

We might seem to be in a stalemate; the way ahead, however, is clearly marked.

3.4. Research and Practice

In psychiatry, clinical research and clinical practice are still too far apart. In clinical research, diagnosis is carefully weighted (standardized interviews), intensity of symptoms followed over time (rating scales), side effects systematically monitored, and pharmacokinetic factors taken into account. In clinical practice, this approach is rare, though most of these methods are far beyond the experimental stage. In medicine, prescribing drugs, for instance antihypertensives, without an adequate diagnosis and monitoring their effect by estimating pulse pressure with one's fingertips instead of with a sphygmomanometer would be considered as malpractice. Prescribing, for instance, antidepressants on the basis of a brief unstructured interview and monitoring their effect without any rating device is not judged as such, but it probably should be.

We know more and can do more than what is being actually applied in clinical practice. This harms the quality of patient care, harms the quality of residency training, and harms the recruitment of potential researchers because they have been insufficiently exposed to the practical fruits of biological psychiatric research and, thus, remain deprived of a powerful motivating factor.

3.5. Posterity

The recruitment of young investigators into biological psychiatry proceeds slowly; I refer to young psychiatrists. The field cannot be developed by pure neurobiologists and experimental psychologists alone. The research psychiatrist, preeminent connoisseur of psychopathology with at least a working knowledge of certain aspects of neurobiology and psychometrics, is an indispensable intermediary between the unimodal brain and behavior researchers.

Interest in human brain and behavior research is, to a great extent, a function of the way it is being taught to medical students and residents in psychiatry. In many medical schools in the USA, as well as in many other countries, this leaves a lot to be desired. The number of hours available to discuss biological aspects of abnormal behavior is too small and the number of competent teachers insufficient. The potential of research psychiatrists is thus insufficiently activated.

In this context, I point to an even more fundamental shortcoming in the teaching of psychiatry in general. In the medical curriculum, the teaching of the basic sciences is meant to acquaint the student with the fundamental processes and functions of the human body. This knowledge serves as the scientific basis for the understanding of disease in terms of malfunction, of pathophysiology, and instills habits of systematic observation. The basic curriculum in most medical schools is exclusively oriented to medicine and surgery. A basic curriculum for the behavioral sciences—which, in a medical school, are mainly represented by psychiatry—is lacking.

The absence of a basic curriculum for the behavioral sciences in the training of physicians leaves the student completely unprepared for the introduction to psychiatry as a clinical science and a practical discipline. This omission, moreover, suggests that psychiatry has no scientific base, perpetuating the stereotype that it remains a discipline based on words rather than on facts, relying on theory rather than on empiricism, a statue without a socle. This state of affairs does serious injustice to the impressive contributions that the biological, psychological, and social sciences have made to our understanding of abnormal behavior. The smaller the exposition, the smaller the chance that interest will be kindled for the scientific aspects of psychiatry.

A psychiatric component should be added to the basic science curriculum of medical students, consisting of a biological, a psychological, and a social science component (van Praag, 1988c). It is about time for academic psychiatry to begin serious discussions on this matter and to formulate concrete proposals for the agencies entrusted with medical education. If not us psychiatrists, who else?

4. DANGERS

4.1. Disadvantages of DSM-III Diagnoses

The first of two dangers related to the DSM-III is misuse. DSM-III diagnoses tend to be used as complete diagnoses instead of what they really are: partial diagnoses. They are partial simply because they are in large measure descriptive—symptomatological—and refrain from etiological judgments. The decision to ignore etiology was made because little is as yet known with certainty about causation of most psychiatric syndromes; hence, there is little to be standardized. This does not preclude, however, the necessity of causation being hypothesized in any given case, because those hypotheses are needed to indicate psychotherapy. Symptoms are currently the targets of psychotropic drugs; etiology is the object of the psychotherapies, to the extent that psychological factors codetermine a given case.

I consider the revival of classical nosological thinking kindled by the DSM-III as its second definitely negative consequence. It presents psychiatric disorders as self-contained entities; circumscribed and precisely definable. Nowadays, one can listen to "academic" discussions on the presence or absence of particular symptoms as if they were of crucial pathognomonic significance, and fancy oneself in a case conference in Germany some 100 odd years ago. Using the DSM-III, it is easy to ignore that many, if not most, psychiatric syndromes overlap with others; that many, if not most, patients show signs of belonging not to one, but to several syndromes; and that very few psychiatric symptoms seem to be pathognomic for a particular behavior disorder.

It is, of course, not the DSM-III itself that should be blamed. It is a categorical system and, as such, rigid and by definition describing separate entities. We psychiatrists are the ones who should be blamed for having failed to appraise that. A dimensional diagnostic system would be much closer to the factual realities of clinical practice, i.e. the recognition that the behavior disorder of a given patient is often a composite of parts of different syndromes. Yet, hardly any attempts have been made to develop dimensional diagnostic systems in psychiatry. Although, it is easy to grasp why—they seem rather cumbersome to handle in actual practice—this negligence is hard to justify if one is aspiring to greater diagnostic sophistication.

4.2. Standardized and Free Interviews

Standardized, structured interviews are indispensable for surveying the occurrence of psychiatric symptoms in a systematic, uniform, and unbiased way. They are relatively powerless in uncovering experiential information, elucidating personal development, or casting light on interpersonal relations, all the particular strengths of free interviewing. The two types of interviews are complementary, but they require different skills. The danger of overrating the standardized approach is real, particularly in research-oriented circles. Even worse, one can witness a standardized interview degenerating into a question-and-answer game: answers being taken on face value, not caring for the meaning behind the words, disregarding the as-yet-unspoken and oblivious to the emotional content of the communication. This is a perversion of a legitimate method and an impoverishment of the psychiatric examination.

4.3. Overreliance on Standardized Assessment

The danger of overreliance on rating scale results has become real despite only minor improvement of the instruments being used. Specifically, there is the danger of the desk researcher studying rating scale and standardized interview results rather than actual patients. These may be data collected not by himself, but by a research assistant with little psychiatric experience and training. The practice is not universal, of course, but is frequent enough to be alarming. Because the precision of psychometric measurements is limited, one needs a solid psychiatric background to score the various items adequately.

As an analogy: One can easily teach a medically untrained person to measure blood pressure, because the method is precise and needs no interpretation. One would be ill advised to try the same with x-ray readings. These data are multi-interpretable and cannot reliably be judged by personnel without profound medical and radiological experience. Research assistants cost less than psychiatrists, but no money is worth compromising the legitimacy of the diagnostic assessment.

4.4. Inflation

The most significant danger of biological psychiatry having been admitted to the circles of mainstream psychiatry is the tendency to inflate the explanatory and therapeutic weight of biological findings. A tendency to onesidedness, to emphasize one approach at the expense of others, seems almost ineradicably ingrained in psychiatry. We have variously lived through periods of inflation of the biological dimension (last part of the 19th century), the psychological vantage point (the first half of this century) and overreliance on the social point of entry to abnormal behavior (the sixties and seventies). Some signs hint at the emergence of a new extremism, this time again biological in nature, albeit in a new attire.

In the 19th century, anatomy was put on the throne. Today, there is a trend toward putting pharmacology there, along with biochemistry and molecular biology. The same hopes are cherished as some 100 years ago. In the end, it is biology that will solve the enigma of mental disorder and will bring salvation to psychiatric patients. The ramifications of this mood set are unmistakable. Psychiatrists set up practices as "psychopharmacologists" and there is perceptible pressure to "medicalize" psychiatry. Some maintain that psychiatrists should be involved only in biological diagnosis and biological treatment, leaving psychological and environmental aspects of diagnosis, as well as psychotherapy, to nonmedical specialists.

This is self-deception, even self-destruction. First, what does "biological diagnosis" mean? Granted, that much "biology" has been found in mental disorders, it is also true that few findings possess diagnostic specificity. Does biology contribute in any way to the diagnosis of, for instance, depression, schizophrenia, anxiety states? As biological diagnosticians, we would maneuver ourselves out of the marketplace; I mean that professionally, not financially. As for becoming a "psychopharmacologist," I would be the last to belittle the importance of drugs, but I also wish to face reality. What can a practicing psychopharmacologist do more than choose between a neuroleptic, an antidepressant, an anxiolytic, and a "mood stabilizer"? If psychiatric practice were to be so reduced, what a boring profession it would be and one could hardly expect it to ignite excitement among medical students.

I add another more fundamental objection. Even in a neurobiological utopia in which the brain as a behavior-regulating organ were fully understood and one had all the drugs necessary to regulate abnormal brain function, it would be inappropriate to sever the ties of psychiatry and of psychiatrists with the psychological and social roots of the human condition. Biological approaches in psychiatry could conceivably elucidate two aspects of the causation of mental disorder (van Praag & Leijnse, 1965; van Praag, 1969, 1979b). The first is pathogenesis, i.e. the conglomerate of abnormal brain functions underlying the occurrence of abnormal behavior. The second is etiology, at least to the extent that it is biological in nature.

I define etiology as the conglomerate of factors that have contributed to the set of brain dysfunctions underlying a particular abnormal behavior. They can be psychological, social, or biological in nature. Biological factors could have been acquired, recently (e.g. a trauma capitis) or in the past (e.g. a birth trauma), or can be hereditary. An example of the latter is an enzyme with a marginal *anlage*, functioning adequately under normal conditions, but failing if demands are increased. The biological approach is not apt to clarify etiological factors of a psychological or social nature, nor does it provide the tools to alleviate them. Those factors should be studied in their own right, i.e. with psychological and sociological methods, and treated with interventions appropriate for the pathology to be addressed, that is with psychotherapy and social intervention.

Several studies indicate that pharmacotherapy alone is less effective than in conjunction with psychotherapy (Weissman et al., 1981; Karasu, 1982; Conte et al., 1986). Why, then, should psychiatrists fight with one hand behind their backs? By no means do I suggest that we should try to regain a monopoly on nonbiological approaches. I do maintain that we should not maneuver ourselves to the sidelines, or allow ourselves to be pushed there. Collaboration with nonmedically trained mental health workers, by all means. Ceding the psychosocial roots of our profession, on no account. With that, we would give up our very identity.

The three pillars of psychiatry—biology, psychology, social sciences—are interdependent and consequently one cannot give up one or two of them without seriously compromising the attractiveness of the field and, much more important, its effectiveness.

5. SUMMARY

Biological psychiatry has significantly contributed to the growth of psychiatry as a whole and to its ongoing scientific maturation. The achievements, however, should not blind us for the darker sites of the biological revolution: the unfulfilled expectations and the outright dangers, the most ominous sign being the inflationary trend seen in the tendency to overrate the explanatory and therapeutic weight of biological findings.

Overzealousness has been a plague of psychiatry since its very inception as a scientific discipline more than a century ago. This time, may common sense prevail.

−11−

Reconquest of the Subjective

1. PREOCCUPATION WITH THE OBJECTIVE

Psychiatric research over the past three decades has now acquired the esteem it clearly deserves. Since empirical research presupposes definition of the object one studies and availability of instruments to measure it, operationalization of diagnosis and development of psychometric instruments have become major concerns for psychiatry. This progress was promoted to a large degree by biological psychiatry. The search for the biological underpinnings of abnormal human behavior and the study of the efficacy and mechanism of action of biological treatments are both contingent on the use of standardized diagnoses and objective measurement. Biological psychiatry moved in recent years from a minority position into the mainstream and its methodological attributes became the standard approach, especially in research.

In itself, this methodological development is to be hailed. Let there be no doubt about my stand as to that. Actually, my collaborators and I contributed at an early time to this development by introducing an operationalized classification of depression (van Praag, 1962), and a standardized structured interview to assess depressive syndromes (van Praag et al., 1965). At the same time, however, I have cautioned against the potential dangers of objectification: coarsening of diagnosis; preoccupation with the obvious; disregard for the subjective constituents of the psychopathological spectrum; horizontalism, i.e. a system of diagnosing mainly grounded on symptoms and detached from etiology, particularly from determinants of a psychological nature; oversimplification, i.e. classification of roughly comparable

This chapter was adapted from van Praag H.M. (1992). Reconquest of the subjective. *British Journal of Psychiatry*, *160*; 266-271.

but actually dissimilar syndromes into broad, general categories (e.g. van Praag, 1969). It is clear from today's diagnostic practices that these dangers have not been avoided.

At present, symptoms are the major currency in psychiatric diagnosis; particularly, well defined and easily demonstrable ones. Etiologically, too, it is the obvious that counts: definite family loading, demonstrable brain lesions, life events with an "absolute valence," that is, with traumatic impact for the average individual. Objectivity is the catchword in psychiatry today. The prevailing classification system, grounded in the DSM-III, and the available measuring instruments, caters to an overly objective approach, while at the same time this approach is consolidated by it. Clearly (at least to my mind), the DSM-III system and the psychometric instruments in use provide no more than rough-draft diagnoses, not only lacking detail and finesse but also disregarding elements essential for proper diagnosis, actually those that are subjective. A painting by Vermeer in which the blues have been left out may be Vermeer-like, but it is not a Vermeer. Similarly, a rough-draft diagnosis, omitting important subjective components, provides not much more than a global diagnostic outline.

2. DEFENSE OF THE SUBJECTIVE

The preoccupation with the objective did not subside over the years; on the contrary, it seems to have intensified. It is no longer seen as a transitory phase on the way to greater diagnostic refinement, but as an endpoint. The so-called subjective is not seen as territory still to be conquered, using empirical methods, and has become synonymous with nonoperationable, nonmeasurable, nonquantifiable, a symbol of soft science, at best. Rating scales developed several decades ago are still universally used (e.g. the Hamilton Depression Scale (Hamilton, 1960) and the Brief Psychiatric Rating Scale (Overall & Gorman, 1962)). The major standardized diagnostic interview, the Schedule for Affective Disorders and Schizophrenia (Endicott & Spitzer, 1978), introduced more than a decade ago, is still in use in its original form and I know of no attempts to refine or extend its scope. The Present State Examination (Wing et al., 1974) has been modified without fundamentally broadening and deepening it. Stagnation has set in, both in putting the diagnostic process on a scientific footing and in the development of appropriate measuring instruments.

Assuming this to be a fair depiction of the prevailing *zeitgeist* in the psychiatric research community, I want to distance myself from it and submit for consideration the following two theses:

1. Subjective psychopathology should not be disregarded lest important diagnostic and therapeutic information be lost.
2. Subjective psychopathology is not by definition unmeasurable and unverifiable. Though certified instruments for that purpose are virtually absent, sustained efforts should be made to develop them.

The term "subjective," moreover, is often misused in psychopathology, being applied to phenomena that are, in essence, quasisubjective. Therefore, before elucidating these theses, I will define the terms *objective* and *subjective* as used in psychopathology.

3. THE OBJECTIVE-SUBJECTIVE DIMENSION IN PSYCHOPATHOLOGY

In psychopathology, the terms objective and subjective are used in two ways: to qualify behavioral phenomena and to indicate methods used to collect and measure these phenomena. Data collection and measurement may be said to be objective if they are minimally influenced by both the patient who exhibits and reports the phenomena and the investigator who registers them. Conversely, the greater the impact of patient and/or investigator, the more subjective the method is.

Obviously, today's objectifying armamentarium—rating scales, questionnaires, standardized interviews, and the like—represents only a first step on the road to objective collection and measurement of psychopathological phenomena, not an endpoint. They generate estimates, but no measurements. A symptom is found to be present or absent and, if present, an estimate is given of its severity. Moreover, these instruments are not wholly objective, registering a fair amount of subjective "noise." To the extent that a symptom is not directly observable, we rely on statements made by the patient, which are translated into diagnostic terms by the interviewer. Neither participant is "bias-free." Statements made by patients are influenced by their willingness to communicate and their ability to recognize and verbalize inner experiences; those statements are likewise influenced by the "transcription process," that is the interviewer's ability to listen and to understand what the patient is communicating, as well as by his attachment to preconceived theoretical biases.

Used to qualify a psychopathological symptom, the term objective refers to the manifestation of phenomena in observable behavior which may be diagnosed independently of verbal communication. Examples are motor unrest and certain components of depressive and anxiety syndromes. Psychopathological symptoms approximate objectivity if they are spontaneously expressed (e.g. "I feel depressed") or unambiguously agreed to upon direct questioning (e.g. "Yes, indeed, I feel depressed").

These symptoms, clearly defined and easy to establish, are the major criteria for today's diagnoses and the main targets of objective psychometric methods. For the sake of convenience, the remaining phenomena are qualified as subjective (a euphemism for "soft") because they are not easily measured and are, therefore, "unscientific." This generalization makes no sense, first, because these remaining phenomena are utterly heterogenous and, second, because the measurability of the so-called subjective symptoms is unexplored and, thus, unknown at present. Let us discuss the heterogeneity of the psychopathological domain that is called "subjective."

4. SUBJECTIVE AND QUASISUBJECTIVE SYMPTOMS

4.1. Subjective Symptoms

Two types of symptoms truly deserve to be called subjective. First are those that are confined to the patient's experiential world, not expressed in observable behavior, and "atmospheric" rather than "factual" in nature, i.e. do not manifest themselves as delineated mental phenomena and are not verbalized as such. The quality of the depressed mood is an example. In the operationalized definition of vital depression (comparable to "endogenous depression" and the

DSM-III concept of "major depression, melancholic type") which we formulated in the early sixties (van Praag, 1962), we included the criterion that the affective anomaly had to be "unmotivated," referring to the absence of a sense of comprehensibility. The mood-lowering is experienced as meaningless (apart from a possible interpretation in a metaphysical sense). The patient says: "I do not know how I came to be this way; it has come over me." The mood-lowering is felt "leibnah" (body-oriented) rather than "geistnah" (psyche-oriented).

"Unmotivated" does *not* mean that precipitating factors of a psychotraumatic nature are necessarily absent. In some cases, precipitating factors are indeed absent and the patient indicates that the origin of his complaints is a mystery to him. If, however, the patient does mention a reason for his complaints, further investigation reveals that this "reason" is no longer experienced as an adequate explanation of the existing condition. The depression has become detached from its original motivation. In other words, the continuity, that is the comprehensible relation between the mood-state and what has prompted it is lost. In such cases, the patient experiences as painful the very fact that he can no longer experience sadness about the original precipitating event. In personal depression, on the other hand (comparable to neurotic depression and the DSM-III concept of dysthymia), the patient experiences a direct connection between mood state and precipitating events.

The DSM-III included in the definition of major depression, melancholic type, "a distinctive quality of mood, i.e. the depressed mood is perceived as distinctly different from the kind of feeling experienced following the death of a loved one." This criterion was retracted in the DSM-III-R for no convincing reason.

Qualitative heterogeneity occurs in other psychopathological domains as well, but systematic studies are virtually nonexistent. Let me mention two examples. Anguish is by no means a monolithic experience. Introspection alone learns that, for instance, fear of failure; fear, induced by external threats; and anxiety without discernible cause are experientially different. How diagnostically important these experiential nuances are remains largely to be explored. In the analysis of pain, they clearly are. Among the components to be known for proper diagnosis is the experiential quality: Is the pain throbbing, burning, shooting, cutting, etc.? Similarly in psychiatry, qualitative differences in mood are also of diagnostic importance, as will be mentioned later.

A second group of psychopathological phenomena can be described as purely subjective not because they are "diffuse" and remain confined to the patient's experiential world, but because they are conceptualized in the interviewer's/observer's mind. The meaning of a particular behavior or utterance, the patient's habitual attitudes, and the construed relationship between present and past experiences are all constructs generated by the interviewer/observer and not communicated, as such, by the patient. The usefulness and plausibility of these constructs depend on the interpretative and synthesizing skills of the interviewer/observer.

4.2. The Universe Between the Objective and the Subjective

Obviously, the terms "objective" and "subjective" mark the end-points of a spectrum. The realms of subjectivity and objectivity blend into one another and they do so on various levels. First, many psychopathological symptoms have both objective and subjective components. Depressed mood, for instance, might be evident in facial expression and manifest as a painful affect. Second, the expression of a psychopathological state in overt behavior might range from clear-cut and unmistakable (i.e. "objective") to ambiguous and in need of interpretation (i.e. "subjective"). The same holds true for symptoms that are verbally communicated. The communication might range from clear-cut to obscure and in need of clarification or interpretation.

Moreover, one can distinguish a category of symptoms to be characterized as "quasisubjective." They are communicated quite straightforwardly, but are not included in today's diagnostic glossary as provided by the DSM-III. In the psychiatric vernacular, they are generally called "subjective," a qualification incorrectly used as a synonym for "vague" or "undefined." Such phenomena are by no means nondescript, but they do not fit the presently "authorized" diagnostic framework. They are not verbally encoded in memory, at least not in directly and succinctly communicable form. They are still to be operationalized and measuring instruments are not available, yet they are no less "objective" or more "subjective" than many symptoms that are officially authorized.

For instance, German psychiatry distinguishes the concept called "Wahn Stimmung," a sub- or pre-delusional state. In this state, the patient is preoccupied with thoughts that might become delusional, but are not crystallized as yet, still somewhat fluid and correctable. Is it true or false, the subject agonizes. Am I on the wrong track, or are the others blinded? This state is accompanied by intense anguish, uncertitude, inner turmoil, and the unsettling conjecture that something is about to go terribly wrong. It is not readily observable, not spontaneously and concisely verbalized, not unmistakably acknowledged when a straightforward question is posed. A standardized interview is unsuitable to trace this indisputably pathological experience. To this end, one needs unrestricted access to the realm of the subjective.

The early stages of vital depression provide further examples of such "apocryphal" symptomatology. Frequently, such patients reject the label of depression as inappropriate to describe their emotional state. In 28 percent of 225 patients we diagnosed as depressed, this appeared to be the case. They felt not so much downhearted as spiritless, full of displeasure and discontent. Without knowing why, they lacked zest in living. This condition might be described as a persistent hangover or, to use Schneider's (1959) words, as a *depressio sine depressione*. Westerman (1922) used the term "korperliche Traurigkeit" (somatic sadness) in this context in order to indicate that these feelings are usually experienced as "leibnah" (body-oriented). The patient often does not give the outsider an impression of marked sadness. Some appear as resigned and others as rather irritable and caustic. Although despondency is not prominent, taedium vitae can be very pronounced.

This *depressio sine depressione* completely slips through the meshes of the current diagnostic net. The same is true for the state of irritable suspiciousness that occurred as an early symptom of depression in 22 percent of the same cohort, and as the major symptom in 18 percent. This is an accentuation of a waiting-guarded attitude—one of the basic attitudes for communication with the surrounding world (van Praag, 1991a). It occurs not only in vital depression, but also as a personality disorder sui generis and as a precursor of paranoid states. The relationship with others or with particular others becomes tense. They are mistrusted and the candor of their intentions is called into question as the patient feels provoked. A gesture, a word, or even a facial expression may suffice to arouse anger, which may or may not be expressed. Again, a yes or no question will not reveal such subaggressive of subparanoid states. An unrestricted form of interviewing is necessary to identify such conditions. Failing to do so can lead to missing the diagnosis.

"Objective" psychopathological phenomena correspond to what are called "signs" in medicine. (Quasi-)subjective psychopathology is comparable to what in this discipline is called a "symptom," that is a pathological phenomenon of which the patient complains and for which what he says is the only evidence. In psychiatry, this distinction is of little help, since most psychopathological phenomena carry both a "symptom" and "sign" component. Moreover, the nature of a "sign" is rarely completely self-evident, usually requiring verbal communication for verification.

5. LACUNAE IN THE CURRENT DIAGNOSTIC PROCESS

Diagnosing is the process of characterizing the phenomenology of a disease state and identifying its origins. The result of that process is a diagnosis. Based on the considerations outlined above, I conclude that the process of diagnosing has withered in psychiatry. A variety of psychopathological symptoms are ignored by the available measuring instruments and are not properly utilized for the diagnosis and classification of mental disorders.

The same can be said of certain psychological factors that might contribute to the morbid state. I allude to what might be called "subjective" or "relative" life events. Like symptom rating scales, existing life-event inventories emphasize obvious, "absolute" events, i.e. incidents that have a traumatic impact on the average individual. In contrast, subjective life events are those that are harmful for susceptible individuals, but are considered innocuous by the average individual. For example, a spouse's gesture, a tactless word by the boss, or a disappointing date can, for some (personality-disordered) individuals, be upsetting, frightening, frustrating, and disheartening to a degree that it qualifies as stressful. Most of these stressors would not be detected by a life-event scale or structured interview. Thoughts may be damaging as well. The thought, for instance, not to be liked, not to find association with others, not to meet expectations (of oneself or others) can be profoundly distressing. These cognitive events, tucked away in everyday life, are missed if one relies exclusively on the assessment methodology presently accepted.

6. IMPORTANCE OF THE SUBJECTIVE

How diagnostically important is subjective and quasisubjective psychopathology? Our own very preliminary studies suggest that its import is considerable. By way of illustration, I mention three examples.

6.1. Quality of Mood

Quality of mood is a predictor of response to antidepressants in that patients with "unmotivated" mood-lowering proved to be more responsive than patients who saw a clear relation between mood-lowering and adversity (see section 4.1).

In the study on which this statement is based, 87 depressed patients were involved, all of whom were interviewed independently by two clinicians. The first interviewer determined the syndromal type of the depression, using a structured, standardized interview (van Praag et al., 1965). The syndromal diagnosis could be vital depression, personal depression, or mixed depression.* The second interviewer was requested to zero in solely on the quality of the depressed mood and to judge the extent to which the mood state was experienced by the patient as comprehensible or incomprehensible, that is as related or unrelated to a particular life event or to a particular cognitive set.

It was first of all demonstrated that "unmotivated" mood-lowering is by far the most common in vital depression. The reverse is true for "motivated" mood-lowering, which was most commonly found in personal depression (Table 11:1).

Next, we studied whether quality of mood is diagnostically relevant, in that it predicts outcome of treatment with antidepressants. For this purpose, the cohort of 98 depressed patients was split into a group with "motivated" (n = 48) and one with "unmotivated"

---

*For those concepts, see Chapter 3, Section 2.2.1.

TABLE 11:1

Presence or Absence of a Comprehensible Relation Between Mood-Lowering and Causative Factor (as Experienced by the Patient) in Various Syndromal Depression Types

| | | *Syndromal Diagnosis* | | |
	N	*Vital (endogenous, melancholic) Depression*	*Personal (neurotic, dysthymic) Depression*	*Mixed (double) Depression*
"Unmotivated" Depression	39	24	5	10
"Motivated" Depression	48	6	30	12

mood lowering (n = 39). In 11 patients clear categorization proved impossible. Patients were treated with either the tricyclic antidepressant imipramine or the monoamine oxidase inhibitors iproniazid or isocarboxazide. The treatment response was considered as "good" if after six weeks the Hamilton depression score had dropped at least 50 percent, the global depression score had risen to 3.5 or more (a score of 5 representing being symptom-free and a score of 1 being deeply depressed), and the well-being score had risen to 7.5 or higher (a score of 10 representing being back to the premorbid level and a score of 1 feeling miserable).

In the group with "unmotivated" mood-lowering, the percentage of good responders (63 percent) was substantially higher than in the group with "motivated" mood-lowering (31 percent) (Table 11:2). The highest predictive value for a good response had the combined presence of "unmotivated" mood lowering and anhedonia (Table 11:3).

We concluded that quality of mood is a relevant variable in the diagnosis of depression.

TABLE 11:2

The Effect of Antidepressants in Depressions with "Motivated" and "Unmotivated" Mood-Lowering

| | | *Percentage of Patients With Good Response to Antidepressants* | |
	N	Tricyclics	MAO Inhibitors
"Unmotivated" Depression	39	62	65
"Motivated" Depression	48	29	33

TABLE 11:3
Psychopathological Predictors of Antidepressant Response

	Percentage of Patients with Good Response to Antidepressants	
	Tricyclics	MAO Inhibitors
"Unmotivated" Mood-Lowering and Anhedonia	81	82
Both Symptoms Absent	27	22
Anhedonia Present Unmotivated Mood-Lowering Absent	52	49
Anhedonia Absent Unmotivated Mood-Lowering Present	62	65
Anorexia Present Anhedonia Absent Unmotivated Mood-Lowering Absent	30	35
Sleep Disturbances Present Anhedonia Absent Unmotivated Mood-Lowering Absent	49	31

6.2. Ego-syntonic Personality Dysfunctions

A "character neurosis" (as Freud called it) co-occurring with depression is also an important predictor of response to antidepressants. In this form of personality disorder, symptoms are ego-syntonic. They are experienced as part of one's self ("just the way I am") rather than as ego-dystonic (pathological). In a study (van Praag, 1989) of the co-occurrence of character neurosis and depression, we concentrated on the patient's inner experiences, exploring whether his or her personality make-up was experienced as a source of dissatisfaction and displeasure. In Chapter 3, Section 2.5.2, I described the criteria used for the diagnosis of character neurosis. I also mentioned that signs of ego-syntonic personality dysfunctioning were frequently found in depression, as compared to a control group, and that they occurred irrespective of syndromal depression type.

We next studied the significance of character neurosis co-occurring with depression for the outcome of treatment with antidepressants. A group of 52 patients with vital depression was divided into those without (n = 31) and those with (n = 21) signs of character neurosis. Severity of depression was comparable in both groups. All patients were treated with imipramine or the monoamine oxidase inhibiting iproniazid or isocarboxazide. After six weeks, the treatment response was considered to be "good" in 80 percent of those with uncomplicated vital depression and in only 42 percent in the

TABLE 11:4

Depression, Ego-syntonic Personality Disorder, and Response to Antidepressants in Vital (Endogenous, Melancholic) Depression

	N	*Percentage of Patients With Good Response to Antidepressants*	
		Tricyclics	MAO Inhibitors
Depression with ego-syntonic personality disorder	21	36	47
Depression without ego-syntonic personality disorder	31	78	81

group with concurrent character neurosis (Table 11:4). In patients with personal or mixed depression, the factor of character neurosis did not influence the outcome of treatment with antidepressants.

We concluded that character neurosis—a common occurrence in depression—is a relevant variable in the diagnosis of depression because, like quality of mood, it is a factor determining the response to antidepressants. It is also important to diagnose character neurosis properly since it is a major indication for psychotherapy.

6.3. Relative Life Events

Egosyntonic personality dysfunctions are common in panic disorder, and in such patients, the panic attack is frequently preceded by relative life events.

According to the official definition, panic attacks appear "out of the blue," that is without apparent cause. If that were so, psychotherapy, at least psychodynamic forms of psychotherapy, would probably be useless. However, if that criterion would be incorrect, one could expect drug treatment without insight–oriented psychotherapy to be an incomplete treatment.

In a group of 25 patients diagnosed as hyperventilation syndrome and meeting the DSM-III-R criteria of panic disorder, we studied the existence of ego-syntonic personality pathology and the occurrence of life events in the 24 hours prior to panic attacks. Character neurosis was defined as mentioned in Chapter 3, Section 2.5.2. Life events were called absolute if they would have been psychotraumatic for the average, normal individual. We called a life event relative that

TABLE 11:5
Co-occurrence of Panic Disorder, Ego-syntonic Personality Disorder, and Life
Events

| | N | Number of Patients Reporting Life Events | |
		Relative Life Events*	Absolute Life Events*
PANIC DISORDER	25		
With Ego-Syntonic Personality Disorder	19	14	1
Without Ego-Syntonic Personality Disorder	6	1	–
MATCHED NORMAL CONTROLS	25		
With Ego-Syntonic Personality Disorder	3	2	–
Without Ego-Syntonic Personality Disorder	22	–	–

*Having occurred 1–48 hours prior to a panic attack that had been experienced in the two preceding months. In the control group, the two months before the interview were examined.

had led to grave and prolonged distress in a particular individual, but that probably would have done no or only very transient harm to normal individuals. Specifically, a relative life event would have been experienced as inducing or reinforcing feelings of alienation (the incident being, for instance, having been a wallflower at a party), feelings of being rejected (for instance, an unhappy date), or feelings of self-doubt or self-depreciation (precipitated by, for example, a derogatory remark from one's employer).

Signs of ego-syntonic personality pathology were found in 19 of 25 panic disorder patients and 14 of them identified relative life events prior to panic attacks that had occurred in the preceding two months. No relative life events were reported by the patients without demonstrable personality pathology. Ego-syntonic personality pathology and related relative life events were much more common in panic disorder than in a normal control group (Table 11:5). Absolute life events we found to be uncommon prior to panic attacks. Only one patient reported a psychotraumatic event 1–24 hours prior to a panic attack that had occurred in the preceding two months.

We concluded from this study (in a tentative way because of the small sample size) that ego-syntonic personality pathology is common in panic disorder and that in patients with the combined pathology relative life events play a role in the precipitation of panic attacks.

It seems fair to assume that in those patients proper treatment would include insight-oriented psychotherapy.

6.4 Methodology

The three studies reported above illustrate that (quasi-) subjective psychopathology is by no means trivial, might contain predictive information regarding treatment response, and might thus contribute to adequate treatment planning.

We may now ask whether the realm of (quasi-) subjective psychopathology is, in principle, accessible to objective methods or doomed to remain unverifiable, "soft," and speculative. As stated above, I believe a structured, standard interview is unsuitable for exploration of this important domain, as are self-rating scales, which are, in fact, standard interview questions committed to paper. It is conceivable that projective tests could be developed for this purpose, but operationalization of relevant materials and their reliable and reproducible assessment will be problematic.

In the studies discussed above, the experiential issues, i.e. quality of mood, ego-syntonic personality dysfunctions, and relative life events, were studied via a *free* interview. The relevant issues to be rated by the interviewer, however, had been defined, discussed, and illustrated in live interviews in advance. In this manner, we were able to reach an acceptable degree of interrater reliability. Though admittedly preliminary, our findings suggest that the realm of (quasi-) subjective psychopathology is principally accessible in a systematic and reproducible way.

7. CONCLUSIONS

The movement toward objectification in psychiatric diagnosing seems to have come to premature closure and thus threatens to become a withering, rather than fertilizing, force. Stagnation is evident, both in diagnosis and measurement of abnormal behavior. In the process of diagnosing, the obvious is overemphasized, i.e. those psychopathological symptoms that are well delineated and ascertainable with little doubt. As a result, the realm of subjective and quasisubjective psychopathology is seriously neglected. The lack of a separate etiological axis in the DSM-III, moreover, has led to an attenuation of etiological deliberations, particularly of psychogenesis. Detailed scrutiny of psychodevelopmental and environmental determinants of abnormal behavior is not a DSM requirement; neither is an analysis of the interaction between (relative) life events and (ego–syntonic) personality imperfections. No hypothesis is requested regarding the etiological contributions of the axis II diagnosis to the axis I pathology.

That which is not mentioned in the DSM-III carries the odium of irrelevance. In reality, today's diagnostic concepts are no more than first-draft diagnoses, lacking both depth and comprehensiveness. Although the DSM-III is multiaxial, it is, at the same time, unidimensional. This rather profound reductionism is acceptable in early stages of scientific development, but should not be considered as an end point. In the successive DSM editions, symptoms have been moved back and forth; refinement of diagnostic concepts, however, has not been forthcoming. What seems to have happened is premature codification of diagnostic concepts and diagnostic terms. The prevalent diagnostic strategy is to count generally crude psychopathological symptoms. This amounts to serious primitivization of the diagnostic process. I do, of course, not contend that a psychiatric diagnosis should refer to all features relevant in a given case. What I do argue is, that one cannot with impunity ignore important domains of psychopathology in the process of arriving at a diagnosis.

A comparable stagnation has occurred in psychometrics. Many of the measuring instruments developed as long as three decades ago are still in use; I know of few attempts to refine, adjust, or extend them. The recent revision of the MMPI is an admirable exception to the rule. By definition, staying put prevents progress. Imagine where radiology would be if the prevailing *zeitgeist* had frozen methodology at the level where it was a decade or more ago.

I consider the realm of (quasi-) subjective psychopathology to be of crucial, not marginal, diagnostic importance. I believe, moreover, that its manifestations are principally accessible to objective, that is reliable and verifiable, measurement. Hence, sustained attempts should be made to expand and refine diagnostic concepts and corresponding psychometric instruments lest we end up with a severely coarsened psychiatry, obsessed with the obvious, detached from the experiential realm, oblivious of nuance and detail—in truth, a mirror image of the psychiatry from bygone times when the *zeitgeist* demanded individual fine tuning, overriding the need for verifiability. If that were to happen, research psychiatry would have won a Pyrrhic victory.

8. SUMMARY

Objectivity is the catchword in psychiatry today. Symptoms are the major diagnostic currency, particularly the well defined and easily demonstrable ones. As a consequence, subjective psychopathology is insufficiently taken into account in psychiatric diagnosing, whereas instruments to measure these features are virtually absent.

Etiologically, too, it is the obvious that counts, such as definite family loading, demonstrable brain lesions, and life events with "absolute valence." Psychological factors that are more subtle, but for certain individuals not less damaging, such as relative life events, are largely ignored.

This state of affairs is discussed and deplored. The following conclusions are reached: (1) Subjective psychopathology should not be disregarded, lest important diagnostic and therapeutic information be lost; (2) subjective psychopathology is not, by definition, immeasurable and unverifiable, and sustained efforts should be made to develop instruments to measure it.

Postscript

Research has been a quintessential aspect of my life. Hence, I have thoroughly enjoyed psychiatry's turn to empiricism; the critical attitude it developed towards theories and theorizing; its increasing willingness to discard unsubstantiated hypotheses; the mistrust it began to demonstrate towards psychiatric sages and gurus; its willingness, eventually, to admit brain and behavior into mainstream psychiatry, reclaiming for psychiatry a rightful place in the family of medicine; the wisdom it displayed in embracing nonindividual and nonanalytical approaches in psychotherapy, thus expanding the profession's therapeutic reach tremendously; the growth of epidemiology it favored and the methods it adopted to study systematically the relation between individuals and the groups to which they belong, by which psychiatry obtained solid anchorpoints in the social sciences.

This signified major progress and I still thoroughly enjoy this sight. Yet this book has not become a song of praise, but a critical commentary. Optimism and belief in progress are not at variance with critical sense. I wrote this book to draw attention to some adverse effects of the psychiatric revolution that could be detrimental to its very achievements and slow down further advancement.

The domain I have emphasized most is diagnosis, pivotal as it is to all psychiatric research efforts. The classification system nowadays most commonly referred to is the DSM III and its progeny. Its introduction in 1980 was a landmark, in that it provided psychiatry for the first time with a detailed and operationalized taxonomy that was readily accepted throughout the world. As a promoter of research, its significance can hardly be overrated. The enthusiasm with which it was received, however, suppressed the notion that this edifice was raised on a precarious basis, i.e., expert opinion. After the introduction of the DSM III, the next step should have been the initiation of systematic studies specifically geared towards validity issues raised by the diagnostic concepts that had been proposed. This happened only sporadically. The main vehicle for change remained expert opinion, carrying us from one revised edition to the other with no end in sight. This creates havoc in the system—and diagnostic disorder and research are incompatible.

The nosological revival ushered in by the rise of modern biological psychiatry and strongly reinforced by the appearance of the DSM III, set forth "a new-disorder-rush." The number of diagnoses exploded. Non-specific symptoms were inflated to true disorders; a particular etiology was blown up to become the cause of a distinct disorder; a particular course was overvalued to support a novel disease concept. The next step, logically, consisted of the search for the origins, or at least for a marker, of such a "disorder." It comes as no surprise that these efforts produced a flurry of non-reproducible results.

Another harmful consequence of the neo-nosological *zeitgeist* is the disregard for other than nosological classification systems and, in particular, for the dimensional approach. I do not deny that we need a categorization of mental disorders to provide a language for easy clinical communication, but I do, at the same time, maintain that that language is crude, often ambiguous and imprecise, and hence utterly unsuitable for research purposes. The necessity to add a functional/dimensional level to the diagnostic process is acute. On that level, the prevailing syndrome would be dissected into its component parts, i.e. the psychological dysfunctions, each of which is assessed and measured separately. In this manner, a science of psychopathology could eventually be built up. On much shorter notice, biological psychiatry would profit because psychological dysfunctions constitute a behavioral focus that is much better defined and transferable than the disorders presently distinguished ever can be.

The process of objectification of psychopathological phenomena, furthermore, is responsible for considerable losses in diagnostic sophistication. In the urge to ascertain psychiatric symptoms with a fair degree of certainty and precision, the attention of psychiatrists moved firmly towards those phenomena that present themselves unambiguously and that are, preferably, accessible for research assistants with little clinical know-how and interview experience. Naturally, then, the experiential, the interpersonal, the emotional aspects of psychopathology and of premorbid personality functioning fared badly in biological psychiatry. They were pushed aside as diagnostically nonessential. This, it seems to me, is no more than a rationalization for diagnostic impotence. In psychiatry, the realm of the subjective cannot be ignored lest the profession be pauperized past redress. Hence, much more effort should be put into developing methods that permit its systematic evaluation. Psychiatry is just masquerading as a science if important components of the psychopathological spectrum are simply ignored because they remain unaccessible.

The 1990s have been officially designated as the Decade of the Brain and by no less than the President of the USA, George Bush. An unfortunate declaration, in that it authorizes the present inclination to overexpose the views on abnormal behavior obtained from the biological vantage point. As in Kraepelin's days, the hope is alive that from biology will come the redemption that is the key to understanding mental disorder. This viewpoint is a misconception. Abnormal behavior will never be fully understood in a biological frame of reference, dissociated from psychological and social considerations. The brain dysfunctions underlying abnormal behavior will never be fully understood if the disrupting effects of psychological and social forces are disregarded. For brain and behavior research to be productive, the spiritual aspects of the human condition have to be systematically explored and analyzed. Psychiatry should not be "medicalized," if that expression means its exclusive orientation on biology and severance of its roots in the psychological and social sciences. In doing that, we would forgo our very identity, not only as researchers, but as diagnosticians and therapists as well, and the human mind and its ailments would have been simplified beyond recognition.

The progress psychiatry has made over the past 25 years is astonishing and admirable, and I am astonished and I do admire. Let there be no misunderstanding about that. Yet this book does not highlight the revenues, but presents an analysis of the price that had to be paid to come so far. In other words, what I did was to highlight the expense side of the ledger in order to suggest ways to keep it down to a minimum. I undertook this task not to spoil the excitement that permeates psychiatry today, but to warn against over-excitement, a process that could damage the very generators of the jubilation.

May the rest not be silence.

References

Ainaes, R., & Torgensen, S. (1988) DSM-III symptom disorders (Axis I) and personality disorders (Axis II) in an outpatient population. *Acta Psychiatrica Scandinavia, 78*, 348–355.

Akil H., Watson, E.J., Young, E., Lewis, M.E., Khachaturian, H., & Walker, J.M. (1984) Endogenous opiods: Biology and function. *Annual Review of Neuroscience, 7*, 223–225.

Akiskal, H.S., Bitar, A.H., Puzantian, V.R., Rosenthal, T.L., & Walker, P.W. (1978) The nosological status of neurotic depression. *Archives of General Psychiatry, 35*, 756–766.

Andreasen, N.C. (1982) Negative symptoms in schizophrenia. *Archives of General Psychiatry, 39*, 784–788.

Andreasen, N.C. (1988) Brain imaging: Applications in psychiatry. *Science, 239*, 1381–1388.

Andreasen, N.C. (1989) The American concept of schizophrenia. *Schizophrenia Bulletin, 15*, 519–531.

Andreasen, N.C., & Flaum, M. (1991) Schizophrenia: The characteristic symptoms. *Schizophrenia Bulletin, 17*, 27–49.

Andreasen, N., Flaum, M., Swayze II, V.W., Tyrell, G., & Arndt, S. (1990) Positive and negative symptoms in schizophrenia. *Archives of General Psychiatry, 47*, 615–621.

Andreasen, N.C. & Olsen, S. (1982) Negative versus positive schizophrenia. *Archives of General Psychiatry, 39*, 789–794.

Andreasen, N.C., Olsen, S.A., Dennert, J.W., & Smith, M.S. (1982) Ventricular enlargement in schizophrenia: Relationship to positive and negative symptoms. *American Journal of Psychiatry, 139*, 297–302.

Angrist, B., Rotrosen, J., & Gershon, S. (1980) Differential effects of amphetamine and neuroleptics on negative vs. positive symptoms in schizophrenia. *Psychopharmacology, 72,* 17–19.

Angst,J., Bastrup,P., Grof, H., Hippius, H., Poldinger, W., & Weis, P. (1973) The course of monopolar depression and biopolar psychoses. *Psychiatrica Neurologia Neurochirurgia, 76,* 489–500.

Antonovsky, A., Maoz, B., Dowty, N., & Wijsenbeek, H. (1971) Twenty-five years later: A limited study of the sequelae of the concentration camp experience. *Social Psychiatry, 6,* 186–193.

Apter, A., Kotler, M., Sevy, S., Plutchik, R., Brown, S.L., Foster, H., Hillbrand, M., Korn, M.L., & van Praag, H.M. (1991) Correlates of risk of suicide in violent and nonviolent psychiatric patients. *American Journal of Psychiatry, 148,* 883–887.

Apter, A., van Praag, H.M., Plutchik, R., Sevy, S., Korn, M., & Brown, S.L. (1990) Interrelationships among anxiety, aggression, impulsivity and mood: A serotonergically linked cluster. *Psychiatry Research, 32,* 191–199.

Arango, V., Ernsberger, P., Marzuk, P.M., Chen, J-S., Tierney, H., Stanley, M., Reis, D.J., & Mann, J. (1990) Autoradiographic demonstration of increased serotonin 5-HT2 and beta adrenergic receptor binding sites in the brain of suicide victims. *Archives of General Psychiatry, 47,* 1038–1047.

Archer, M. (1987) The post-viral syndrome: A review. *Journal of the Royal College of General Practitioners, 37,* 212–214.

Arndt, S., Alliger, R.J., & Andreasen, N.C. (1991) The distinction of positive and negative symptoms. The failure of a two-dimensional model. *British Journal of Psychiatry, 158,* 317–322.

Aronson, T.A. (1987) Is panic disorder a distinct diagnostic entity? *The Journal of Nervous and Mental Disease, 175,* 584–594.

Arora, R.C.,& Meltzer, H.Y. (1989) Increased serotonin (5–HT2) receptor binding as measured by H-lysergic acid diethylamide (3H-LSD) in the blood platelets of depressed patients. *Life Sciences, 44,* 734–735.

Asakura, M., Tsukamoto, T., Kubota, H., Imafuku, I.M., Nishizaki, J., Sata, A., Shinbo, K., & Hasegawa, K. (1987) Role of serotonin in the regulation of β-adrenoceptors by antidepressants. *European Journal of Pharmacology, 141,* 95–100.

Asberg, M., Nordstrom, P., & Traskman-Bendz, L. (1986) Biological factors in suicide. In: A. Roy (Ed.), *Suicide.* Baltimore: Wilkins and Wilkins.

Asberg, M., Schalling, D., Traskman-Bendz, L., & Wagner, A. (1987) Psychobiology of suicide, impulsivity, and related phenomena. In: H.Y.

Meltzer (Ed.), *Psychopharmacology: The Third Generation of Progress*. New York: Raven Press.

Asberg, M., Traskman, L., & Thoren, P. (1976) 5-HIAA in the cerebrospinal fluid: A biochemical suicide predictor? *Archives of General Psychiatry, 33*, 1193–1197.

Ashton, H. (1987) *Brain or Systems Disorders and Psychotropic Drugs*. Oxford: Oxford University Press.

Asnis, G.M., Halbreich, U., Rabinovich, H., Ryan, N.D., Sachar, E.J., Nelson, B., Puig-Antich, J., & Novacenko, H. (1985) The cortisol response to desipramine in endogenous depressives and normal controls: Preliminary findings. *Psychiatry Research, 14*, 225–233.

Bahnson, C.B., & Smith, K. (1975) Autonomic changes in a multiple personality. *Psychosomatic Medicine, 37*, 85–86.

Banki, C.M. (1977a) Correlation between CSF metabolites and psychomotor activity in affective disorders. *Journal of Neurochemistry, 28*, 255–257.

Banki, C.M. (1977b) Correlation of anxiety and related symptoms with cerebrospinal fluid 5-hydroxyindoleacetic acid in depressed women. *Journal of Neural Transmission, 41*, 135–143.

Banki, C.M., Molnar, G., & Vojnik, M. (1981) Cerebrospinal fluid amine metabolites, tryptophan and clinical parameters in depression. *Journal of Affective Disorders, 3*, 91–99.

Barlow, D.H. (1988) *Anxiety and its Disorders: The Nature and Treatment of Anxiety and Panic*. New York: Guilford Press.

Barlow, D.H., DiNardo, P.A., Vermilyea, B.B., Vermilyea, J.A., & Blanchard, E.B. (1986) Co-morbidity and depression among the anxiety disorders: Issues in classification and diagnosis. *Journal of Nervous and Mental Disease, 174*, 63–72.

Bartholini, G., Haefely, W., Jalfre, M., Keller, H.H., & Pletscher, A. (1972) Effects of clozapine on cerebral catecholaminergic neurone systems. *British Journal of Pharmacology, 46*, 736–740.

Bartholini, G., Keller, H.H., & Pletscher, A. (1973) Effect of neuroleptics on endogenous norepinephrine in rat brain. *Neuropharmacology, 12*, 751–756.

Bateson, G., Jackson, D., Haley, J., & Weakland, J. (1956) Towards a theory of schizophrenia. *Behavioral Science, 1*, 251–264.

Beasley Jr., C.M., Dornseif, B.E., Bosomworth, J.C., Sayler, M.E., Rampey Jr., A.H., Heiligenstein, J.H., Thompson, V.L., Murphy, D.J., & Masica, D.N. (1991) Fluoxetine and suicide: A meta-analysis of controlled trials of treatment for depression. *British Medical Journal, 303*, 685–692.

Bell, D.S., & Bell, K.M. (1988) The chronic fatigue syndrome. *Annals of Internal Medicine, 108,* 167.

Bell, E.J., Riding, M.H., & McCartney, R.A. (1988) Coxsackie B viruses and myalgic encephalomyelitis. *Journal of the Royal Society of Medicine, 81,* 329–331.

Berg, E., Lindelius, R., Petterson, U., & Salum, I. (1983) Schizoaffective psychoses. *Acta Psychiatrica Scandinavica, 67,* 389–398.

Bick, P.A. (1986) Seasonal major affective disorder. *American Journal of Psychiatry, 143,* 90–91.

Bielski, R.J., & Friedel, R.O. (1976) Prediction of tricyclic antidepressant response. *Archives of General Psychiatry, 33,* 1479–1489.

Bilder, R.M., Sukdeb, M., Rieder, R.O., & Pandurangi, A.K. (1985) Symptomatic and neuropsychological components of defect states. *Schizophrenia Bulletin, 11,* 409–419.

Bioulac, B., Benezich, M., Renaud, B., Noel, B., & Roche, D. (1980) Serotonergic functions in the 47, XYZ syndrome. *Biological Psychiatry, 15,* 917–923.

Blehar, M.C., & Lewy, A.J. (1990) Seasonal mood disorders: Consensus and controversy. *Psychopharmacology Bulletin, 26,* 465–494.

Blehar, M.C., & Rosenthal, N.E. (1989) Seasonal affective disorders and phototherapy. *Archives of General Psychiatry, 46,* 469–474.

Bleuler, E. (1911) *Dementia praecox oder die Gruppe der Schizophrenien.* Leipzig: F. Deuticke.

Bleuler, M. (1978) *The Schizophrenic Disorders: Long-term Patient and Family Studies.* New Haven: Yale University Press.

Bliss, E.L. (1983) Multiple personalities, related disorders and hypnosis. *American Journal of Clinical Hypnosis, 26,* 114–123.

Bogerts, B., Meertz, E., & Schonfeldt-Bausch, R. (1985) Basal ganglia and limbic system pathology in schizophrenia. *Archives of General Psychiatry, 42,* 784–791.

Boor, M. (1982) The multiple personality epidemic. *Journal of Nervous and Mental Disease, 170,* 302–304.

Bouman, T.K., Niemantsverdiet-van Kampen, J.G., Ormel, J., & Slooff, C.J. (1986) The effectiveness of lithium prophylaxis in bipolar and unipolar depressions and schizo-affective disorders. *Journal of Affective Disorders, 11,* 275–280.

Boyd, J.H., Burke, Jr., J.D., Gruenberg, E.,Holzer, III, C.E., Rae, D.S., George, L.K., Karno, M., Stoltzman, R., McEvoy, L., & Nestadt, G. (1984) Exclusion criteria of DSM-III. A study of co-occurrence of hierarchy-free syndromes. *Archives of General Psychiatry, 41,* 983–989.

Brewerton, T.D. (1991) Fluoxetine-induced suicidality, serotonin, and seasonality. *Biological Psychiatry, 30,* 190–196.

Brockington, I.F., & Leff, J.P. (1978) Definitions of schizophrenia: Concordance and prediction of outcome. *Psychological Medicine, 8,* 387–398.

Brown, W.A. (1988) Predictors of placebo response in depression. *Psychopharmacology Bulletin, 24,* 14–17.

Brown, W.A. (1990) Is light treatment a placebo? *Psychopharmacology Bulletin, 26,* 527–530.

Brown, G.L., Ebert, M.E., Goyer, P.F., Jimerson, D.C., Klein, W.J., Bunney, W.E., & Goodwin, F.K. (1982) Aggression, suicide and serotonin: Relationships to CSF amine metabolites. *American Journal of Psychiatry, 139,* 741–746.

Brown, G.L., Goodwin, F.K., Ballenger, J.C., Goyer, P.F., & Major, L.F. (1979) Aggression in humans correlates with cerebrospinal fluid metabolites. *Psychiatry Research, 1,* 131–139.

Brown, G.W., Ni Bhrolchain, M., & Harris, T.O. (1979) Psychotic and neurotic depression. Part 3. Aetiological and background factors. *Journal of Affective Disorders, 1,* 195–211.

Brown, J.W., & Harris, T.O. (1978) *Social Origins of Depression.* London, Tavistock.

Brown, R., Colter, N., Corsellis, J.A.N., Crow, T.J., Frith, C.D., Jagoe, R., Johnstone, E.C., & Marsh, L. (1986) Postmortem evidence of structural brain changes in schizophrenia. *Archives of General Psychiatry, 43,* 36–42.

Brown, S.L., Bleich, A., & van Praag, H.M. (1991) The monoamine hypothesis of depression: The case for serotonin. In: S.L. Brown & H.M. van Praag (Eds.), *The Role of Serotonin in the Psychiatric Disorders,* pp. 91–128. New York: Brunner/Mazel.

Bruton, C.J., Crow, T.J., Frith, C.D., Johnstone, E.C., Owens, D.G.C., & Roberts, G.W. (1990) Schizophrenia and the brain: A prospective clinico-neuropathology study. *Psychological Medicine, 20,* 285–304.

Burki, H.R., Ruch, W., Asper, H., Baggiolini, M., & Stille, G. (1974) Effect of single and repeated administration of clozapine on the metabolism of dopamine and noradrenaline in the brain of the rat. *European Journal of Pharmacology, 27,* 180–190.

Buus Lassen, J. (1974) Evidence of noradrenaline (NA)—and dopamine (DA)—receptor blockade by clozapine. *Journal of Pharmacology, 5,* 14.

Caine, E.D., & Joynt, R.J. (1986) Neuropsychiatry again. *Archives of Neurology, 43,* 325–329.

Carpenter, W.T., Heinrichs, D.W., & Wagman, A.M.I. (1988) Deficit and nondeficit forms of schizophrenia: The concept. *American Journal of Psychiatry, 145,* 578–583.

Carpenter, W.T., Strauss, J.S., & Mulec, S. (1973) Are there pathognomic symptoms in schizophrenia? *Archives of General Psychiatry, 28,* 846–852.

Carroll, B.J. (1983) Neurobiologic dimensions of depression and mania. In: J. Angst (Ed.), *The Origins of Depression: Current Concepts and Approaches.* New York: Springer Verlag.

Carroll, B.J. (1984) Problems with diagnostic criteria for depression. *Journal of Clinical Psychiatry, 45,* 14–18.

Ceulemans, D.L.S., Hoppenbrouwers, M.I.J.A., Gelders, Y.G., & Reyntjens, A.J.M. (1985) The influence of ritanserin, a serotonin antagonist, in anxiety disorders: A double-blind placebo-controlled study versus lorazepam. *Pharmacopsychiatry, 18,* 303–305.

Charney, D.S., Woods, S.W., Goodman, W.K., & Heninger, G.R. (1987) Serotonin function in anxiety. II. Effects of the serotonin agonist MCPP in panic disorder patients and healthy subjects. *Psychopharmacology, 92,* 14–24.

Checkley, S.A., Glass, I.B., Thompson, C., Corn, T., & Robinson, P. (1984) The GH response to clonidine in endogenous as compared with reactive depression. *Psychological Medicine, 14,* 773–777.

Cleghorn, J.M., Garnett, E.S., Nahmias, C., Firnau, G., Brown, G.M., Kaplan, R., Szechtman, H., & Szechtman, B. (1989) Increased frontal and reduced parietal glucose metabolism in acute untreated schizophrenia. *Psychiatry Research, 28,* 119–133.

Cloninger, C.R. (1986) A unified biosocial theory of personality and its role in the development of anxiety states. *Psychiatric Development, 3,* 167–226.

Cloninger, C.R. (1987) A systematic method for clinical description and classification of personality variants. *Archives of General Psychiatry, 44,* 573–588.

Coccaro, E.F. (1989) Central serotonin and impulsive aggression. *British Journal of Psychiatry, 155,* 52–62.

Coccaro, E.F., Siever, L.F., Klar, H.M., Maurer, G., Cochrane, K., Cooper, T.B., Mohs, R.C., & Davis, K.L. (1989) Serotonergic studies in patients with affective and personality disorders. *Archives of General Psychiatry, 46,* 587–599.

Cohn, J.B., Bowden, C.L., Fisher, J.G., & Rodos, J.J. (1986) Double-blind comparison of buspirone and clorazepate in anxious outpatients. *The American Journal of Medicine, 80,* 10–16. (Suppl 3B).

Conte, H.R., Plutchik, R., Wild, K.V., & Karasu, T.B. (1986) Combined psychotherapy and pharmacotherapy for depression. *Archives of General Psychiatry, 43,* 471–479.

Coons, P.M., Bowman, E.S., & Milstein, V. (1988) Multiple personality disorder. A clinical investigation of 50 cases. *The Journal of Nervous and Mental Disease, 176,* 519–527.

Coons, P.M., Milstein, V., & Marley, C. (1982) EEG studies of two multiple personalities and a control. *Archives of General Psychiatry, 39,* 823–825.

Coryell, W., & Zimmerman, M. (1988a) The heritability of schizophrenia and schizoaffective disorder. *Archives of General Psychiatry, 45,* 323–327.

Coryell, W., & Zimmerman, M. (1988b) Diagnosis and outcome in schizo-affective depression: A replication. *Journal of Affective Disorders, 15,* 21–27.

Costa, E. & Guidotti, A. (1985) Commentary. Endogenous ligands for benzodiazepine recognition sites. *Biochemical Pharmacology, 34,* 3399–3403.

Costall, B., Domeney, A.M., Gerrard, P.A., Kelly, M.E., & Naylor, R.J. (1988) Zacopride: Anxiolytic profiles in rodent and primate models of anxiety. *Journal of Pharmacy and Pharmacology, 49,* 302–305.

Cowley, G., Hager, M., & Joseph, N. (1990) Chronic fatigue syndrome. *Newsweek.* November 12, 34–40.

Crow, T.J. (1973) Catecholamine-containing neurones and electrical self-stimulation: 2. A theoretical interpretation and some psychiatric implications. *Psychological Medicine, 3,* 66–73.

Crow, T.J. (1977) A general catecholamine hypothesis. *Neuroscience Research Progress Bulletin, 15,* 195–205.

Crow, T.J. (1980) Molecular pathology of schizophrenia: More than one disease process? *British Medical Journal, 280,* 66–68.

Crow, T.J. (1984) A re-evaluation of the viral hypothesis: Is psychosis the result of retroviral integration at a site close to the cerebral dominance gene? *British Journal of Psychiatry, 145,* 243–253.

Crow, T.J., & Deakin, J.F.W. (1985) Neurohormonal transmission, behaviour and mental disorder. In: M. Shepherd (Ed.), *Handbook of Psychiatry, Part 5.* Cambridge: Cambridge University Press.

Crowe, R.R., Noyes, Jr., R., Pauls, D.L., Slymen, D. (1983) A family study of panic disorder. *Archives of General Psychiatry, 40,* 1065–1069.

Curzon, G., Hutson, P.H., Kantamaneni, B.D., Sahakian, B.J., & Sarna, G.S. (1985) 3,4-Dihydroxyphenylethylamine and 5-hydroxytryptamine metabolism in the rat: Acidic metabolites in cisternal cerebrospinal fluid before and after giving probenecid. *Journal of Neurochemistry, 45,* 508–513.

Dalen, P., & Hays, P. (1990) Aetiological heterogeneity of schizophrenia:

The problem and the evidence. *British Journal of Psychiatry, 157,* 119–122.

Davis, K.L., & Greenwald, B. (1991) Biology of schizophrenia. In: K. Davis, H. Klar & J.T. Coyle (Eds.), *Foundations of Psychiatry.* Philadelphia: W.B. Saunders.

Davison, K., & Bagley, C. (1969) Schizophrenia-like psychoses associated with organic disorders of the CNS: A review of the literature. In: R.N. Herrington (Ed.), Current problems in neuropsychiatry. *British Journal of Psychiatry Special Publications.*

Den Boer, J.A., & Westenberg, H.G.M. (1988) Effect of a serotonin and noradrenaline uptake inhibitor in panic disorder: A double-blind comparative study with fluoxamine and maprotiline. *International Clinical Psychopharmacology, 3,* 59–74.

Den Boer, J.A., & Westenberg, H.G.M. (1990) Serotonin function in panic disorders: A double-blind placebo-controlled study of fluvoxamine and ritanserin. *Psychopharmacology, 102,* 85–94.

Den Boer, J.A., Westenberg, H.G.M., Kamerbeek, W.D.J., Verhoeven, W.M.A., & Kahn, R.S. (1987) Effect of serotonin uptake inhibitors in anxiety disorders: A double-blind comparison of clomipramine and fluvoxamine. *International Clinical Psychopharmacology, 2,* 21–32.

Denicoff, K.D., Rubinow, D.R., Papa, M.Z., Simpson, C., Seipp, C.A., Lotze, M.T., Chang, A.E., Rosenstein, D., & Rosenberg, S.A. (1987) The neuropsychiatric effects of treatment with interleukin-2 and lymphokine-activated killer cells. *Annals of Internal Medicine, 107,* 293–300.

de Ruiter, C., Ruken, H., Garssen, B., van Schaik, A., & Kraaimaat, F. (1989) Comorbidity among the anxiety disorders. *Journal of Anxiety Disorders, 3,* 57–68.

Detera-Wadleigh, S.D., Berrettini, W.H., Goldin, L.R., Boorman, D., Anderson, S., & Gershon, E.S. (1987) Close linkage of c-Harvey-ras-I and the insulin gene to affective disorder is ruled out in three North American pedigrees. *Nature, 325,* 806–808.

Deutsch, S.I., & Davis, K.L. (1983) Schizophrenia: A review of diagnostic and biological issues I. Diagnosis and Prognosis. *Hospital and Community Psychiatry, 34,* 313–322.

Devau, G., Multon, M.F., Pujol, J.F., & Buda, M. (1987) Inhibition of tyrosine hydroxylase activity by serotonin in explants of newborn rat locus ceruleus. *Journal of Neurochemistry, 49,* 665–670.

DeWied, D. (1978) Psychopathology as a neuropeptide dysfunction. In: J.M. van Ree & L. Terenius (Eds.), *Characteristics and Functions of Opioids.* North Holland: Biomedical Press.

DeWied, D., Kovacs, J.L., Bohus, B., Van Ree, J.M., & Griven, H.M. (1978) Neuroleptic activity of the neuropeptide β-LPH-62-77 ([destyr]-β-endorphin; DTγE). *European Journal of Pharmacology, 49*, 427–436.

Dietzel, M., Saletu, B., Lesch, O.M., Sieghart, W., & Schjerve, M. (1986) Light treatment in depressive illness. *European Neurology, 25*, 93–103.

DiNardo, P.A., & Barlow, D.H. (1990) Syndrome and symptom co-morbidity in the anxiety disorders. In: J.D. Maser & C.R. Cloninger (Eds.), *Comorbidity in Anxiety and Mood Disorders.* Washington, D.C.: American Psychiatric Press.

Doran, A., Pickar, D., Boronow, J., Breier, A., Wolkowitz, O., & Goodwin, F. (1985) CT scans in schizophrenia patients, medical and normal controls: Replication and new findings abstracted (p. 140). American College of Neuropsychopharmacology Annual Meeting: Abstracts of Panels and Posters.

Dunner, D.L., Ishiki, D., Avery, D.H., Wilson, L.G., & Hyde, T.S. (1986) Effect of alprazolam and diazepam on anxiety and panic attacks on panic disorder: A controlled study. *Journal of Clinical Psychiatry, 47*, 458–460.

Eastwood, M.R., & Peacocke, J. (1976) Seasonal patterns of suicide, depression and electroconvulsive therapy. *British Journal of Psychiatry, 129*, 472–475.

Eastwood, M.R., & Stiasny, S. (1978) Psychiatric disorder, hospital admission, and season. *Archives of General Psychiatry, 35*, 769–771.

Eaton, W.W., Sigal, J.J., & Weinfeld, M. (1982) Impairment in holocaust survivors after 33 years: Data from an unbiased community sample. *American Journal of Psychiatry, 139*, 773–777.

Egeland, J.A., Gerhard, D.S., Pauls, D.L., Sussex, J.N., Kidd, K.K., Allen, C.R., Hoffstetter, A.M., & Housman, D.E. (1987) Bipolar affective disorders linked to DNA markers on chromosome 11. *Nature, 325*, 783–787.

Egeland, J.A., & Hoffstetter, A.M. (1983) Amish study. I. Affective disorder among the Amish 1976–1980. *American Journal of Psychiatry, 140*, 56–61.

Elk, R., Dickman, B.J., & Teggin, A.F. (1986) Depression in schizophrenia: A study of prevalence and treatment. *British Journal of Psychiatry, 149*, 228–229.

Ellenberger, H.F. (1970) *The Discovery of the Unconscious.* New York: Basic Books.

Endicott, J., Nee,J., Cohen, J., Fleiss, J., Williams, J.B.W., & Simon, R.

(1982) Diagnostic criteria for schizophrenia: Reliabilities and agreement between systems. *Archives of General Psychiatry, 39*, 884–889.

Endicott, J., Nee, J., Cohen,J., Fleiss, J.L., & Simon, R. (1986) Diagnosis of schizophrenia. *Archives of General Psychiatry, 43*, 13–19.

Endicott, J., & Spitzer, R.L. (1978) A diagnostic interview. The schedule for affective disorders and schizophrenia. *Archives of General Psychiatry, 35*, 837–844.

Epstein, H. (1979) *Children of the Holocaust. Conversations with Sons and Daughters of Survivors.* New York: J.P. Putnam's Sons.

Eriksson, E., Westberg, P., Alling, C., Thuresson, K., & Modigh, K. (1991) Cerebrospinal fluid levels of monoamine metabolites in panic disorder. *Psychiatry Research, 36*, 243–251.

Evans, L., Kenardy, J., Schneider, P., & Hoey, H. (1986) Effect of a selective serotonin uptake inhibitor in agoraphobia with panic attacks. *Acta Psychiatrica Scandinavica, 73*, 49–53.

Evans, L., & Moore, G. (1981) The treatment of phobic anxiety by zimeldine. *Acta Psychiatrica Scandinavica, 63*, (Suppl 290), 342–345.

Eysenck, H.J. (1947) *Dimensions of Personality.* London: Routlege & Kegan Paul.

Faergeman, P.M. (1963) *Psychogenic Psychoses.* London: Butterworth.

Fahy, T.A. (1988) The diagnosis of multiple personality disorder. A critical review. *British Journal of Psychiatry, 153*, 597–606.

Fahy, T.A., Abas, M., & Brown, J.C. (1989) Multiple personality. A symptom of psychiatric disorder. *British Journal of Psychiatry, 154*, 99–101.

Fallon, I.R., Boyd, J.L., McGill, C.W., Razani, J., Moss, H.B., & Gilderman, A.M. (1982) Family management and the prevention of exacerbation of schizophrenia. *New England Journal of Medicine, 306*, 1437–1440.

Farmer, A., Jackson, R., McGuffin, P., & Storey, P. (1987) Cerebral ventricular enlargements in chronic schizophrenia: Consistencies and contradictions. *British Journal of Psychiatry, 150*, 324–330.

Fava, G.A., Grandi, S., Canestrari, R., & Molnar, G. (1990) Prodromal symptoms in primary major depressive disorder. *Journal of Affective Disorders, 19*, 149–152.

Fawcett, J., Clark, D.C., Scheftner, W.A., & Gibbons, R.D. (1983) Assessing anhedonia in psychiatric patients. The pleasure scale. *Archives of General Psychiatry, 40*, 79–84.

Feighner, J.P., Robins, E., Guze, S.B., Woodruff, R.A., Winokur, G., & Munoz, R. (1972) Diagnostic criteria for use in psychiatric research. *Archives of General Psychiatry, 25*, 57–63.

Feinberg, M., & Carroll, B.J. (1982) Separation of subtypes of depression using discriminant analysis. I. Separation of unipolar endogenous depression from non-endogenous depression. *British Journal of Psychiatry, 140,* 384–391.

Ferron, A., Descarries, L., & Reader, T.A. (1982) Altered neuronal responsiveness to biogenic amines in rat cerebral cortex after serotonin denervation or depletion. *Brain Research, 231,* 93–108.

Feuerstein, T.J., & Hertting, G. (1986) Serotonin (5-HT) enhances hippocampal noradrenaline (NA) release: Evidence for facilitatory 5-HT receptors within the CNS. *Nanunyn-Schmiedeberg's Archives of Pharmacology, 333,* 191–197.

Fink, M. (1979) *Convulsive therapy. Theory and practice.* New York: Raven Press.

Foulds, J.A. (1976) *The Hierarchical Nature of Personal Illness.* London: Academic Press.

Frances, A., Pincus, H.A., Widiger, T.A., David, W.W., & First, M.B. (1990) DSM-IV: Work in progress. *American Journal of Psychiatry, 147,* 1439–1448.

Franklin, K.B.J. (1978) Catecholamines and self-stimulation: Reward and performance effects dissociated. *Pharmacology, Biochemistry, and Behavior, 9,* 813–820.

Freed, C.R., & Yamamoto, B.K. (1985) Regional brain dopamine metabolism: A marker for the speed, direction and posture of moving animals. *Science, 229,* 62.

Freeman, H. (1988) Progress in antidepressant therapy. Fluoxetine: A comprehensive overview. *British Journal of Psychiatry, 153,* 1–112. (Suppl 3).

Friedman, M., & Rosenman, R. (1959) Association of specific overt behavior pattern with blood and cardiovascular findings. *Journal of the American Medical Association, 169,* 1286–1291.

Frith, C.K., Dowdy, J., Ferrier, I.N., & Crow, T.J. (1985) Selective impairment of paired associate learning after administration of a centrally-acting adrenergic agonist (clonidine). *Psychopharmacology, 87,* 490–493.

Fuccila, J.C. (1990) Commedia Dell'arte. *Encyclopedia Americana, 7,* 377–378.

Fuenmayor, L.D., & Bermudez, M. (1985) Effect of the cerebral tryptaminergic system on the turnover of dopamine in the striatum of the rat. *Journal of Neurochemistry, 44,* 670–674.

Garfield, E. (1988) Current research on seasonal affective disorder and phototherapy. *Current Contents Life Science, 31,* 3–9.

Garvey, M.J., Wesner, R., & Godes, M. (1988) Comparison of seasonal and nonseasonal affective disorders. *American Journal of Psychiatry, 145,* 100–102.

Gay, M., & Shulman, S. (1978) Comparison of children of holocaust survivors with children of the general population of Israel: Are children of Holocaust survivors more disturbed than others? *Mental Health and Society, 5,* 252–256.

Gelder, M.G. (1986) Panic attacks: New approaches to an old problem. *British Journal of Psychiatry, 149,* 346–352.

George, A., & Soloff, P.H. (1986) Schizotypal symptoms in patients with borderline personality disorders. *American Journal of Psychiatry, 143,* 212–215.

Gillespie, R.D. (1929) The clinical differentiation of types of depression. *Guy's Hospital Reports, 79,* 306–344.

Glennon, R.A., Ismaiel, A.E., McCarthy, B.G., & Peroutka, S.J. (1989) Binding of arylpiperazines to 5-HT3 serotonin receptors: Results of a structure affinity study. *European Journal of Pharmacology, 168,* 387–392.

Goetz, K., & van Kammen, D. (1986) Computerized axial tomography scans and subtypes of schizophrenia: A review of the literature. *Journal of Nervous and Mental Disease, 174,* 31–41.

Gold, D., Bowden, R., Sixbey, J., Riggs, R., Katon, W.J., Ashley, R., Obrigewitch, R., & Corey, L. (1990) Chronic fatigue. *Journal of the American Medical Association, 264,* 48–53.

Golden, C., Moses, J., Zelazowski, R., Graber, B., Zatz, L., Horvath, T., & Berger, P. (1980) Cerebral ventricular size and neuropsychological battery. *Archives of General Psychiatry, 37,* 619–623.

Gonzalez-Heydrich, J., & Peroutka, S.J. (1990) Serotonin receptor and reuptake sites: Pharmacologic significance. *Journal of Clinical Psychiatry, 51,* (Suppl. 4) 5–12.

Goodwin, F.K., & Jamison, K.R. (1990) *Manic Depressive Illness.* New York: Oxford University Press.

Goodwin, F.K., Murphy, D.L., Brodie, H.K.H., & Bunney, W.E. (1970) L-DOPA, catecholamines and behaviour: A clinical and biochemical study in depressed patients. *Biological Psychiatry, 2,* 341–366.

Goodwin, F.K., & Post, R.M. (1983) 5-hydroxytryptamine and depression: A model for the interaction of normal variances and pathology. *British Journal of Clinical Pharmacology, 15,* 393–405.

Greaves, G.B. (1980) Multiple personality: 165 years after Mary Reynolds. *Journal of Nervous and Mental Disease, 168,* 577–596.

Green, A.R., & Deakin, J.F.W. (1980) Brain noradrenaline depletion prevents ECS-induced enhancement of serotonin- and dopamine-mediated behaviour. *Nature, 285,* 232–233.

Gross, S. (1988) The relationship of severity of the Holocaust conditions to survivors' child-rearing abilities and their offsprings' mental health. *Family Therapy, 15,* 211–222.

Guesella, J.F., Wexler, N.S., Conneally, P.M., Naylor, S.L., Anderson, M.A., Tanzi, R.E., Watkins, P.C., Ottina, K., Wallace, M.R., Sakaguchi, A.Y., Young, A.B., Shoulson, I., Bonilla, E., & Martin, J.B. (1983) A polymorphic DNA marker genetically linked to Huntington's disease. *Nature, 306,* 234–238.

Guldberg, C.A., Dahl, A.A., Hansen, H., & Bergem, M. (1990) Predictative value of the four good prognostic features in the DSM III-R schizophreniform disorder. *Acta Psychiatrica Scandinavica, 82,* 23–25.

Gurney, C., Roth, M., Garside, R.F., Kerr, T.A., & Schapira, K. (1972) Studies in the classification of affective disorders. The relationship between anxiety states and depressive illness II. *British Journal of Psychiatry, 121,* 162–166.

Hamilton, M. (1960) A rating scale for depression. *Journal of Neurology, Neurosurgery, & Psychiatry, 23,* 56–62.

Hamilton, M. (1982) Symptoms and assessment of depression. In: E.S. Paykel (Ed.), *Handbook of Affective Disorders.* Edinburgh: Churchill Livingstone.

Hanksworth, H., & Schwarz, T. (1977) *The Five of Me.* New York: Pocket Books.

Harding, C.M., Brooks, G.W., Ashikaga, T., Strauss, J.D., & Breier, A.A. (1987) The Vermont longitudinal study of persons with severe mental illness-1: Methodology, study sample, and overall status 32 years later. *American Journal of Psychiatry, 144,* 718–726.

Harding, C.M., & Strauss, J.S. (1984) How serious is schizophrenia? Comments on prognosis. *Biological Psychiatry, 19,* 1597–1600.

Hardy, D.W., Daghestani, A.N., & Egan, W.H. (1988) Multiple personality disorder: Failure to diagnose and the potential for malpractice liability. *Psychiatric Annals, 18,* 543–548.

Heal, D.J., Philpot, K.M., O'Shaughnessy, K.M., & Davies, C.L. (1986) The influence of central noradrenergic function on 5-HT2-mediated head-twitch responses in mice: Possible implications for the actions of antidepressant drugs. *Psychopharmacology, 89,* 414–420.

Heim, M. (1988) Zur effizienz der bright-light-therapie bei zyklothymen achsensyndromen –eine cross-over studie. *Psychiatrie, Neurologie und Medizinische Psychologie, 40,* 269–277.

Herman, J.B., Rosenbaum, J.F., & Brotman, A.W. (1987) The alprazolam to clonazepam switch for the treatment of panic disorder. *Journal of Clinical Psychopharmacology, 7,* 175–178.

Heston, L.L. (1966) Psychiatric disorders in foster home reared children of schizophrenic mothers. *British Journal of Psychiatry, 112*, 819–825.

Hickie, I., Lloyd, A., Wakefield, D., & Parker, G. (1990) The psychiatric status of patients with the chronic fatigue syndrome. *British Journal of Psychiatry, 156*, 534–540.

Hirschfeld, R., Klerman, G.L., Clayton, P.J., Keller, M.B., McDonald-Scott, P., & Larkin, B.H. (1983a) Assessing personality: Effects of the depressive state on trait measurement. *American Journal of Psychiatry, 140*, 695–699.

Hirschfeld, R.M., Klerman, G.L., Clayton, P.J., & Keller, M.B. (1983b) Personality and depression. Empirical findings. *Archives of General Psychiatry, 40*, 993–998.

Holmes, G.P., Kaplan, J.E., Nelson, M., Gantz, N.M., Komaroff, A.L., Schonberger, L.B., Strauss, S.E., Jones, J.F., Dubois, R.E., Cunningham-Rundles, C., Pahwa, S., Tosato, G., Zegans, L.S., Purtilo, D.T., Brown, N., Schooley, R.T., & Brus, I. (1988) Chronic fatigue syndrome: A working case definition. *Annals of Internal Medicine, 108*, 387–389.

Holzman, P.S., Kringlen, E., Matthysse, S., Flanagan, S.D., Lipton, R.B., Cramer, G., Levin, S., Lange, K., & Levy, D.L. (1988) A single dominant gene can account for eye tracking dysfunctions and schizophrenia in offspring of discordant twins. *Archives of General Psychiatry, 45*, 641–647.

Horevitz, R.P., & Braun, B.G. (1983) Are multiple personality disorder patients borderline? An analysis of 33 patients. *Psychiatric Clinics of North America, 7*, 69–87.

Hunt, G.E., Atrens, D.M., Chesher, G.B., & Becker, F.T. (1976) α-Noradrenergic modulation of hypothalamic self-stimulation: Studies employing clonidine, 1-phenylephrine and α-methyl-O-tyrosine. *European Journal of Pharmacology, 37*, 105–111.

Imboden, J., Canter, A., & Cluff, L.E. (1961) Convalescence from influenza. *Archives of Internal Medicine, 108*, 393–399.

Iqbal, N., Asnis, G.M., Wetzler, S., Kahn, R., Kay, S.R., & van Praag, H.M. (1991b) The MCPP challenge test in schizophrenia: Hormonal and behavioral responses. *Biological Psychiatry, 30*, 770–778.

Iqbal, N., Asnis, G.M., Wetzler, S., Kay, S.R., & van Praag, H.M. (1991a) The role of serotonin in schizophrenia: New findings. *Schizophrenia Research, 5*, 181–182.

Irving, J.B., Soursey, R.D., Buchsbaum, M.S., & Murphy, D.L. (1989) Platelet monoamine oxidase activity and life stress as predictors of psychopathology and coping in a community sample. *Psychological Medicine, 19,* 79–90.

Jaspers, K. (1948) *Allgemeine Psychopathologie.* Heidelberg: Springer.

Jauch, D.A., & Carpenter, W.T. (1988a) Reactive psychosis I. Does the pre-DSM III concept define a third psychosis? *Journal of Nervous and Mental Disease, 176,* 72–81.

Jauch, D.A., & Carpenter, W.T. (1988b) Reactive psychosis II. Does DSM-III-R define a third psychosis? *Journal of Nervous and Mental Diseases, 176,* 82–86.

Javitt, D.C., & Zukin, S.R. (1991) Recent advances in the phencyclidine (PCP) model of schizophrenia. *American Journal of Psychiatry, 148,* 1301–1308.

Jenike, M.A., Baer, L., & Greist, J.H. (1990) Clomipramine versus fluoxetine in obsessive-compulsive disorder: A retrospective comparison of side effects and efficacy. *Journal of Clinical Psychopharmacology, 10,* 122–124.

Jernigan, T. (1986) Anatomical and CT scan studies of psychiatric disorders. In: P. Berger, & H.K.H. Brodie (Eds.), *American Handbook of Psychiatry* (pp. 213–235). New York: Basic Books.

Johnstone, E.C., Cunningham-Owens, D.G., Frith, C.D., McPherson, K., Dowie, C., Riley, G., & Gold, A. (1980) Neurotic illness and its response to anxiolytic and antidepressant treatment. *Psychological Medicine, 10,* 321–328.

Jones, B.J., Costall, B., Domeney, A.M., Kelly, M.E., Naylor, R.J., Oakley, N.R., & Tyers, M.B. (1988) The potential anxiolytic activity of GR38032F, a 5-HT3-receptor antagonist. *British Journal of Pharmacology, 93,* 985–993.

Jones, J.F., Fay, G., Minnich, L.L., Hicks, M.J., Kibler, R., & Lucas, D.O. (1985) Evidence for active Epstein–Barr virus infection in patients with persistent, unexplained illnesses: elevated anti-early antigen antibodies. *Annals of Internal Medicine, 102,* 1–7.

Kahn, J., McNair, D.M., Lipman, R.S., Covi, L., Rickels, K., Downing, R., Fisher, S., & Frankenthaler, L.M. (1986) Imipramine and chlordiazepoxide in depressive and anxiety disorders: II. Efficacy in anxious outpatients. *Archives of General Psychiatry, 43,* 79–85.

Kahn, R.S., Davidson, M., Siever, L., DuMont, K., Kerman, B., Apter, S., & Davis, K.L. (1991b) Serotonin function in treatment of refractory schizophrenia. 144th Annual Meeting, American Psychiatric Association, New Orleans.

Kahn, R.S., Dubie, C., & van Praag, H.M. (1992) Panic disorder: A biological overview. *European Journal of Neuropsychopharmacology, 2,* 1–20.

Kahn, R.S., Kalus, O., Wetzler, S., Cahn, W., Asnis, G.M., & van Praag, H.M.(1990) Effects of serotonin antagonists on m-chlorophenyl-piperazine mediated responses in normal subjects. *Psychiatry Research, 33,* 189–198.

Kahn, R.S., & van Praag, H.M. (1988) A serotonin hypothesis of panic disorder. *Human Psychopharmacology, 3,* 285–288.

Kahn, R.S.,& van Praag, H.M., (1992) Panic disorder: A biological perspective. *European Neuropsychopharmacology, 2,* 1–20.

Kahn, R.S., van Praag, H.M., Wetzler, S., Asnis, G.M., & Barr, G. (1988c) Serotonin and anxiety revisited. *Biological Psychiatry, 23,* 189–208.

Kahn, R.S., & Westenberg, H.G.M. (1985) L-5-Hydroxytryptophan in the treatment of anxiety disorders. *Journal of Affective Disorders, 8,* 197–200.

Kahn, R.S., Westenberg, H.G.M., & Jolles, J. (1984) Zimelidine treatment of obsessive-compulsive disorder. *Acta Psychiatrica Scandinavica, 69,* 259–261.

Kahn, R.S., Westenberg, H.G.M., Verhoeven, W.M.A., Gispen-de Wied, C.C., & Kamerbeek, W.D.J. (1987) Effect of a serotonin precursor and uptake inhibitor in anxiety disorders: A double-blind comparison of 5-hydroxytryptophan, clomipramine and placebo. *International Clinical Psychopharmacology, 2,* 33–45.

Kahn, R.S., Wetzler, S., Asnis, G.M., Kling, M.A., Suckow, R.F., & van Praag, H.M. (1991a) Pituitary hormone response to meta-chlorophenylpiperazine in panic disorder and healthy control subjects. *Psychiatry Research, 37,* 25–34.

Kahn, R.S., Wetzler, S., van Praag, H.M., & Asnis, G.M. (1988a) Neuroendocrine evidence for 5-HT receptor hypersensitivity in patients with panic disorder. *Psychopharmacology, 96,* 360–364.

Kahn, R.S., Wetzler, S., van Praag, H.M., & Asnis, G.M. (1988b) Behavioral indications for receptor hypersensitivity in panic disorder. *Psychiatry Research, 25,* 101–104.

Kalus, O., Wetzler, S., Kahn, R., Asnis, G.M., & van Praag, H.M. (1992) A dose response study of M-chlorophenylpiperazine in normal subjects. *Psychopharmacology, 106,* 388–390.

Kanofsky, J.D., Sandyk, R., Kaplan, S., & Yaryura-Tobias, J.A. (1991) Seasonal panic disorder responsive to light therapy. *Lancet, 337,* 1103–1104.

Karasu, T.B. (1982) Psychotherapy and pharmacotherapy: Towards an integrative mode. *American Journal of Psychiatry, 139,* 1102–1113.

Katz, M.M., Koslow, S.H., Maas, J.W., Frazer, A., Kocsis, J., Secunda, S., Bowden, C.L., & Casper, R.C. (1991) Identifying the specific clinical actions of amitriptyline: Interrelationships of behaviour, affect and plasma levels in depression. *Psychological Medicine, 21*, 599–611.

Katz, M.M., Koslow, S., Maas, J.W., Frazer, A., Rowden, C., Casper, R.C., Croughan, J., Kocsis, J., & Redmond, E. (1987) The timing and specificity and clinical prediction of tricyclic drug effects in depression. *Psychological Medicine, 17*, 297–309.

Katz, M.M., & Wetzler, S. (1991) Behavior measurement in psychobiological research. *Encyclopedia of Human Biology, 1*, 607–614.

Kay, S.R. (1991) *Positive and Negative Syndromes in Schizophrenia: Assessment and Research.* New York: Brunner/Mazel.

Kay, S.R. (1992) New perspectives on the positive-negative distinction in schizophrenia. In: J.P. Lindenmayer & S.R. Kay (Eds.), *New Biological Vistas on Schizophrenia.* New York: Brunner/Mazel.

Kay, S.R., Opler, L.A., & Fiszbein, A. (1990) *Positive and Negative Syndrome Scales (PANSS). Rating Manuel.* Toronto: Multi Health Systems Inc.

Kay, S.R., Opler, L.A., & Fiszbein, A. (1993) *Positive and Negative Syndrome Scales (PANSS).* Toronto: Multi Health Systems Inc.

Kay, S.R., & Sevy, S. (1991) Pyramidical model of schizophrenia. *Schizophrenia Bulletin, 16*, 653–662.

Kay, S.R., & Singh, M.M. (1989) The positive-negative distinction in drug-free schizophrenic patients: Stability, response to neuroleptics, and prognostic significance. *Archives of General Psychiatry, 46*, 711–718.

Keinan, J., Mikulincer, M., & Rybnicki, A. (1988) Perception of self and parents by second-generation Holocaust survivors. *Behavioral Medicine, 84*, 6–12.

Keller, S.R. (1988) Children of Jewish Holocaust survivors: Relationship of family communication to family cohesion, adaptability and satisfaction. *Family Therapy, 15*, 223–237.

Kelsoe, J.R., Ginns, E.I., Egeland, J.A., Gerhard, D.S., Goldstein, A.M., Bale, S.J., Pauls, D.L., Long, R.T., Kidd, K.K., Conte, G., Housman, D.E., & Paul, S.E. (1989) Re-evaluation of the linkage relationship between chromosome 11p loci and the gene for bipolar affective disorder in the Old Order Amish. *Nature, 342*, 238–243.

Kendell, R.E. (1976) The classification of depression: A review of contemporary confusion. *British Journal of Psychiatry, 129*, 15–20.

Kendell, R.E. (1987) Schizophrenia: Clinical features. In: R. Michels, J.O. Chvenar, Jr., H. Keith, H. Brodie, A.M. Cooper, S.B. Guze, L.L. Judd, G.L. Klerman, & A.J. Solnit (Eds.), *Psychiatry* (Vol. 1). New York: Basic Books.

Kendell, R.E., & Brockington, I.F. (1980) The identification of disease entities and the relationship between schizophrenic and affective psychoses. *British Journal of Psychiatry, 137,* 324–331.

Kendell, R.E., Brockington, I.F., & Leff, J.P. (1979) Prognostic implications of six alternative definitions of schizophrenia. *Archives of General Psychiatry, 36,* 25–31.

Kendler, K.S. (1988) Familial aggregation of schizophrenia and schizophrenia spectrum disorders. *Archives of General Psychiatry, 45,* 377–383.

Kendler, K.S. (1990) Toward a scientific psychiatric nosology. *Archives of General Psychiatry, 47,* 969–973.

Kendler, K.S., & Davis, K.L. (1981) The genetics and biochemistry of paranoid schizophrenia and other paranoid psychoses. *Schizophrenia Bulletin, 7,* 689–709.

Kendler, K.S., Gruenberg, A.M., & Strauss, T.S. (1981) An independent analysis of the Danish adoption study of schizophrenia. *Archives of General Psychiatry, 38,* 973–987.

Kendler, K.S., Gruenberg, A.M., & Tsuang, M.T. (1984) Outcome of schizophrenic subtypes defined by four diagnostic systems. *Archives of General Psychiatry, 41,* 149–154.

Kennedy, H.G. (1988) Fatigue and fatigability. *British Journal of Psychiatry, 153,* 1–5.

Kety, S.S. (1983) Mental illness in the biological and adoptive relations of schizophrenic adoptees. *American Journal of Psychiatry, 140,* 720–727.

Kety, S.S., Rosenthal, D., Wender, P.H., Schulsinger, F., & Jacobson, B. (1978) The biological and adoptive families of adopted individuals who became schizophrenic: Prevalence of mental illness and other characteristics. In: L.C. Wynne, R.L. Cromwell, & S. Matthysse (Eds.), *The Nature of Schizophrenia: New Approaches to Research and Treatment.* New York: Wiley.

Kihlstrom, J.F. (1987) The cognitive unconscious. *Science, 237,* 1445–1452.

Kirch, D.G., & Weinberger, D.R. (1986) Anatomical neuropathology in schizophrenia: Post-mortem findings. In: H.A. Nasrallah & D.R. Weinberger (Eds.), *The Neurology of Schizophrenia* (pp. 325–348). Amsterdam: Elsevier Science Publishers.

Klein, D.F. (1964) Delineation of two drug-responsive anxiety syndromes. *Psychopharmacologia, 5,* 397–408.

Klein, D.F. (1974) Endogenomorphic depression: A conceptual and terminological revision. *Archives of General Psychiatry, 31,* 447–454.

Klein, D.F. (1980) Anxiety reconceptualized. *Comprehensive Psychiatry, 21,* 411–427.

Klein, D., Gittelman, R., Quitkin, F., & Riskin, A. (1980) *Diagnosis and*

Drug Treatment of Psychiatric Disorders in Adults and Children. Baltimore: Williams and Wilkins, Second Edition.

Koczkas, S., Holmberg, G., & Wedin, L. (1981) A pilot study of the effect of the 5-HT uptake inhibitor, zimelidine, on phobic anxiety. *Acta Psychiatrica Scandinavica, 63* (Suppl 290), 328–341.

Kraepelin, E. (1899) *Psychiatrie. Ein Lehrbuch fur Studirende und Aerzte.* II Band: Sechste Auflage, Leipzig, Verlag von Johann Ambrosius Barth.

Kraepelin, E. (1919) *Dementia Praecox and Paraphrenia.* Edinburgh: Livingstone.

Kraines, S. (1957) *Mental Depressions and Their Treatment.* Macmillan: New York.

Kretschmer, E. (1951) *Korperbau und Charakter.* Berlin: Springer Verlag.

Kripke, D.R., Mullaney, D.J., Savides, T.J., & Gillin, J.C. (1989) Phototherapy for nonseasonal major depressive disorders. In: N.E. Rosenthal & M.C. Blehar (Eds.), *Seasonal Affective Disorders and Phototherapy.* Guilford Press: New York.

Kruesi, M., Dale, J., & Straus, S. (1989) Psychiatric diagnoses in patients who have chronic fatigue syndrome. *Journal of Clinical Psychiatry, 50,* 53–56.

Krystal, H. (1968) *Massive Psychic Trauma.* New York: International Universities Press.

Langfeldt, G. (1939) *The Prognosis in Schizophrenia and the Factors Influencing the Course of the Disease.* London: Melford.

Last, U. (1988) The transgenerational impact of holocaust trauma: Current state of the evidence. *International Journal of Mental Health, 17,* 72–89.

Last, U., & Klein, H. (1984) Holocaust traumatization: The transgenerational impact. In: I. Guttman (Ed.), *The Nazi Concentration Camps and the Condition of Jewish Prisoners.* Jerusalem: Yad Vashem.

Lemberger, L., Fuller, R.W., & Zerbe, R.L. (1985) Use of specific serotonin uptake inhibitor as antidepressants. *Clinical Neuropharmacology, 8,* 229–317.

Leon, G.R., Butcher, J.N., Kleinman, M., Goldberg, A., & Almagor, M. (1981) Survivors of the holocaust and their children: Current status and adjustment. *Journal of Personality and Social Psychiatry, 41,* 503–516.

Leonhard, K. (1960) Die atypischen Psychosen und Kleists Lehre vond den endogenen Psychosen. In: H.W. Gruhle, R. Jung, W. Mayer-Gross, & M. Muller (Eds.), *Psychiatrie der Gegenwart Band II: Klinische Psychiatrie.* Berlin: Springer Verlag.

Leuthold, G.H. (1940) Jahreszeit und phasenbeginn manisch-depressiever psychosen. *Archive fur Psychiatrie und Nervenkrankheiten, 111,* 55–61.

Levav, I., & Abramson, J.H. (1984) Emotional distress among concentration camp survivors—a community study in Jerusalem. *Psychological Medicine, 14*, 215–218.

Leventhal, G., & Ontell, M.K. (1989) A descriptive demographic and personality study of second-generation Jewish holocaust survivors. *Psychological Reports, 64*, 1067–1073.

Levitt, J.J., & Tsuang, M.T. (1988) The heterogeneity of schizoaffective disorder: Implications for treatment. *American Journal of Psychiatry, 145*, 926–936.

Lewine, R.J.J., Fogg, L., & Meltzer, H.Y. (1983) Assessment of negative and positive symptoms in schizophrenia. *Schizophrenia Bulletin, 9*, 368–376.

Lewis, A. (1934) Melancholia: A clinical survey of depressive states. *Journal of Mental Sciences, 80*, 277–378.

Lewy, A.J., Sack, R.I., Frederickson, R.H., Reaves, M., Denney, D., & Zietske, D.R. (1983) The use of bright light in the treatment of chronobiologic sleep and mood disorders: The phase-response curve. *Psychopharmacology Bulletin, 19*, 523–525.

Lidberg, L., Asberg, M., & Sundquist-Stensman, U.B. (1984) 5-Hydroxyindoleacetic acid in attempted suicides who have killed their children. *Lancet, ii*, 928.

Lidberg, L., Tuck, J.R., Asberg, M., Scalia-Tomba, G.P., & Bertilsson, L. (1985) Homicide, suicide and CSF 5-HIAA. *Acta Psychiatrica Scandinavica, 71*, 230–236.

Liebowitz, M.R., Fyer, A.J., Gorman, J.M., Campeas, R.B., Sandberg, D.P., Hollander, E., Papp, L.A., & Klein, D.F. (1988) Tricyclic therapy of the DSM-III anxiety disorders: A review with implications for further research. *Journal of Psychiatric Research, 22*, 7–31.

Lindstrom, L.H. (1985) Low HVA and normal 5-HIAA CSF levels in drug free schizophrenia patients, compared to healthy volunteers: Correlations to symptomatology and heredity. *Psychiatry Research, 14*, 265–274.

Linnoila, M., Virkhunen, M., Scheinin, M., Nuutila, A., Rimon, R., & Goodwin, F.K. (1983) Low cerebrospinal fluid 5-hydroxyindoleacetic acid concentration differentiates impulsive from nonimpulsive violent behavior. *Life Science, 33*, 2609–2614.

Losonczy, M.F., Davidson, M., & Davis, K.L. (1987) The dopamine hypothesis of schizophrenia. In: H.Y. Meltzer (Ed.), *Psychopharmacology: The Third Generation of Progress*. New York: Raven Press.

Luchins, D., & Meltzer, H. (1986) A comparison of CT findings in acute and chronic ward schizophrenics. *Psychiatry Research, 17*, 7–14.

Ludolph, P.S. (1985) How prevalent is multiple personality. *American Journal of Psychiatry, 142,* 1526–1527.

Lukoff, N., Snyder, K., Ventura, J., & Neuchterlein, K.H. (1981) Life events, familial stress and coping in the development course of schizophrenia. *Schizophrenia Bulletin, 10,* 258–292.

Mackert, A., Volz, H.P., Stieglitz, R-D, & Muller-Oerlinghausen, B. (1991) Phototherapy in nonseasonal depression. *Biological Psychiatry, 30,* 257–268.

Manchanda, R., Hirsch, S.R., & Barnes, T.R.E. (1988) Criteria for evaluating improvement in schizophrenia in psychopharmacological research. (With special reference to gamma endorphin fragments). *British Journal of Psychiatry, 153,* 354–358.

Manier, D.H., Gillespie, D.D., Steranka, L.R., & Sulser, F. (1984) A pivotal role for serotonin (5-HT) in the regulation of beta-adrenoceptors by antidepressants: Reversibility of the action of parachlorophenylalanine by 5-hydroxytryptophan. *Experientia, 40,* 1223–1226.

Manu, P., Matthews, D.A., & Lane, T.J. (1988) The mental health of patients with a chief complaint of chronic fatigue. *Archives of Internal Medicine, 148,* 2213–2217.

Mapother, E. (1926) Discussion on manic-depressive psychosis. *British Medical Journal, 2,* 872–876.

Marneros, A., Deister, A., Rhode, A., Steinmeyer, E.M., & Junemann, H. (1989) Long-term outcome of schizoaffective and schizophrenic disorders: A comparative study. *European Archives of Psychiatry and Neurological Sciences, 238,* 118–125.

Mason, S.T. (1984) *Catecholamines and Behaviour.* Cambridge: Cambridge University Press.

Mathews, R.J., Jack, R.A., & West, W.S. (1985) Regional blood flow in a patient with multiple personality. *American Journal of Psychiatry, 142,* 504–505.

Matussek, P. (1975) *Internment in Concentration Camp and its Consequences.* New York: Springer.

Matussek, P., & Feil, W.B. (1983) Personality attributes of depressive patients. Results of group comparisons. *Archives of General Psychiatry, 40,* 783–790.

Mayer-Gross, W., Slater, E., & Roth, M. (1955) *Clinical Psychiatry.* Cassell and Company: London.

McDonald, E.M., Mann, A.H., & Thomas, H.C. (1987) Interferons as mediators of psychiatric morbidity. *The Lancet, 2,* 1175–1177.

McGorry, P.D., Copolov, D.L., & Singh, B.S. (1990) Current concepts in functional psychosis. The case for a loosening of associations. *Schizophrenia Research, 3*, 221–234.

McGrath, R.E., Buckwald, B., & Resnick, E.V. (1990) The effect of L-tryptophan on seasonal affective disorder. *Journal of Clinical Psychiatry, 51*, 162–163.

McGuffin, P., Farmer, A., & Gutterman, I.I. (1987) Is there really a split in schizophrenia? The genetic evidence. *British Journal of Psychiatry, 150*, 581–592.

McGuffin, P., Sargeant, M., Hetti, G., Tidmarsh, S., Wheatley, S., & Marchbanks, R.M. (1990) Exclusion of a schizophrenia susceptibility gene from the chromosome 5q11-q13 region: New data and a reanalysis of previous reports. *American Journal of Human Genetics, 47*, 524–535.

McKegney, F.P., & Schwartz, C.E. (1986) Behavioral medicine: Treatment and organizational issues. *General Hospital Psychiatry, 8*, 330–339.

McNair, D.M., Lorr, M., & Droppelman, L.F. (1990) *Manual for the Profile of Mood States.* San Diego: Educational and Industrial Teaching Service.

Meares, R., Mendelsohn, F.A.D., & Milgrom-Friedman, L. (1981) A sex difference in the seasonal variation of suicide rate: A single cycle for men, two cycles for women. *British Journal of Psychiatry, 138*, 321–325.

Mellor, C.S. (1970) First rank symptoms of schizophrenia: I. The frequency in schizophrenics on admission to hospital: II. Difference between individual first rank symptoms. *British Journal of Psychiatry, 117*, 15–23.

Meltzer, H.Y. (1991) The mechanism of action of novel antipsychotic drugs. *Schizophrenia Bulletin, 17*, 263–287.

Meltzer, H.Y., Perline, R., Tricou, B.J., Lowy, A., & Robertson, A. (1984) Effect of 5-hydroxytryptophan on serum cortisol levels in major affective disorders. II. Relation to suicide, psychosis and depressive symptoms. *Archives of General Psychiatry, 41*, 379–387.

Meltzer, H.Y., Sommers, A.A., & Luchins, D.J. (1988) The effect of neuroleptics and other psychotropic drugs on negative symptoms in schizophrenia. *Journal of Clinical Psychopharmacology, 6*, 329–338.

Meltzer, H.Y., & Zureich, J.L. (1987) Relationship of auditory hallucinations and paranoia to platelet MAO activity in schizophrenics: Sex and race interactions. *Psychiatry Research, 22*, 99–109.

Merikangas, K.R., Spence, A., & Kupfer, D.J. (1989) Linkage studies of bipolar disorder: Methodological and analytic issues. *Archives of General Psychiatry, 46*, 1137–1141.

Mesulam, M-M. (1990) Schizophrenia and the brain. *New England Journal of Medicine, 322*, 842–844.

Mitchill, S.L. (1816) A double consciousness, or duality of person in the same individual. *Medical Repository, 3,* 185–186.

Moller, H.J., Schmid-Bode, W., Cording-Tommel, C., Wittchen, H.U., Zaudig, M., & von Zerssen, D. (1988) Psychopathological and social outcome in schizophrenia versus affective/schizoaffective psychoses and prediction of poor outcome in schizophrenia. *Acta Psychiatrica Scandinavica, 77,* 379–389.

Moller, H.J., von Zerssen, D., Werner-Eilert, K.,& Wuschner-Stockeim, M. (1982) Outcome in schizophrenia and similar paranoid psychoses. *Schizophrenia Bulletin, 8,* 99–108.

Morand, C., Young, N., & Ervin, F.R. (1983) Clinical response of aggressive schizophrenics to oral tryptophan. *Biological Psychiatry, 18,* 576–578.

Morey, L.C. (1988) Personality disorders in DSM-III and DSM-III-R: Convergence, coverage, and internal consistency. *American Journal of Psychiatry, 145,* 573–577.

Nadler, A., Kay-Venaki, S., & Gleitman, R. (1985) Transgenerational effects of the Holocaust: Externalization of aggression in second generation Holocaust survivors. *Journal Consulting Clinical Psychology, 53,* 365–369.

Nelson, J.C., & Charney, D.S. (1981) The symptoms of major depressive illness. *American Journal of Psychiatry, 138,* 1–13.

Niederland, G. (1968) Clinical observations on the "survivor-syndrome." *International Journal of Psychoanalysis, 49,* 313–315.

Ninan, P.T., van Kammen, D.P., Scheinin, M., Linnoila, M., Bunney, W.E., & Goodwin, F.K. (1984) CSF 5-hydroxyindoleacetic acid levels in suicidal schizophrenic patients. *American Journal of Psychiatry, 141,* 566–569.

Noyes, Jr., R., Anderson, D.J., Clancy, J., Crowe, R.R., Slymen, D.J., Ghoneim, M.M., & Hinrichs, J.V. (1984) Diazepam and propranolol in panic disorder and agoraphobia. *Archives of General Psychiatry, 41,* 287–292.

O'Callaghan, E., Sham, P., Takei, N., Glover, G., & Murray, R.M. (1991) Schizophrenia after prenatal exposure to 1957 A2 influenza epidemic. *The Lancet, 337,* 1248–1250.

O'Grady, J.C. (1990) The prevalence and diagnostic significance of schneiderian first-rank symptoms in a random sample of acute psychiatric inpatients. *British Journal of Psychiatry, 156,* 496–500.

Olds, J., & Milner, P. (1954) Positive reinforcement produced by electrical stimulation of the septal area and other regions of the rat brain. *Journal of Comparative Physiological Psychology, 47,* 419–427.

Olivier, B., Mos, J., Hartog, J., & Rasmussen, D. (1990) Serenics. *Drug News and Perspectives, 3*, 261–271.

Orne, M.T., Dinges, D.F., & Orne, E.C. (1984) The differential diagnosis of multiple personality disorder in the forensic context. *International Journal of Clinical and Experimental Hypnosis, 32*, 118–167.

O'Rourke, D., Wurtman, J.J., Wurtman, R.J., Chebli, R., & Gleason, R. (1989) Treatment of seasonal depression with *d*-fenfluramine. *Journal of Clinical Psychiatry, 50*, 343–347.

Overall, J.E., & Gorman, D.R. (1962) The brief psychiatric rating scale. *Psychological Reports, 10*, 798–812.

Owen, M.J., & Mullan, M.J. (1990) Molecular genetic studies of manic-depression and schizophrenia. *Trends in Neuroscience, 13*, 29–31.

Pakkenberg, B. (1987) Post-mortem study of chronic schizophrenic brains. *British Journal of Psychiatry, 151*, 744–752.

Palca, J. (1990) Does a retrovirus explain fatigue syndrome puzzle? *Science, 249*, 1240–1241.

Pandey, G.N., Pandey, S.C., Janicak, P.G., Marks, R.C., & Davis, J.M. (1990) Platelet serotonin-2 receptor binding sites in depression and suicide. *Biological Psychiatry, 28*, 215–222.

Papeschi, R., & McClure, D.J. (1971) Homovanillic and 5-hydroxyindoleacetic acid in cerebrospinal fluid in depressed patients. *Archives of General Psychiatry, 25*, 354–358.

Parker, G., & Walter, S. (1982) Seasonal variation in depressive disorders and suicidal deaths in New South Wales. *British Journal of Psychiatry, 140*, 626–632.

Paykel, E.S. (1971) Classification of depressed patients: A cluster analysis derived grouping. *British Journal of Psychiatry, 118*, 275–288.

Paykel, E.S. (1979) Predictors of treatment response. In: E. Paykel & S. Paykel (Eds.), *Psychopharmacology of Affective Disorders*. Oxford: A. Coppeneds Oxford University Press, pp. 193–220.

Paykel, E.S. (1987) Melancholia. *Journal of Psychopharmacology, 2*, 67–70.

Paykel, E.S., Rao, B.M., & Taylor, C.M. (1984) Life stress and symptom pattern in out-patient depression. *Psychological Medicine, 14*, 559–568.

Peabody, C.A., Faull, K.F., King, R.J., Whiteford, H.A., Barchas, J.D., & Berger, P.A. (1987) CSF amine metabolites and depression. *Psychiatry Research, 21*, 1–7.

Pearlson, G.D., Garbacz, D.J., Tompkins, R.H., Ahn, H.S., Gutterman, D.F., Veroff, A.E., & DePaulo, J.R. (1984) Clinical correlates of lateral ventricular enlargement in bipolar affective disorder. *American Journal of Psychiatry, 141*, 253–256.

Perse, T.L., Greist, J.H., Jefferson, J.W., Rosenfeld, R., & Dar, R. (1987)

Fluvoxamine treatment of obsessive-compulsive disorder. *American Journal of Psychiatry, 144,* 1543–1548.

Peter, K., Rabiger, U., & Kowalik, A. (1986) Erste ergebnisse mit bright-light (phototherapie) bei affektive psychosen. *Psychiatrie, Neurologie und Medizinische Psychologie, 38,* 384–390.

Pfefferbaum, A., Rosenbloom, M., Crusan, K., & Jernigan, T. (1988a) Brain CT changes in alcoholics: The effects of age and alcohol consumption. *Alcoholism Clinical Experiential Research, 12,* 81–87.

Pfefferbaum, A., Zipursky, R.B., Lim, K.O., Zatz, L.M., Stahl, S.M., & Jernigan, T.L. (1988b) Computed tomographic evidence for generalized sulcal and ventricular enlargement in schizophrenia. *Archives of General Psychiatry, 45,* 633–640.

Pfohl, B., Coryell, W., Zimmerman, M., & Stangl, D. (1986) DSM-III personality disorders: Diagnostic overlap and internal consistency of individual DSM-III criteria. *Comprehensive Psychiatry, 27,* 21–34.

Pilkonis, P.A., & Frank, E. (1988) Personality pathology in recurrent depression: Nature, prevalence, and relationship to treatment response. *American Journal of Psychiatry, 145,* 435–441.

Plutchik, R., van Praag, H.M., & Conte, H.R. (1988) Correlates of suicide and violence risk, III. A 2-stage model of countervailing forces. *Psychiatry Research, 28,* 215–225.

Plutchik, R., van Praag, H.M., Picard, S., Conte, H.R., & Korn, M. (1989) Is there a relation between seriousness of suicide intent and the lethality of the suicide attempt? *Psychiatry Research, 29,* 71–79.

Posey, T.B., & Losch, M.E. (1983) Auditory hallucinations of hearing voices in 375 normal subjects. *Imagination, Cognition and Personality, 2,* 99–113.

Putnam, F.W. (1987) Multiple personality disorder? *Journal of Clinical Psychiatry, 48,* 174.

Putnam, F.W., Guroff, J.J., Silberman, E.K., Barban, L., & Post, R.M. (1986) The clinical phenomenology of multiple personality disorder: Review of 100 recent cases. *Journal of Clinical Psychiatry, 47,* 285–293.

Radford, C. (1988) The chronic fatigue syndrome. *Annals of Internal Medicine, 108,* 166.

Radhakrishnan, J., Mathew, K., Richard, J., & Verghese, A. (1983) Schneider's first rank symptoms—Prevalence, diagnostic use and prognostic implications. *British Journal of Psychiatry, 142,* 557–559.

Raleigh, M.J. (1987) Differential behavioral effects of tryptophan and 5-hydroxytryptophan in vervet monkeys: Influence of catecholaminergic systems. *Psychopharmacology, 93,* 44–50.

Ramsay, M. (1986) *Postviral Disease Syndrome: The Saga of Royal Free Disease.* Gower Medical: London.

Raskin, M., Peeke, H.V.S., Dickman, W., & Pinsker, W. (1982) Panic and generalized anxiety disorder: Developmental antecedents and precipitants. *Archives of General Psychiatry, 39,* 687–689.

Redmond, R.C., & Huang, Y.H. (1979) New evidence for a locus coeruleus-norepinephrine connection with anxiety. *Life Science, 25,* 2149–2162.

Reich, J. (1990) Relationship between DSM-III avoidant and dependent personality disorders. *Psychiatry Research, 34,* 281–292.

Reich, J.H., & Noyes, R. (1988) A comparison of DSM III personality disorders in recovered depressed and panic disorder patients. *Journal of Nervous and Mental Disease, 176,* 300–304.

Reinhard, J.F., Jr., Galloway, M.P., & Roth, R.H. (1983) Noradrenergic modulation of serotonin synthesis and metabolism. II. Stimulation by 3-Isobutyle-1-methylxanthine. *Journal of Pharmacology and Experimental Therapeutics, 226,* 764–769.

Robbins, T.W., Everitt, B.J., Cole, B.J., Archer, T., & Mohammed, A. (1985) Functions of the coeruleo-cortical noradrenergic projection: A review of recent experimentation and theory. *Physiological Psychology, 13,* 390–397.

Roberts, G.W. (1990) Schizophrenia: The cellular biology of a functional psychosis. *Trends in Neurosciences, 13,* 207–211.

Roberts, G.W. (1991) Schizophrenia: A neuropathological perspective. *British Journal of Psychiatry, 158,* 8–17.

Robins, L.N., Helzer, J.E., Weissman, M.M., Orvaschel, H., Gruenberg, E., Burke, J.D., & Regier, D.A. (1984) Lifetime prevalence of specific psychiatric disorders in three sites. *Archives of General Psychiatry, 41,* 949–958.

Robinson, D.S., Alms, D.R., Shrotriya, R.C., Messina, M., & Wickramarapne, P. (1989) Serotonergic anxiolytics and treatment of depression. *Psychopathology, 22,* 27–36. (Suppl 1).

Rodgers, R.J., & Cooper, J.Y. (1991) *5-HT1A Agonists, 5-HT3 Antagonists and Benzodiazepines.* London: Wiley.

Rose, S.L., & Garske, J. (1987) Family environment, adjustment, and coping among children of holocaust survivors: A comparative investigation. *American Journal of Orthopsychiatry, 51,* 332–344.

Rosen, W.G., Mohs, R.C., Johns, C.A., Small, N.S., Kendler, K.S., Horvath, T.B., & Davis, K.L. (1984) Positive and negative symptoms in schizophrenia. *Psychiatry Research, 13,* 277–284.

Rosenberg, R., Beck, P., Mellergard, M. Ottosson, J. (1991) Alprazolam,

Imipramine and placebo treatment of panic disorder: Predicting therapeutic response. *Acta Psychiatrica Scandinavica 365, 46–52.*

Rosenheck, R., & Nathan, P. (1985) Secondary traumatization in the children of Vietnam veterans with posttraumatic stress disorder. *Hospital Community Psychiatry, 36,* 538–539.

Rosenthal, N.E., Sack, D.A., Skwerer, R.G., Jacobsen, F.M., & Wehr, T.A. (1988) Phototherapy for seasonal affective disorder. *Journal of Biological Rhythms, 3,* 101-120.

Rosenthal, N.E., Sack, D.A., Gillin, J.C., Lewy, A.J., Goodwin, F.K., Davenport, Y., Mueller, P.S., Newsome, D.A., & Wehr, T.A. (1984) Seasonal affective disorder. *Archives of General Psychiatry, 41,* 72–80.

Rosenthal, S.H., & Klerman, G.L. (1966) Content and consistency in the endogenous depressive pattern. *British Journal of Psychiatry, 112,* 471–484.

Ross, C.A., Norton, G.R., & Wozney, K. (1989a) Multiple personality disorder: An analysis of 236 cases. *Canadian Journal of Psychiatry, 34,* 413–418.

Ross, C.A., Heber, S., Norton, G., & Anderson, G. (1989b) Differences between multiple personality disorder and other diagnostic groups on structured interview. *The Journal of Nervous and Mental Disease, 177,* 487–491.

Ross, C.A., Miller, S.D., Reagor, P., Bjornson, L., Fraser, G.A., & Anderson, G. (1990) Structured interview data on 102 cases of multiple personality disorder from four centers. *American Journal of Psychiatry, 147,* 596–601.

Roth, M., Gurney, C., Garside, R.F., & Kerr, T.A. (1972) Studies in the classification of affective disorders: The relationship between anxiety states and depressive illness I. *British Journal of Psychiatry, 121,* 147–161.

Roth, M., & Mountjoy, C.Q. (1982) The distinction between anxiety states and depressive disorders. In: E.S. Paykel (Ed.), *Handbook of Affective Disorders.* Edinburgh: Churchill Livingstone, pp. 70–92.

Roy, A., DeJong, J., & Linnoila, M. (1989) Cerebrospinal fluid monoamine metabolites and suicidal behavior in depressed patients. *Archives of General Psychiatry, 46,* 609–612.

Roy, A., & Linnoila, M. (1988) Suicidal behavior, impulsiveness and serotonin. *Acta Psychiatrica Scandinavia, 78,* 529–535.

Rudorfer, M.V., & Potter, W.Z. (1989) Antidepressants. A comparative review of the clinical pharmacology and therapeutic use of the "newer" versus the "older" drugs. *Drugs, 37,* 713–738.

Rümke, H.C. (1960) *Psychiatrie II.* Amsterdam: Scheltema and Holkema.

Rümke, H.C. (1967) About schizophrenia (German). In: H.C. Rümke (Ed.), *Eine bluehende Psychiatrie in Gefahr.* Berlin: Springer.

Rydin, E., Schalling, D., & Asberg, M. (1982) Rorschach ratings in depressed and suicidal patients with low CSF 5-HIAA. *Psychiatry Research, 7,* 229–243.

Sanderson, W.C., Beck, A.T., & Beck, J. (1990) Syndrome comorbidity in patients with major depression: Prevalence and temporal relationships. *American Journal of Psychiatry, 147,* 1025–1028.

Sanderson, W.C., & Wetzler, S. (1990) Five percent carbon dioxide challenge: Valid analogue and marker of panic disorder? *Biological Psychiatry, 27,* 689–701.

Sanderson, W.C., & Wetzler, S. (1991) Chronic anxiety and generalized anxiety disorder: Issues in comorbidity. In: R.M. Rapee & D.H. Barlow (Eds.), *Chronic Anxiety and Generalized Anxiety Disorder and Mixed-Anxiety Depression.* New York: Guilford Press.

Sanderson, W.C., Wetzler, S., Beck, A.T., & Betz, F. (1992) Prevalence of personality disorders in patients with major depression and dysthymia. *Psychiatry Research, 42,* 93–99

Sartorius, N., Jablensky, A., Korten, A., Ernberg, G., Anker, M., Cooper, J.E., & Day, R. (1986) Early manifestations and first-contact incidence of schizophrenia in different cultures. *Psychological Medicine, 16,* 909–928.

Schneider, F.R., Liebowitz, M.R., Davies, S.O., Fairbanks, J., Hollander, E., Campeas, R., & Klein, D.F. (1990) Fluoxetine in panic disorder. *Journal of Clinical Psychopharmacology, 10,* 119–121.

Schneider, K. (1959) *Klinische Psychopathologie.* Stuttgart: J Thieme Verlag.

Schreiber, F.R. (1973) *Sybil.* Chicago: Regnery.

Schwartz, M.N. (1988) The chronic fatigue syndrome—one entity or many. *New England Journal of Medicine, 319,* 1726–1728.

Scott, J. (1988) Chronic depression. *British Journal of Psychiatry, 153,* 287–297.

Segonzac, A., Shoemake, H., Tateishi, T., & Langer, S.Z. (1985) 5-methoxytryptoline, a competitive endocoid acting at (3H) imipramine recognition sites in human platelets. *Journal of Neurochemistry, 45,* 249–256.

Shear, M.K., & Fyer, M.R. (1988) Biological and psychopathological findings in panic disorder. In: A.J. Frances, & R.E. Hales (Eds.), *American Psychiatric Press Review,* (Vol. 7), Washington, D.C.: American Psychiatric Press.

Sheehan, D.V., Ballenger, J., & Jacobsen, G. (1980) Treatment of endogenous anxiety with phobic, hysterical and hypochondriacal symptoms. *Archives of General Psychiatry, 34,* 51–59.

Shepherd, M., Watt, D., Falloon, I., & Smeeton, N. (1989) The natural history of schizophrenia. A five-year follow-up. *Psychological Medicine*, 1–45.

Sheppard, G., Gruzella, J., Manchadra, R., & Hirsch, S.R. (1983) 150 positron emission tomograhic scanning in predominately never-treated patients. *Lancet,2*, 1448–1452.

Sherrington, R., Brynjolffson, J., Petursson, H., Potter, M., Dudleston, K., Barraclough, B., & Wasmuth, J. (1988) Localization of a susceptibility locus for schizophrenia on chromosome 5. *Nature, 336*, 164–167.

Siever, L.J. (1989) Role of noradrenergic mechanisms in the etiology of affective disorders. In: H.Y. Meltzer (Ed.), *Psychopharmacology, The Third Generation of Progress* (pp. 493–504). New York: Raven Press.

Siever, L.J., Coursey, R.D., Alterman, I.S., Zahn, T., Brody, L., Bernad, P., Buchsbaum, M., Lake, C.R., & Murphy, D.L. (1980) Clinical, psychophysiological, and neurological characteristics of volunteers with impaired smooth pursuit eye movements. *Biological Psychiatry, 26*, 35–51.

Sigal, J.J., DiNicola, V.F., & Buonvino, M. (1988) Grandchildren of survivors: Can negative effects of prolonged exposure to excessive stress be observed two generations later? *Canadian Journal of Psychiatry, 33*, 207–212.

Sigal, J.J., & Weinfeld, M. (1987) Mutual involvement and alienation in families of holocaust survivors. *Psychiatry, 50*, 280–288.

Sigal, J.J., & Weinfeld, M. (1989) *Trauma and Rebirth. Intergenerational Effects of the Holocaust*. New York: Praeger.

Siris, S.G., Adan, F., Cohen, M., Mandeli, J., Aronson, A., & Casey, E. (1988) Postpsychotic depression and negative symptoms: An investigation of syndromal overlap. *American Journal of Psychiatry, 145*, 1532–1537.

Slater, E. (1938) Zur periodik des manisch–depressiven irreseins. *Zeitschrift fur Neurologie und Psychiatrie, 162*, 794–801.

Solkoff, N. (1981) Children of survivors of the Nazi holocaust: A critical review of the literature. *American Journal of Orthopsychiatry, 51*, 29–42.

Solomon, Z., Kotler, M., & Mikulincer, M. (1988) Combat-related posttraumatic stress disorder among second-generation holocaust survivors: Preliminary findings. *American Journal of Psychiatry, 145*, 865–868.

Spitzer, D.L., Endicott, J., & Robins, E. (1977) *Research Diagnostic Criteria (RDC) for a Selected Group of Functional Disorders*. Third Edition. New York: New York State Psychiatric Institute.

St. George-Hyslop, P.H., Tanzi, R.E., Polinsky, R.J., Haines, J.L., Nee,

L., Watkins, P.C., Myers, R.H., Feldman, R.G., Pollen, D., Drachman, D., Growdon, J., Bruni, A., Foncin, J-F., Salmon, D., Frommelt, P., Amaducci, L., Sorbi, S., Piacentini, S., Stewart, G.D., Hobbs, W.J., Conneally, M., & Gusella, J.F. (1987) The genetic defect causing familial Alzheimer's disease maps on chromosome 21. *Science, 235*, 885–890.

Stein, L. (1978) Reward transmitters: Catecholamines and opioid peptides. In M.A. Lipton, A. DiMascio, & K.F. Killam (Eds.), *Psychopharmacology: A Generation of Progress* (pp. 569–581). New York: Raven Press.

Stevens, J.R. (1982) Neuropathology of schizophrenia. *Archives of General Psychiatry, 39*, 1131–1139.

Stinson, D., & Thompson, C. (1990) Clinical experience with phototherapy. *Journal of Affective Disorders, 18*, 129–135.

Stockmeier, C.A., & Meltzer, H.Y. (1991) Beta adrenergic receptor binding in frontal cortex of suicide victims. *Biological Psychiatry, 29*, 183–191.

Stokes, M.J., Cooper, R.G., & Edwards, R.H.T. (1988) Normal muscle strength and fatigability in patients with effort syndromes. *British Medical Journal, 297*, 1014–1017.

Straus, S.E., Dale, J.K., Tobi, M., Lawley, T., Preble, O., Blaese, R.M., Hallahan, M.S., & Henle, W. (1988) Acyclovir treatment of the chronic fatigue syndrome. *New England Journal of Medicine, 319*, 1692–1698.

Straus, S.E., Tosato, G., Armstrong, G., Lawley, T., Preble, O.T., Henle, W., Davey, R., Pearson, G., Epstein, J., Brus, I., & Blaese, R.M. (1985) Persisting illness and fatigue in adults with evidence of Epstein-Barr virus infection. *Annals of Internal Medicine, 102*, 7–16.

Strauss, J.S., Carpenter, Jr., W.T., & Bartko, J.J. (1974) The diagnosis and understanding of schizophrenia: II. Speculations on the processes that underlie schizophrenic symptoms and signs. *Schizophrenia Bulletin, 11*, 61–76.

Suddath, R.L., Casanova, M.F., Goldberg, T.E., Daniel, D.G., Kelsoe, J.R., & Weinberger, D.R. (1989) Temporal lobe pathology in schizophrenia: A quantative magnetic resonance imaging study. *American Journal of Psychiatry, 146*, 464–472.

Suddath, R.L., Christison, G.W., Torrey, E.F., Casanova, M.F., & Weinberger, D.R. (1990) Anatomical abnormalities in the brains of monozygotic twins discordant for schizophrenia. *New England Journal of Medicine, 322*, 789–794.

Swinscow, D. (1951) Some suicide statistics. *British Medical Journal, i,* 1417–1425.

Szymanski, S., Kane, J.M., & Lieberman, J.A. (1991) A selective review of biological markers in schizophrenia. *Schizophrenia Bulletin, 17*, 99–111.

Taerk, G.S., Toner, B.B., Salit, I.E., Garfinkel, P.E., & Ozersky, S. (1987) Depression in patients with neuromyasthenia (benign myalgic encephalomyelitis). *International Journal of Psychiatry in Medicine, 17,* 49–56.

Takahashi, K., Asano, Y., Kohsaka, M., Okawa, M., Sasaki, M. Honda, Y., Higuchi, T., Yamazaki, J., Ishizuka, Y., Kawaguchi, K., Ohta, T., Hanada, K., Sugita, Y., Maeda, K., Nagayama, H., Kortori, T., Egashira, K., & Takahashi, S. (1991) Multi-center study of seasonal affective disorders in Japan. A preliminary report. *Journal of Affective Disorders, 21,* 57–65.

Targum, S.D. (1991) Panic attack frequency and vulnerability to anxiogenic challenge studies. *Psychiatry Research, 36,* 75–83.

Taylor, D.P., Eison, M.S., Riblet, L.A., & Vandermaelen, C.P. (1985) Pharmacological and clinical effects of buspirone. *Pharmacology, Biochemistry, and Behavior, 23,* 687–694.

Taylor, M. (1972) Schneiderian first-rank symptoms and clinical prognostic features in schizophrenia. *Archives of General Psychiatry, 26,* 64–67.

Taylor, W.S., & Martin, M.F. (1944) Multiple personality. *Journal of Abnormal and Social Psychology, 39,* 281–300.

Teicher, M.H., & Glod, C. (1990) Seasonal affective disorder: Rapid resolution by low-dose alprazolam. *Psychopharmacology Bulletin, 26,* 197–202.

Teicher, M.H., Glod, C., & Cole, J.O. (1990) Emergence of intense suicidal preoccupation during fluoxetine treatment. *American Journal of Psychiatry, 147,* 207–210.

Terman, M., Terman, J.S., Quitkin, F.M., McGrath, P.J., Stewart, J.W., & Rafferty, B. (1989) Light therapy for seasonal affective disorder. *Neuropsychopharmacology, 2,* 1–22.

Thase, M.E. (1986) Defining and treating seasonal affective disorder. *Psychiatric Annals, 16,* 733–737.

Thase, M.E. (1989) Comparison between seasonal affective disorder and other forms of recurrent depression. In: N.E. Rosenthal & M.C. Blehar (Eds.) *Seasonal Affective Disorders and Phototherapy.* New York: Guilford Press.

Thigpen, C.H., & Cleckley, H. (1954) A case of multiple personality. *Journal of Abnormal and Social Psychology, 49,* 135–151.

Thompson, C., & Isaacs, G. (1988) Seasonal affective disorder—a British sample. *Journal of Affective Disorders, 14,* 1–11.

Torgersen, S. (1983) Genetic factors in anxiety disorders. *Archives of General Psychiatry, 40,* 1085–1089.

Traskman, L., Asberg, M., Bertilsson, L., & Sjostrand, L. (1981) Monoamine metabolites in CSF and suicidal behavior. *Archives of General Psychiatry, 38,* 631–636.

Trimble, M.R. (1991) *The Psychoses of Epilepsy.* New York: Raven Press.

Turner, S., Toone, B., & Brett-Jones, J. (1986) Computerized tomographic scan changes in early schizophrenia: Preliminary findings. *Psychological Medicine, 16,* 219–225.

van Kammen, D.P., Peters, J., van Kammen, W.B., Nugent, A., Goetz, K.L., Yao, J., & Linnoila, M. (1989) CSF norepinephrine in schizophrenia is elevated prior to relapse after haloperidol withdrawal. *Biological Psychiatry, 26,* 176–188.

van Praag, H.M. (1962) A critical investigation of the importance of monoamine oxidase inhibition as a therapeutic principle in the treatment of depression. *Thesis.* Utrecht.

van Praag, H.M. (1965) The treatment of depression with antidepressants. *Ned T.v. Geneesk, 109,* 2123–2129. (Dutch).

van Praag, H.M. (1966) Psychotropic Drugs. A Guide for the Practicing Physician. Van Gorcum: Assen. (Dutch).

van Praag, H.M. (1969) The complementary aspects in the relation between biological and psychodynamic psychiatry. *Psychiatria Clinica, 2,* 307–318.

van Praag, H.M. (1971) The position of biological psychiatry among the psychiatric disciplines. *Comprehensive Psychiatry, 12,* 1–7.

van Praag, H.M. (1972) Biologic psychiatry in perspective: The dangers of sectarianism in psychiatry. *Comprehensive Psychiatry, 13,* 401–410.

van Praag, H.M. (1976) About the impossible concept of schizophrenia. *Comprehensive Psychiatry, 17,* 481–497.

van Praag, H.M. (1977a) *Depression and schizophrenia. A Contribution on Their Chemical Pathologies.* New York: Spectrum Publications.

van Praag, H.M. (1977b) Significance of biochemical parameters in the diagnosis, treatment and prevention of depressive disorders. *Biological Psychiatry, 12,* 101–131.

van Praag, H.M. (1978a) *Psychotropic drugs. A Guide for the Practitioner.* New York: Brunner/Mazel.

van Praag, H.M. (1978b) The scientific foundation of antipsychiatry. *Acta Psychiatrica Scandinavica, 58,* 113–141.

van Praag, H.M. (1979a) Psychopsychiatry: Can psychosocial factors cause psychiatric disorders? *Comprehensive Psychiatry, 20,* 215–225.

van Praag, H.M. (1979b) Tablets and talking. A spurious contrast in psychiatry. *Comprehensive Psychiatry, 6,* 502–510.

van Praag, H.M. (1981) Socio-biological psychiatry. *Comprehensive Psychiatry, 22,* 441–450.

van Praag, H.M. (1982a) A transatlantic view of the diagnosis of depression according to the DSM-III. 1. Controversies and misunderstandings in depression diagnosis. *Comprehensive Psychiatry, 23*, 315–329.

van Praag, H.M. (1982b) A transatlantic view of the diagnosis of depression according to the DSM-III. II. Did the DSM-III solve the problem of depression diagnosis. *Comprehensive Psychiatry, 23*, 330–337.

van Praag, H.M. (1982c) Neurotransmitters and CNS disease: Depression. *Lancet, 11*, 1259–1264.

van Praag, H.M. (1982d) Depression, suicide and the metabolism of serotonin in the brain. *Journal of Affective Disorders, 4*, 275–290.

van Praag, H.M. (1983a) CSF 5-HIAA and suicide in non depressed schizophrenic. *Lancet, i*, 977–978.

van Praag, H.M. (1983b) In search of the mode of action of antidepressants: 5-HT-tyrosine mixtures in depressions. *Neuropharmacology, 22*, 433–440.

van Praag, H.M. (1984) Studies in the mechanism of action of serotonin precursors in depression. *Psychopharmacology Bulletin, 20*, 599–602.

van Praag, H.M. (1986a) (Auto) aggression and CSF 5-HIAA in depression and schizophrenia. *Psychopharmacology Bulletin, 22*, 669–673.

van Praag, H.M. (1986b) Biological suicide research. Outcome and limitations. *Biological Psychiatry, 21*, 1305–1323.

van Praag, H.M. (1986c) Psychiatrists, beware of dichotomies! *Biological Psychiatry, 21*, 247–248.

van Praag, H.M. (1986d) Serotonin precursors with and without tyrosine in the treatment of depression. In: C. Shagrass, R. Josias, W. Bridger, K. Weiss, D. Stoff, & J. Simpson (Eds.), *Biological Psychiatry.* New York: Elsevier Science Publishers, Inc.

van Praag, H.M. (1988a) Biological psychiatry audited. *Journal of Nervous and Mental Disease, 176*, 195–199.

van Praag, H.M. (1988b) Serotonergic mechanisms and suicidal behavior. *Psychiatry and Psychobiology, 3*, 335–346.

van Praag, H.M. (1988c) The teaching of psychiatry: A statue rwithout a socle. *Biological Psychiatry, 24*, 863–864.

van Praag, H.M. (1989) Diagnosing depression—Looking backward into the future. *Psychiatric Developments, 7*, 375–394.

van Praag, H.M. (1990a) (Re)-minding our business. *Human Psychopharmacology, 5*, 1–2.

van Praag, H.M. (1990b) Two-tier diagnosing in psychiatry. *Psychiatry Research, 34*, 1–11.

van Praag, H.M. (1991a) Malice or maladie? About the evil deeds of the great Herod. In: H.M. van Praag, (Ed.), *Minds in distress. Psychiatric reflections on biblical and post-biblical figures.* (In preparation).

van Praag, H.M. (1991b) The present and the future of serotonergic drugs. *Human Psychopharmacology, 6,* 13–19.

van Praag, H.M. (1992a) Reconquest of the subjective. Against the waning of psychiatric diagnosing. *British Journal of Psychiatry, 160,* 266–271.

van Praag, H.M. (1992b) Serotonergic mechanisms in the pathogenesis of schizophrenia. In: J.P. Lindenmayer & S.R. Kay, *New Biological Vistas on Schizophrenia,* New York: Brunner/Mazel.

van Praag, H.M., Asnis, G.M., Brown, S.L., Korn, M., Harkavy Friedman, J.M., & Wetzler, S. (1991) Beyond serotonin. A multi-aminergic perspective on abnormal behavior. In: S.L. Brown & H.M. van Praag (Eds.), *The Role of Serotonin in Psychiatric Disorders* pp. 302–332. New York: Brunner/Mazel.

van Praag, H.M., Asnis, G.M., Kahn, R.S., Brown, S.L., Korn, M., Harkavy Friedman, J.M., & Wetzler, S. (1990) Monoamines and abnormal behavior. A multi-aminergic perspective. *British Journal of Psychiatry, 157,* 723–734.

van Praag, H.M., & de Haan, S. (1979) Central serotonin metabolism and frequency of depression. *Psychiatry Research, 1,* 219–224.

van Praag, H.M., & de Haan, S. (1980) Depression vulnerability and 5-hydroxytryptophan prophylaxis. *Psychiatry Research, 3,* 75–83.

van Praag, H.M., Kahn, R., Asnis, G.M., Lemus, C.Z., & Brown, S.L. (1987b) Therapeutic indications for serotonin potentiating compounds. A hypothesis. *Biological Psychiatry, 22,* 205–212.

van Praag, H.M., Kahn, R.S., Asnis, G.M., Wetzler, S., Brown, S.L., Bleich, A., & Korn, M.L. (1987c) Denosologization of biological psychiatry or the specificity of 5-HT disturbances in rrpsychiatric disorders. *Journal of Affective Disorders, 13,* 1–8.

van Praag, H.M., & Korf, J. (1971a) Endogenous depressions with and without disturbances in the 5-hydroxytryptamine metabolism: A biochemical classification? *Psychopharmacology, 19,* 148–152.

van Praag, H.M., & Korf, J. (1971b) Retarded depression and the dopamine metabolism. *Psychopharmacologia, 19,* 199–203.

van Praag, H.M., & Korf, J. (1975) Central monoamine deficiency in depression: Causative or secondary phenomenon? *Pharmakopsychiatria, 8,* 321–326.

van Praag, H.M., Korf, J., & Dols, L.C.W. (1976) Clozapine versus perphenazine: The value of the biochemical mode of action of neuroleptics in predicting their therapeutic activity. *British Journal of Psychiatry, 129,* 547–555.

van Praag, H.M., Korf, J., Lakke, J.P.W.F., & Schut, T. (1975) Dopamine metabolism in depression, psychoses and Parkinson's disease: The problem of the specificity of biological variables in behavioral disorders. *Psychological Medicine, 5,* 138–146.

van Praag, H.M., Korf, J., & Puite, J. (1970) 5-hydroxyindoleacetic acid levels in the cerebrospinal fluid of depressive patients treated with probenecid. *Nature, 225,* 1259–1260.

van Praag, H.M., Korf, J., & Schut, T. (1973) Cerebral monoamines and depression. An investigation with the probenecid technique. *Archives of General Psychiatry, 28,* 827–831.

van Praag, H.M., & Leijnse, B. (1964) Die Bedeutung der Psychopharmakologie fur die klinische Psychiatrie. Systematik als notwendiger Ausgangspunkt. *Nervenarzt, 34,* 530–537.

van Praag, H.M., & Leijnse, B. (1965) Neubewertung des Syndroms. Skizze einer funktionellen Pathologie. *Psychiatria Neurologia Neurochirurgia, 68,* 50–66.

van Praag, H.M. & Lemus, C. (1986) Monoamine precursors in the treatment of psychiatric disorders. In: R.J. Wurtman & J.J. Wurtman (Eds.), *Nutrition and the Brain,* pp. 89–138. New York: Raven Press.

van Praag, H.M., Lemus, C., & Kahn, R. (1987a) Hormonal probes of central serotonergic activity. Do they really exist? *Biological Psychiatry, 22,* 86–98.

van Praag, H.M., & Nijo, L. (1984) About the course of schizoaffective psychoses. *Comprehensive Psychiatry, 25,* 9–22.

van Praag, H.M., Plutchik, R., & Conte, H. (1986) The serotonin-hypothesis of (auto) aggression. Critical appraisal of the evidence. *Annals of the New York Academy of Science, 487,* 150–167.

van Praag, H.M., Uleman, A.M., & Spitz, J.C. (1965) The vital syndrome interview. A structured standard interview for the recognition and registration of the vital depression symptom complex. *Psychiatria Neurologia Neurochirurgia, 68,* 329–346.

van Praag, H.M., Verhoeven, W.M.A., & Kahn, R.S. (1988) *Psychofarmaca.* Third Edition. Assen/Maastricht: Van Gorcum.

Ventura, J., Nuechtelein, K.H., Lukoff, D., & Hardesty, J.P. (1989) A prospective study of stressful life events and schizophrenic relapse. *Journal of Abnormal Psychology, 98,* 407–411.

Verhoeven, W.M.A., & Van Ree, J.M. (1988) Neuropeptides and schizophrenia: The current status of their therapeutic action. *New Trends in Experimental and Clinical Psychiatry, 4,* 135–142.

Verhoeven, W.M.A., van Ree, J.M., & de Wied, D. (1986) Neuroleptic-like peptides in schizophrenia. In: A.K. Sen, & T. Lee (Eds.), *Receptor and*

Ligands in Psychiatry and Neurology. London: Cambridge University Press.

Virkkunen, M., Nuutila, A., Goodwin, F.K., & Linnoila, M. (1987) Cerebrospinal fluid monoamine metabolite levels in male arsonists. *Archives of General Psychiatry, 44,* 241–247.

Volavka, J., Crowner, M., Brizer, D., Convit, A., van Praag, H.M., & Suckow, R.F. (1990) Tryptophan treatment of aggressive psychiatric inpatients. *Biological Psychiatry, 28,* 728–732.

Volz, H.P., Mackert, A., Stieglitz, R.D., & Muller-Oerlinghausen, B. (1990) Effect of bright light therapy on non-seasonal depressive disorder. *Journal of Affective Disorders, 19,* 15–21.

von Gebsattel, V.E. (1937a) On the question of depersonalization (German). *Nervenarzt, 10,* 169–178.

von Gebsattel, V.E. (1937b) A contribution to the theory of melancholia (German). *Nervenarzt, 10,* 248–257.

Wehr, T.A. (1989) Seasonal affective disorders: A historical overview. In: N.E. Rosenthal & M.C. Blehar (Eds.), *Seasonal Affective Disorders and Phototherapy.* New York: Guilford Press.

Wehr, T.A., & Rosenthal, N.E. (1989) Seasonality and affective illness. *American Journal of Psychiatry, 146,* 829–839.

Wehr, T.A., Sack, D.A., & Rosenthal, N.E. (1987) Seasonal affective disorder with summer depression and winter hypomania. *American Journal of Psychiatry, 144,* 1602–1603.

Weinberger, D.R. (1987) Implications of normal brain development for the pathogenesis of schizophrenia. *Archives of General Psychiatry, 44,* 660–669.

Weinberger, D.R., Bigelow, L.B., Kleinmann, J.E., Klein, S.T., Rosenblatt, J.E., & Wyatt, R.J. (1980a) Cerebral ventricular enlargement in chronic schizophrenia. *Archives of General Psychiatry, 37,* 11–13.

Weinberger, D.R., Cannon-Spoor, E., Potkin, S.G., & Wyatt, R.J. (1980b) Poor premorbid adjustment and CT scan abnormalities in chronic schizophrenia. *American Journal of Psychiatry, 137,* 1410–1413.

Weinberger, D.R., & Kleinman, J.E. (1986) Observations on the brain in schizophrenia. In: A.J. Frances & R.E. Hales (Eds.), *Psychiatry Update: The American Psychiatric Association Annual Review* (Vol. 5). Washington, D.C.: American Psychiatric Press.

Weiss, E., O'Connell, A.N., & Siiter, R. (1986) Comparisons of second-generation holocaust survivors, immigrants, and nonimmigrants on measures of mental health. *Journal of Personality and Social Psychology, 50,* 828–831.

Weiss, M.D. (1988) Parental uses of authority and discipline by Holocaust survivors. *Family Therapy, 15*, 199–209.

Weissman, M.M., Klerman, G.L., Pousoff, B.A., Sholdmskas, G., & Padran, N. (1981) Depressed outpatients: One year after treatment with drugs and/or interpersonal therapy. *Archives of General Psychiatry, 38*, 51–55.

Wessely, S. (1990) Old wine in new bottles: Neurasthenia and 'ME'. *Psychological Medicine, 20*, 35–53.

Wessely, S., & Powell, R. (1989) Fatigue syndromes: A comparison of chronic "postviral" fatigue with neuromuscular and affective disorders. *Journal of Neurology, Neurosurgery, and Psychiatry, 52*, 940–958.

Wessely, S., & Thomas, P.K. (1989) The chronic fatigue syndrome ('myalgicencephalomyelitis' or 'postviral fatigue'). In: C. Kennard (Ed.), *Recent Advances in Neurology*, London: Churchill Livingstone.

Westenberg, H.J.M., & Verhoeven, W.M.A. (1988) CSF monoamine metabolites in patients and controls: Support for a bimodel distribution in major affective disorders. *Acta Psychiatrica Scandinavia, 78*, 541–549.

Westerman, N. (1922) Ueber die vitale Depression. *Zeitschrift fur die Gesammte Neurologie und Psychiatrie, 77*, 391–398.

Wetzler, S., Kahn, R.S., Asnis, G.M., Korn, M., & van Praag, H.M. (1991) Serotonin receptor sensitivity and aggression. *Psychiatry Research, 37*, 271–279.

Wetzler, S., Kahn, R.S., Cahn, W., van Praag, H.M., & Asnis, G.M. (1990) Psychological test characteristics of depressed and panic patients. *Psychiatry Research, 31*, 179–192.

White, D.M., Lewy, A.J., Sack, R.L., Blood, M.L., & Wesche, D.L. (1990) Is winter depression a bipolar disorder? *Comprehensive Psychiatry, 31*, 196–204.

Wickham, E.A., & Reed, J.V. (1987) Lithium for the control of aggressive and self-mulilating behaviour. *International Clinical Psychopharmacology, 2*, 181–190.

Wieland, S., & Lucki, I. (1990) Antidepressant-like activity of 5-HT1A agonists measured with the forced swim test. *Psychopharmacology, 101*, 497–504.

Williams, A., Reveley, A., Kolakowska, T., Arden, M., & Mandlebrote, B. (1986) Schizophrenia with good and poor outcome: II. Cerebral ventricular size and its clinical significance. *British Journal of Psychiatry, 146*, 239–246.

Williams, J., & Davies, J.A. (1983) The involvement of 5-hydroxytryptamine in the release of dendritic dopamine from slices of rat substantia nigra. *Journal of Pharmacy and Pharmacology, 35*, 734–737.

Wing, Y.K., Cooper, J.E., & Sartorius, N. (1974) *The Measurement and Classification of Psychiatric Symptoms. An Introductory Manual for the Present State Examination and CATEGO Program.* Cambridge: Cambridge University Press.

Wirz-Justice, A., Bucheli, C., Graw, P., Kielholz, P., Fisch, H.U., & Woggon, B. (1986) Light treatment of seasonal affective disorder in Switzerland. *Acta Psychiatrica Scandinavica, 74,* 193–204.

Wise, R.A. (1982) Neuroleptics and operant behavior. The anhedonia hypothesis. *Behavioral and Brain Sciences, 5,* 39–87.

Woods, B.T., Yurgelun-Todd, D., Benes, F.M., Frankenburg, F.R., Pope, Jr., H.G., & McSparren, J. (1990) Progressive ventricular enlargement in schizophrenia: Comparison to bipolar affective disorder and correlation with clinical course. *Biological Psychiatry, 27,* 341–352.

Wyatt, R.J., Alexander, R.C., Egan, M.F., & Kirch, D.G. (1988) Schizophrenia, just the facts. What do we know, how well do we know it? *Schizophrenia Research, 18,* 3–18.

Yerevanian, B.I., Anderson, J.L., Grota, L.J., & Bray, M. (1986) Effects of bright incandescent light on seasonal and nonseasonal depressive order. *Psychiatry Research, 18,* 355–364.

Zegans, L.S., Purtilo, D.T., Brown, N., Schooley, R.T., & Brus, I. (1988) Chronic fatigue syndrome: A working case definition. *Annals of Internal Medicine, 108,* 387–389.

Zimmerman, M., Black, D.W., & Coryell, W. (1989) Diagnostic criteria for melancholia. *Archives of General Psychiatry, 46,* 361–368.

Zimmerman, M., & Coryell, W.H. (1990) DSM-III personality disorder dimensions. *Journal of Nervous and Mental Disease, 178,* 686–692.

Zimmerman, M., Pfohl, B., Coryell, W., Stangl, D., & Corenthal, C. (1988) Diagnosing personality disorder in depressed patients. *Archives of General Psychiatry, 45,* 733–737.

Zis, A.P., & Goodwin, F.K. (1982) The amine hypothesis. In: F.S. Paykel (Ed.), *Handbook of Affective Disorders.* New York: Guilford Press.

Zlotogorski, Z. (1985) Offspring of concentration camp survivors: A study of levels of ego functioning. *Israel Journal of Psychiatry and Related Sciences, 22,* 201.

Zohar, J., Mueller, E.A., Insel, T.R., Zohar-Kadouch, R.C., & Murphy, D.L. (1987) Serotonergic responsivity in obsessive-compulsive disorder. *Archives of General Psychiatry, 44,* 946–951.

Zubin, J., Magaziner, J., & Steinhauer, S.R. (1983) The metamorphosis of schizophrenia: From chronicity to vulnerability. *Psychological Medicine, 13,* 551–571.

Zukin, S.R., Vale, W., Zukin, R.S., & Johnson, K.M. (1986) The brain sigma opioid/phencyclidine receptor and its endogenous neuropeptide ligand: Psychiatric implication. In: C. Shagrass, R. Josias, W. Bridger, K. Weiss, D. Stoff, & J. Simpson (Eds.), *Biological Psychiatry.* New York: Elsevier Science Publisher.

Zung, W.W.K., & Green, R.L. (1974) Seasonal variation of suicide and depression. *Archives of General Psychiatry, 30,* 89–91.

Name Index

292

Subject Index